This book aims to link the Communist experience to the theoretical debates on modernity. The most influential theories of modernity have taken surprisingly little interest in the problematic of Soviet-type societies, and recent events have highlighted the lack of a conceptual framework for the interpretation of their history.

The author tries to show that a revised concept of totalitarianism can be used to clarify the distinctive characteristics of the Soviet model as a pattern of modernity and thus to open up new perspectives for modernization theory.

This line of argument is developed in relation to four main themes: the historical origins of the Soviet model, its institutional core, the differences between its original version and later variants (with particular reference to China and Eastern Europe), and the combination of structural and historical factors which brought about its terminal crisis. The theoretical model used throughout focuses on the changing configurations of economic, political and cultural patterns.

The book is addressed to students in Political Science, Sociology and Comparative History.

Johann P. Arnason is Reader in Sociology at La Trobe University, Melbourne.

The future that failed

Origins and destinies of the
Soviet model

Johann P. Arnason

London and New York

First published in 1993
by Routledge
11 New Fetter Lane, London EC4P 4EE

Simultaneously published in the USA and Canada by Routledge
29 West 35th Street, New York, NY 10001

© 1993 Johann P. Arnason
Typeset in Times by
NWL Editorial Services, Langport, Somerset

Printed and bound in Great Britain by
Biddles Ltd, Guildford and King's Lynn

British Library Cataloguing in Publication Data
A catalogue record for this book is available from the British
Library.

Library of Congress Cataloging in Publication Data
Arnason, Jóhann Páll, 1940–
    The future that failed: origins and destinies of the Soviet
    model/Johann P. Arnason.
    p.   cm. (Routledge social futures series)
    Includes bibliographical references and index.
    1. Communism – Soviet Union.   2. Communism and society.
    3. Communist state.   4. Totalitarianism.   I. Title.   II. Series.
    HX313.A783 1993   93–14819
    321.9′2′0947 – dc20   CIP

ISBN 0–415–06226–8 (hbk)
ISBN 0–415–06227–6 (pbk)

In memoriam Stefán Bjarman
1894–1974

Les humains se trompent à tout coup; l'histoire le montre. On dit 'de deux choses l'une', et c'est toujours la troisième.

Claude Lévi-Strauss

(History shows that human beings get it wrong, time and again. We think it must be one thing or the other, and it is always a third one.)

Contents

Preface

The aim of this essay is to explore some of the border areas between social theory and sovietology, and thus to aid the absorption of the latter discipline – now struggling to survive the extinction of its object – by historical sociology. My main themes and concerns are those of a social theorist, but I have tried to link them to sovietological issues.

More precisely, the following analysis seeks to contextualize the Soviet phenomenon in several interconnected ways. It must, to begin with, be seen as the outcome of long-term processes, particularly those of Russian history. The Soviet model was a Russian creation, and none of its derivative non-Russian versions has had an impact comparable to the original. A closer look at the Russian background suggests that the dynamic of state formation is particularly central to the prehistory of the Soviet regime. Somewhat surprisingly, there seems to have been no attempt to relate this dominant feature of Russian history to Norbert Elias's path-breaking work on state formation in the West. I have tried to indicate some points of contact and possibilities of comparative analysis.

On the other hand, the historical experience of Soviet-type societies has far-reaching implications for the theory of modernity. Recent interpretations, both neo-Marxist and non-Marxist, have tended towards the view that they represent a distinctive pattern of modernity rather than a deviant path or transitional phase of modernization; the difference between Parsonian and Habermasian approaches to this question exemplifies the shift. In retrospect, it would seem that this analysis was – in very general terms – on the right track. There were good reasons to emphasize the specificity and originality of the Soviet version of modernity, and recent events should not raise any new doubts about that. But it goes without saying that we now have to consider the issue from a new angle: an interpretation of the Soviet model *après le déluge* must do justice to the strengths which explain its impact on twentieth-century history as well as to the weaknesses which brought about its unexpected collapse, and try to understand the interconnections between these two aspects of the phenomenon. The argument developed here focuses on the characteristics of economic, political and cultural patterns, as well as the relationships between them; a revised version of the concept of totalitarianism is used as a key to the Soviet configuration of these three dimensions of the social world.

The totalitarian project took shape in an imperial context. It is now a commonplace that the Soviet Union was an empire. But it is easier to recognize this fact than to theorize it. Empires in general – or, in other words, imperial patterns of culture and power – and imperial modernizing processes in particular are still an under-theorized aspect of social development. As I have tried to show in an introductory chapter, this problematic can be linked to the rethinking of modernity that is one of the main concerns of contemporary social theory (a confrontation with 'postmodernism' is beyond the scope of this book, but it might be suggested in passing that it is best understood as a detour – sometimes rewarding, sometimes misguided – towards such a rethinking).

To describe the Soviet model as a pattern of modernity is not to suggest that it can be reduced to self-contained and unvarying structures. Rather, its diffusion beyond its original boundaries entailed its adaptation to different historical contexts and resulted in more or less significant modifications. The reconstruction of the model must therefore be combined with a comparative analysis of its variants. In the present context, however, this part of the argument must be limited to a brief discussion of the two most significant cases: China and Eastern Europe. Finally, the last chapter deals with the terminal crisis of the Soviet model, but is more concerned with its historical background than with the details and direct causes of the collapse.

In more general terms, the purpose of the book is to develop an interpretive framework rather than an explanatory model. As argued below, this framework cannot take the form of a general and systematic theory of Soviet-type societies: their core structures are too context-dependent for that. Historical interpretations are therefore an essential part of the argument, but given the limits of the book, they cannot be backed up by more detailed case studies. The resultant mixture of theory and history may be unpalatable to those who insist on a clear-cut division of labour, but it is in my opinion the only way to make sense of the subject.

Acknowledgements

I have drawn extensively on the work of many sociologists, historians and political scientists as well as a few economists, but given the format of a theoretical essay, detailed acknowledgements are impossible. The bibliography is therefore far from exhaustive; the sources quoted and listed are those most directly relevant to the argument.

Although the historical perspective of the book reflects the events of the last few years, its theoretical core has been in the making for a much longer time and benefited from contact with other projects. Discussions with the Australian branch of the Budapest School were particularly useful; my interpretation of the Soviet phenomenon differs from theirs in fundamental respects, but it took shape in dialogue with the analysis developed in *Dictatorship over Needs*. It should also be noted that the book owes more to the work of Cornelius Castoriadis than direct references might suggest. His analyses of the Soviet regime and the Communist movement are open to question, but his pioneering contribution to a radical critique of the Soviet model and a reorientation of social theory in the light of the Soviet experience is beyond dispute.

Thanks are due to Barry Smart for a suggestion which helped to bring a diffuse project into focus, and to Chris Rojek for his patient and constructive approach to the publishing process; to the Department of Sociology, La Trobe University, for many-sided support, and particularly to Therese Lennox, Beth Robertson and Elaine Young for typing the manuscript; last but not least, to Maria and Jan for their help in completing the work.

Chapter 1

Introduction
Theoretical perspectives

What was this thing called Communism? There are two ways of tackling the question: we can either treat the Communist phenomenon as a movement which rose to power in some states but failed to achieve its global aims, or as a regime which first emerged out of the ruins of a collapsed empire but was later imposed on other states and translated into an international model for anti-systemic movements. The first approach has some obvious merits. An analysis of the cultural orientations and the power-centred dynamics of Communism as a movement can throw light on the phenomenon as a whole (cf., for example, Westoby 1988). Moreover, it can be argued that the regime always retained some characteristics of a movement, and that they were never fully integrated into an institutional framework. If the following reflections are nevertheless more in line with the second approach, the underlying assumption is that the impact of the regime – its built-in aspirations as well as its structural transformations – on the movement which it controlled was more decisive than the traces left within the regime by the movement that had paved the way for it. The focus is, in other words, on the Soviet model as a social regime (in the broad sense suggested by Castoriadis, i.e. a comprehensive institutional pattern) with global ramifications and universal pretensions; its ability to absorb and instrumentalize the legacy of a social movement, as well as to control or at least influence a whole spectrum of movements outside its domestic arena, is only one aspect of a more complex picture, and not the most directly relevant to the present discussion.

This choice of perspective will seem less arbitrary if we can back it up with a historical analysis. But before going on to look at the constitution, development and diffusion of the Soviet model, more must be said about the interpretive context. The complexity and novelty of the phenomenon in question is reflected in the extreme diversity of the attempts to make sense of it. During the more dynamic phase of the Soviet regime, it could be seen as a mode of economic development, and more specific interpretations could focus on contrasts or affinities with Western capitalism. For Marxist critics (at least those who moved beyond the intellectual transit house of Trotskyism), it was tempting to describe the Stalinist system as the most extreme variant of capitalism; the concentration and bureaucratization of capital, the primacy of accumulation and the exploitation of labour were, as they saw it, taken far beyond the limits that had been characteristic of the bourgeois order. Such arguments led to more or less explicit conclusions about a new class structure and a new road to social revolution. On the other hand, those who saw more clearly the difference between Soviet institutions and those of classical capitalism could still try to explain it in terms of an alternative strategy of industrialization and then establish at least a partial functional equivalence of the two systems. Both conceptions – the notion of a super-capitalism as well as that of a substitute for capitalism – have been discredited by the decline and fall of the Soviet model; more generally speaking, the idea of an economy-centred mode of development now seems less plausible than that of a de-differentiating regression which negated the autonomy and specificity of the economic sphere. But the latter point of view is also open to different interpretations. For some observers, the Soviet experience exemplifies the self-defeating utopia of an ethical and political regulation of the economy, whereas others stress the all-too-successful *étatisation* of economic life and the subordination of economic rationality to the imperatives of state- and empire-building.

The claim that the Soviet model was an anti-economy, rather than a distinctive economic system, thus shifts the line of argument towards political factors and strengthens the case for some earlier interpretations that were more directly concerned with this aspect of the Communist experience. The agreement on an elementary premise – the primacy of the political sphere – should not, however, obscure the fundamental differences between the theories which shared it. For some of them, the central place and dominant role of politics in Soviet society was the outcome of a restoration of traditional patterns, while others explained it as a result of the radicalization of modern trends. One version of the former approach is the interpretation of the Bolshevik revolution and its sequel as a reimposition of state control over civil society and – at least in this respect – a reversal of the modernizing process that had been going on since 1861; another is the assumption of an essential continuity between the Russian empire – beginning with its Muscovite origins – and the post-revolutionary regime which rebuilt it. On the other side, those who saw the Soviet power structure as a distinctively modern phenomenon were *eo ipso* attracted to the notion of totalitarianism, but it was easier to agree on its relevance than on its proper use. The relationship between the totalitarian project and its institutional embodiments was controversial, and some definitions of the concept missed the point that 'really existing totalitarianism' – as distinct from the ideal type – was capable of change and adaptation; most importantly, the totalitarian phenomenon could either be explained in terms of general tendencies inherent in the development of the modern state and likely to manifest themselves in an extreme form under certain circumstances, or related – with a stronger emphasis on its radical novelty – to the dynamic of modern revolutions and their imaginary extensions.

The more ambitious theories of totalitarianism also tried to do justice to the cultural and ideological aspects of the phenomenon. But further work on this problematic opened up another field of conflicting interpretations. If the sources of the Soviet model were to be located within modern culture, a plausible case could be made for the more extreme undercurrents and offshoots of the Enlightenment. The simplifying and absolutistic interpretations that accompanied the rise of modern science seemed to prefigure the claims of Marxism-Leninism as a 'scientific world-view'; on a less explicitly ideological level, the idea of a comprehensive, exclusive, uncontestable and universally applicable scientific rationality could be linked to the Bolshevik version of scientific socialism. For others it was the humanistic rather than the scientistic delusion of the Enlightenment that was to blame for its totalitarian deviation. The catastrophe was, in other words, brought about by misguided notions of freedom as a complete and conflictless self-realization, rather than by a misunderstanding of rationality or an over-ambitious quest for rational mastery. In this view, the utopian attempt to translate the 'essential powers of man' into new forms of social life could only end in despotism; more precisely, the essentialist vision had turned into an ideological straitjacket and the supposedly radical project of liberation shrunk to a strategy of total control. Despite broad agreement on the most important and objectionable features of Soviet Marxism as an ideology, both diagnoses differ from those that stress its pre-modern roots. The latter view is encapsulated in the concept of a secular or political religion, at least when the term is given its proper meaning: the modern contents can then be reduced to a disguise of more traditional forces. But the religious genealogy of Communism is no less controversial than the search for secular causes. Some analysts have compared the Soviet challenge to the conquering and universal religions of the past. J. Monnerot's (1953) description of Communism as the Islam of the twentieth century is a case in point; the common characteristic was, as he saw it, the fusion of a new and militant religion with an equally ambitious imperial project. Many authors have tried to link the spirit of Bolshevism more directly to the religious culture of Orthodox Christianity. Others have, by contrast, traced the prehistory of Communism (and, more generally speaking, of the modern revolutionary project) back to Gnostic origins and thus stressed the breakthrough of a marginal tradition, rather than the continuity of a dominant one.

None of these interpretations can be dismissed out of hand. The following discussion will draw on some of them more extensively than others, and although its main thrust will in an important sense be closest to those who single out the political sources and determinants of the Soviet model (more precisely: the long-term dynamics and directions of state formation), I will also try to set this aspect against a broader background. But a systematic comparison of theoretical perspectives is beyond the scope of this book. For present purposes, it is enough to note some more general lessons that can be drawn from the above sketch. First, the conflicting interpretations tend to stress either traditional or modern features of the phenomenon in question. It would therefore be one of the most basic tasks of a more balanced theory to clarify both the contrast and the connection between these two frames of reference. Second, the distinction between economic, political and cultural levels or components is not only a way of locating the starting-points of alternative theories; it also helps to lay down the guidelines for an explicitly multi-dimensional approach. If each of the three levels has given rise to its own set of totalizing interpretations, this already tells us something about the complexity of their interrelations and the need for a correspondingly complex theory. The second point is closely related to the first: analyses of the modernizing process and attempts to distinguish between traditional and modern societies have mostly centred on the concept of differentiation, and our tripartite division is one of many versions of the latter. The view of the social field as a configuration of economic, political and cultural spheres should therefore be formulated more clearly and related to other recent developments in differentiation theory. Finally, there can be no discussion of differentiation without some reference to the complementary problem of integration. For the classical version of modernization theory, the emergence of more complex mechanisms of integration was no less important than the progress of differentiation, and a reconceptualization of the latter aspect must affect our understanding of the former.

To begin with, we should note some attempts to make sense of the Soviet phenomenon within a more general conception of modernity, its sources and its problems. They can, broadly speaking, be divided into three categories: the emphasis is on a particular road to modernity, a distinctive version of modernity, or – in a much less explicit and conclusive fashion – on a mixture of both. In all cases, the argument is to some extent concerned with the plurality of spheres as well as with the unity of the overall configuration.

The first approach is characteristic of the most conventional theory of modernization, and the most succinct formulation can probably be found in the work of Talcott Parsons. In this view, the Soviet model was simply a historically conditioned strategy of modernization, and further progress in this direction would involve a rapprochement with the 'main pattern', i.e. the more balanced and adaptable Western model. There was, strictly speaking, no distinctively Soviet version of modern society, only a less coherent and thoroughgoing form of the modernizing process. As in the West, it brought about changes in economic and political structures, legal norms and cultural patterns; the development of some components was more limited or one-sided than that of others, and the shortcomings of the backward parts are reflected in the structure of the whole.

Habermas's analysis of Soviet-type (or, as he puts it, 'state socialist') societies is perhaps the most clear-cut example of the second viewpoint. The underlying conception of modernity is, by comparison with Parsons, much more flexible and sensitive to structural deformations; the critical function of the theory thus becomes more pronounced and its positive criteria less dependent on existing models. Habermas distinguishes two types of modern society, each of them characterized by a specific imbalance and therefore confined to an impoverished version of the 'project of modernity'. The Western type is dominated by the capitalist economy and its monetary mechanisms, the Soviet alternative by the bureaucratic state and the corresponding medium of administrative power. This systemic difference is significant enough to bring about a bifurcation of the modernizing process, but although the absolutization of power is more directly and thoroughly destructive than the absolutization of money, the long-term socio-cultural consequences are comparable: both lines of development lead to a 'colonization of the lifeworld', i.e. to a progressive erosion of the cultural basis of collective will-formation and democratic initiative. For Habermas, these structural contrasts and affinities are analytically separable from the historical background; the

Russian sources of the Soviet model are thus irrelevant to its internal logic. In the light of recent events, the Parsonian position might seem more convincing: the Soviet model can no longer be regarded as a viable and self-reproducing version of modern society. However, the catastrophic collapse that is now taking place should not be mistaken for the evolutionary convergence which Parsons expected, and the failure of the Soviet model to establish itself as an alternative to Western capitalism does not mean that its emergence and expansion was of no importance for the fate of modernity. On the other hand (and independently of the confrontation with Parsons), Habermas's analysis is, as I have tried to show elsewhere (Arnason 1991: 181–213) open to two major objections: the notion of power as an overextended medium cannot explain the dynamics of the Soviet form of domination, and the search for more adequate keys cannot ignore its historical antecedents.

The third line of argument – a combination of historical and structural perspectives – proved more difficult to develop than the other two. One of the more interesting suggestions was put forward by Alain Touraine. He sees capitalism and Soviet-style socialism as durable patterns of development (one of them dominated by an entrepreneurial but exploitative ruling class, the other by an interventionist but bureaucratic state), reflected not only in different strategies of industrialization and institutional frameworks for industrial society, but also in the respective preconditions for a transition to the post-industrial epoch. On the other hand, the most basic organizational principles and structural conflicts of industrial society prevail within both types. Modern societies can thus be analysed as more or less viable mixtures of the basic but adaptable structures of modernity (industrial or post-industrial) and the more contingent but distinctive and self-perpetuating processes of modern-ization; the mode of development should, according to Touraine (1981: 102–9), not be confused with the mode of production. But if this interpretive hypothesis were to be applied to Soviet-type societies, a more detailed account of the historical origins and characteristics of the Soviet mode of development would be needed, and this might – as I shall later try to show – lead to further revisions of the received idea of modernity.

We have to turn to the work of historians, rather than sociologists, to find more detailed analyses of the historical context of the Soviet model. They have shown that the Soviet phase – and the Soviet form – of the modernization of Russia was in many ways conditioned and prefigured by earlier developments. Their genealogical constructions differ on more specific points; for example, Richard Pipes (or at least one strand of his work) traces the prehistory of Soviet totalitarianism back to the late nineteenth-century Tsarist police state and its efforts to block a democratic transformation while adjusting to the modernizing processes that were going on in other areas, whereas Robert Tucker explains the Stalinist strategy of revolution from above as a revival of the tradition of despotic state intervention, exemplified by Ivan the Terrible and Peter the Great. In both cases, more theoretical questions regarding the role and place of the Soviet model in the modern world are left open, but the implicit links to the above discussion are obvious: if the reference to the Russian past and to its impact on the Soviet present is to be more than an intuitive shortcut, it must lead to a closer examination of both cultural and political traditions, and the evidence for continuity on both levels must be weighed against the massive economic transformation brought about by the post-revolutionary regime.

One of the main aims of the following reflections is to bring the interpretation of Russian history into closer contact with the agenda of social theory. But further clarification of the conceptual framework of this project is needed before we can confront the more substantive issues.

The close connection between the problematic of modernity and the concept of differentiation has already been noted. It is easy to show that the arguments for and against the notion of a specific Soviet version of modernity reflect some underlying assumptions about differentiation, its scope and its historical flexibility. If Habermas goes beyond Parsons in his typology of advanced modern societies, this is mainly because he works with a less rigid model of differentiation and can therefore allow for greater diversity in the relations between various dimensions of the modernizing process. There are, however, limits to this progress. The two societal types are analysed in terms of deviations from a common normative orientation; it is thus only in the light of the 'pathologies' of modernity that structural contrasts between its alternative versions become discernible. Analogously, Touraine's distinction between the two modes of development is based on the observation that the role of the state as a 'complex actor' is in one case dominant enough to block the differentiation of social spheres and actors that is most characteristic of the other. We are thus, in the last instance, dealing with a contrast between historical configurations, rather than between societal types: one of them restricts the logic of society, i.e. the scope of its self-constitution and self-differentiation, much more than the other.

If we can speak about some major innovations in the interpretation of modernity, they are so far more noticeable on the level of general presuppositions than in the context of comparative studies or typologies. As far as basic concepts are concerned, the main trend can perhaps be described as a radicalization of the idea of differentiation, most importantly in relation to components of the socio-cultural world and their role in the modernizing process. The common starting-point is a critique of theories of functional differentiation, whether they are based on a base–superstructure model or on more flexible notions of interconnected subsystems, and an interest in developing the potential of the concept of differentiation beyond this received and restrictive framework, but further steps vary from case to case. The most elaborate model of trans-functional differentiation is the Habermasian conception of three cultural spheres (cognitive, moral and aesthetic), each of which is the embodiment of learning processes that are rooted in the linguistic determinants of the human condition, irreducible to the more specific constraints and demands of social systems, and capable of counterbalancing the functional rationalization that has hitherto set the course of the modernizing process. Another example is Anthony Giddens's analysis of the different 'institutional clusters' (industrial-ization, capitalism, surveillance and warfare) that make up the modern constellation; each of them has its own dynamic, irreducible to that of the others, and their unity can only be the result of partial and temporary coordination, rather than the overall and a priori integration postulated by functionalist theory. Here the emphasis is on historical diversity and openness, rather than anthropological horizons. A combination of both points of view is characteristic of those who follow Max Weber's lead in thematizing the radical internal conflicts of modernity; the tensions between cultural orientations and institutional orders can only be adequately understood in the light of their impact on the human condition. The conflictual relationship between capitalism and democracy is one of several Weberian themes that lend themselves to such an interpretation. As Castoriadis has shown, its significance becomes clearer if the cultural premises and imaginary horizons of both sides are taken into account: capitalist development is inseparable from the vision of an unlimited expansion of rational mastery, and the democratic transformation presupposes the project of an autonomous society. If the former line of development translates an imaginary absolutization of power into a progressive instrumentalization of social life, the latter makes it possible to subject this dominant tendency to critical questioning and confront it with the alternative of collective self-determination and self-limitation.

This brief comparison shows how far the new trends in differentiation theory can diverge, and the differentiation paradigm that will be used here should be set against this background. The trans-functional division of the social field into economic, political and cultural spheres will, as already indicated, be central to our analysis, but I am not suggesting that this perspective can replace or absorb all other models of differentiation. Some further ramifications of the problem will be explored below, while others are beyond the scope of the present book. And it should be noted that the tripartite division itself needs some qualifications. The autonomy of the economic and the political sphere can only be articulated on the basis of cultural contents, i.e. patterns of meaning that are specific to each sphere and conducive to its far-reaching but necessarily incomplete separation from the broader cultural context. These built-in cultural orientations can, in turn, function as sources of further differentiation: the more autonomous the spheres become, the more clearly they emerge as arenas of conflicting interpretations, rather than domains of unequivocal and uncontested principles. Finally, the cultural constitution of economy and politics as separate spheres is accompanied by different projects of reintegration. This last point – integrative models as roots of conflict and differentiation – will be of particular importance for the following discussion.

To describe the tripartite division (or at least its present version) as trans-functional is, above all, to stress two interconnected aspects: the de-centring and pluralizing dynamic inherent in the division as well as the tendency of each sphere to constitute itself as a world in its own right and project its logic onto the social field as a whole. The overall configuration of the spheres lacks the unity and coherence of a system, and each sphere is too autonomous and multi-faceted to be reducible to a subsystem. Such a view of differentiation is, as suggested above, one of the most pronounced traits of recent theorizing about modernity, and it was clearly prefigured by Max Weber's conception of the 'world orders' as interconnected but conflicting ways of synthesizing social and cultural life from a specific perspective. But the present version of differentiation theory can also draw on other sources and other efforts to conceptualize the three spheres in a way that would reflect both their global reach and their insertion into a more complex structure. Some of them should be briefly mentioned.

Marx's work was an epoch-making attempt to grasp the totalizing logic of the modern capitalist economy, but his conceptual apparatus lagged behind his most pioneering insights, and his more critical followers – from Lukács to Wallerstein – have therefore faced a double task: to develop a theory that would on the one hand give a more adequate and comprehensive account of the 'great transformation' (Polanyi 1957) of the economic sphere, and on the other hand take more seriously the question of its cultural and political preconditions. As for the political sphere, Norbert Elias's analysis of state formation as a long-term and multi-dimensional process is the most energetic attempt to reconstruct the genesis of modernity from this angle. The limitations of his paradigm have, however, become more visible with its application to later phases; it oversimplifies the relationship between state formation and capitalist development, tends to treat modern democracy as a mere by-product of the state-building process, and neglects the role of cultural interpretations in the historical transformations of power. These criticisms can also be read as an outline of the agenda for an alternative theory that would incorporate some of Elias's core ideas. Finally, the search for a new concept of culture, more emphatic and at the same time more flexible, is at the centre of current debates in this area. The previously dominant theories, both those associated with the Marxist concept of ideology and those inspired by the less obviously reductionist notion of culture as a programming subsystem, are criticized for denying or limiting the autonomy of culture, but also – paradoxically – for their excessively rigid conception of the cultural input into other spheres. This reaction against over-systematized and over-functionalized ideas of culture is common to many authors who otherwise differ on both premises and conclusions; for our present purposes, it is enough to note two implications of one of the alternatives that have been explored. If we think of culture as an open-ended, understructured and imperfectly integrated complex of interpretive patterns, rather than as a value system or an ideological machine (Castoriadis's analysis of 'imaginary significations' is the most ambitious and challenging version of this view), it is easier to accept that it can neither be completely in control nor under control. On the one hand, it transcends the social field through its articulation of the world as the ultimate context of meaning; the forms of articulation may be susceptible to social uses, but not reducible to the interplay of social forces. On the other hand, cultural interpretations of power appear in a new light: their impact on the space and direction of political and economic developments is important, but less straightforward than the notions of normative programming or ideological representation would suggest. Both points are, as we shall see, relevant to the problematic of political culture.

The aim of this book is to use the model of the three spheres to analyse the Soviet phenomenon and thus to test its applicability to a particular area, rather than to spell out its theoretical implications. It may, however, be useful to indicate the general direction that a theoretical argument would take. It would, to be brief, follow the general and well-known pattern of a 'double hermeneutic'. In the present case, this means that an interpretation of modernity must first of all come to grips with the legacy of earlier interpretations that have both drawn on and in turn influenced the self-thematization of its object. The distinction between the three spheres can thus be grounded in the dialectic of the sociological tradition. The most significant aspect of Durkheim's and Weber's work was their insistence on – or, more precisely, their progressive discovery of – the radical autonomy of culture and politics, and their critique of the economistic reductionism that had not only overshadowed the critical potential of classical Marxism, but also shaped the liberal image of society, as theorized by Spencer (and, arguably, by later functionalists who claimed to have assimilated the insights of Durkheim and Weber). Similar conclusions can be drawn from a retrospective on the Marxist tradition. Tensions between a reductionist view of politics and culture and the need to take them more seriously have been characteristic of both its political and its intellectual history; a recent and particularly striking case is the failure of structuralist Marxism and its attempts to develop a systematic theory of politics and ideology (the latter notion functioning as a codeword for a materialist approach to culture) within the framework of the base–superstructure model. Post-Marxist theories of modernity confront the same problematic on a more advanced level. Habermas's reformulation of critical theory through a synthesis of classical traditions is perhaps the most representative case; his analysis of the connections and conflicts between the lifeworld and the coordinating media of money and power can be read as a clear-cut but questionable version of the tripartite model. Both the reliance on systems theory to explain political and economic dynamics and the equation of the cultural context with the lifeworld are open to objections.

Finally, it should be noted that the distinction between the three spheres is closely related to the central theme of post-functionalist social theory: the self-constitution of society. This idea is open to variations (an inventory might start with Castoriadis, Touraine and Unger), but in general terms it has emerged in contrast to models of systemic closure and structural determination, and its main concern is with the specificity, autonomy and historicity of the social field. These general guidelines are, of course, closely linked to the more particular task of rethinking modernity. If the structure of the self-constituting process is to be analysed further, three aspects stand out: it involves the mobilization and allocation of resources, the exercise and distribution of power, and the articulation and institutionalization of meaning. We can, in other words, distinguish between economic, political and cultural components of social life; the form and degree of their institutional differentiation depends on more specific factors.

From the viewpoint of theories of modernity, the question of socio-cultural spheres and their interrelations is closely linked to two other dimensions of differentiation. There is, first, the global context within which the new configurations of the social field emerge and develop. Several versions of 'globalization theory' (Robertson 1992) have focused on the constitution of a world society as the most fundamental change brought about by the modernizing process. Their primary concern is, however, mostly with the new horizons and mechanisms of integration and their main disagreements are related to this issue (the most developed and detailed version, Wallerstein's world-system theory, stresses the oligarchic, exploitative and self-destabilizing character of global integration). It may be more appropriate to treat this problematic, in the first instance, as another offshoot of differentiation theory: the globalizing process brings different civilizational complexes into contact with each other, throws their contrasts into relief and provokes divergent responses to the new constellation. The new integrative mechanisms are superimposed on this context, but they never absorb it, and their variety is a source of further differentiation and conflict. They include patterns of the international division of labour and accumulation on a worldwide scale as well as imperial projects, international regimes, and cultural or ideological models with a global reach.

It may be objected that this view of the globalizing process obscures its dominant trend: the dynamic of Western expansion and the imposition of Western hegemony. But neither the concrete forms and consequences of Western hegemony, nor the limits to it, can be explained without taking into account the reactions and counter-projects of the civilizations on which it was imposed. The most fundamental aspects of Western modernity were co-determined by its interaction with the world beyond its original domain. The world market was one of the formative conditions of capitalist development; the expansion into other regions affected the dynamics of the European state system and was, in particular, conducive to the invention or reactivation of imperial projects; finally, both legitimizing and contestatory ideologies acquired new dimensions through the articulation of a global horizon. A more detailed analysis would have to trace the specific effects of the several 'inter-civilizational encounters' (Nelson 1973) that took place in the course of Western expansion.

This view of modernity as a global field leads to a third perspective on differentiation. If the globalizing process involves the interaction of different civilizational centres and complexes, we must at least consider the possibility that it might give rise to different versions of modernity, co-determined by the respective historical backgrounds and traditions. It would, in other words, result in a differentiation of the overall patterns of modernity. This suggestion presupposes that we can distinguish between Westernization and modernization, and that the former can be regarded as a particular case or phase of the latter. Some analysts reject such claims on the grounds that the global transformation is inseparable from the expansion and hegemony of the West and should therefore be described as a 'world revolution of Westernization' (Laue 1988). In this view, it has proved impossible to resist the West without imitating its most tangible innovations, and the apparent alternatives to the Western model of development (including, in particular, the totalitarian regimes) are only improvised (and sometimes self-defeating) substitutes for its more elusive and less easily imitable aspects. It is – to mention only the most obvious case – becoming more and more difficult to fit the Japanese trajectory into this picture. And as far as the Soviet model is concerned, the following analysis should show that it was both more and less than a developmental detour – more in terms of the project and its global if temporary impact, less in terms of the lasting achievements and its aftermath. More generally speaking, we should not impose a conceptual framework that prejudges the question whether the strategic substitutes can – for better or worse – develop into structural alternatives; if the possibility of modernizing processes that would include limits, counterweights and alternatives to Westernization is to be envisaged, we need the appropriate analytical distinctions.

Earlier theories of modernization tended to rely on a more or less explicit belief in universal implications of the Western breakthrough. The distinction between Westernization and modernization was thus reduced to a self-transcending dynamic of Western civilization; its specific line of development had led to results that could – as Weber assumed – claim universal sense and validity. There was, moreover, a strong temptation to go beyond Weber's cautious formulations and ground this universal reference in an evolutionary vision of history. As evolutionary explanations became less plausible and the idea of a universalizing logic of development more problematic, the relationship between Westernization and modernization had to be reconsidered. Two ways of doing so seem particularly relevant to our concerns. On the one hand, some authors have proposed to redefine modernity as industrialization and its preconditions; the modernizing process is thus reduced to a part of the Western breakthrough, but it is the part that is most effectively diffused beyond the borders of the West and is most directly conducive to the same dynamic in other contexts. Non-Western civilizations can then be compared with each other and with the West with regard to their compatibility with the imperatives of industrialization. Some of them may turn out to be in some respects more compatible or capable of inventing their own functional equivalents (Murakami 1987). The problem with this approach is that it takes for granted an unchanging functional primacy of industrialization and a uniform functional logic that links it to other areas of social life. As we shall see, the analysis of the Soviet model can serve to illustrate the point: patterns of modernity differ, among other things, with regard to the role and relative weight of industrialization as well as to the way in which it is linked to other goals and processes.

On the other hand, it has been argued (Eisenstadt 1978, 1987) that modernity constitutes a new tradition or a comprehensive civilizational pattern, comparable to the universal religions of the past, and that in this capacity it transcends – in principle and from the outset – the Western background from which it first emerges. Its concrete forms and developmental directions depend on the socio-cultural contexts with which it interacts and to which it has to be adapted; such combinations vary not only from one region of the world to another, but also from one area of social life to another. While this view is no doubt more attuned to the multidimensionality and diversity of the modern constellation, its way of distinguishing between Westernization and modernization (or, rather, of disposing of this problem) is less satisfactory. This is not simply a matter of separating a universal pattern from a historical background. Rather, we need a conceptual framework that would also do justice to the permanent but conflictual connection between Westernizing and modernizing processes. It might therefore be useful to distinguish a civilizational *paradigm* from a civilizational *horizon*; Western expansion imposes the former and in doing so opens up the latter. In other words: if the transition to modernity can be defined in terms of new, more dynamic and more rationalized forms of accumulating wealth and power, together with a cultural context that can generate new frameworks of legitimation as well as new ways of questioning and contestation, it must be added that the successive Western configurations do not exhaust the possibilities inherent in this epochal shift. Non-Western civilizations are under pressure to adopt the models and arrangements that have most effectively contributed to Western hegemony, but at the same time, their distinctive legacies can – to a greater or lesser degree – be translated into alternative forms within the same horizon. In terms of the above shorthand definition, both the relationship between the two dimensions of accumulation and their relationship to the cultural context is subject to such variations. Whether – or under what conditions – they can develop into relatively coherent and durable counter-paradigms of modernity is a question that will be taken up below and serve – together with some others – as a guideline for our analysis of the Soviet model. But at this point, a more general comment should be added: the contributions of diverse traditions to the patterns of modernity can only be understood if both sides of the relationship are taken into account, i.e. not only the shaping of modernity by tradition, but also the re-shaping of tradition by the modernizing process. The latter aspect is sometimes described as 'an invention of tradition', but this is a needlessly extremist formulation; it would be more appropriate to speak about a selective reactivation and reinterpretation, and this process affects different levels of traditions in different ways.

The divergent patterns of modernity are, from another point of view, forms of integration: they impose a unifying framework, more or less coherent and comprehensive, on the plurality of socio-cultural spheres. In this case, it is particularly obvious that a new approach to the problematic of integration must complement the above-mentioned developments in differentiation theory. To make the point in more general terms, it may be useful to contrast the present perspective with a traditional one. In the Parsonian image of modernity (because of its wide-ranging direct and indirect influence on modernization theories, it must be regarded as a paradigmatic case), the primacy of integration is established in two ways. It is, first, built into the conceptual basis: the processes of differentiation are confined within a systemic framework, and the latter is construed as an integrated totality of interdependent functions. Second, the more specifically integrative function is singled out and identified with a corresponding subsystem which then becomes – through the twin concepts of social system and society – the focus of sociological theory. As later critics of Parsonian theory have convincingly shown, these categories serve to transfigure a much more complex and ambivalent historical reality: the nation-state. By contrast, the multiple paradigm shifts summarized above change the balance between differentiation and integration: modernity is, in a very fundamental sense, less integrated and less integrable than some of its most influential interpreters have assumed. The other side of the coin, though, is that we have to allow for a much greater variety of the forms of relative, partial and temporary integration. No systematic inventory will be attempted here, but a brief glance at some of the most salient historical landmarks may help to situate the phenomenon which will subsequently be our main concern.

On the level of institutional integration, the achievements of liberal capitalist democracy have been thrown into relief by the demise of its main rival, and its advocates are now attributing to it some of the virtues and promises that used to be associated with more utopian projects. For all its success, however, it has not become – nor is it about to become – a universal pattern of modernity, and it can certainly not be described as a 'normal' state of things. Its strength and significance consist, above all, in the ability to coordinate and at the same time contain the development of autonomous socio-cultural spheres. The dynamic of capitalist development is – to a varying extent – counterbalanced by an institution-alized capacity to regulate the social conflict that is the obverse of economic rationality and to adapt the logic of the market to other principles of organization. In the political sphere, this pattern has incorporated counterweights and imposed normative limits to the growth of the modern state, but the development of democracy has been contained within institutions that limit the possibilities of its radicalization. And in the cultural sphere, the pluralism of worldviews, ideologies and subcultures is recognized but defused in such a way that neither the imaginary infrastructure nor the explicit ground rules of core institutions are seriously threatened. This version of modernity has, moreover, proved flexible enough to adjust to further changes and respond to new challenges in all three spheres, but also malleable enough to undergo major transformations of the kind that is best exemplified by the Japanese line of development. In the light of these considerations, it seems obvious that liberal capitalist democracy should be described as a constellation rather than as a system (to talk about the victory of one system over another is therefore misleading), and that its logic should be reconstructed in terms of practices rather than principles. To claim that it has exhausted its adaptive potential would be as arbitrary as to assume that it has become immune to radical challenges, and to celebrate it as the end of history is absurd beyond belief. For one thing, the institutions of liberal capitalist democracy were created and consolidated within the framework of the nation-state, and their changing relationship to this basis raises questions about their future: neither their compatibility with higher levels of global interdependence nor their ability to keep in step with the proliferation of nation-states and to cope with the resurgence of ethnic particularism can be taken for granted.

Over-systemized images of liberal capitalist democracy conflate the institutional level with that of interpretive integration. This term is used here to describe the search for a unifying and constitutive principle of modernity – be it individualism, rationality or subjectivity. Such constructions, grounded in the cultural self-thematization of modern societies and more explicitly developed on the level of social theory, are best understood as secondary attempts to unify the diverse figures of individuality, rationality or subjectivity that emerge within different socio-cultural spheres and in the course of their historical transformations. The unifying categories and theories focus on their affinities, rather than their context-dependent pluralism and mutual irreducibility, and thus tend to convert them into self-contained principles that can be applied to different domains or embodied in separate subsystems. The more ambitious versions of interpretive integration, however, frequently combine this approach with another perspective. We can speak about utopian integration when a future development or transformation of modernity is expected to overcome its tensions and conflicts and culminate in a more adequately integrated society. At its most moderate (e.g. in the Parsonian theory of modernity), this vision of the future does not go beyond a more balanced development of the existing pattern, but it may also entail revolutionary changes and even a de-differentiating reversal of the modernizing process. The significance and appeal – but also the difficulties and paradoxes – of Marx's theory of modernity are particularly obvious if we regard it as a strategy of utopian integration. His definition of the classless communist society as a 'free association of the producers' presupposes the absorption of the bureaucratic state and the market economy into a unified but unspecified mainstream of social life. This radical de-differentiation of society is, however, combined with an unqualified acceptance of differentiation as progress on the more fundamental level of the human condition. For Marx, the diversification of the relations between humans and the world is an important part of the civilizing role of capitalism, and post-capitalist humanity will pursue the same goal in a more conscious and coordinated way. At the same time, Marx has his own version of a constitutive principle of modernity: the continuous and self-accelerating growth of the productive forces. This interpretive device allows him to link the analysis of the capitalist version of modernity to the prognosis of its self-destruction and the project of a post-capitalist alternative.

The Marxian image of modernity lends itself to many interpretations, and some of them will be touched upon below. But our main concern here is not with the practical or interpretive patterns of Western modernity. Rather, the aim is to analyse and to contextualize one of the reactive patterns; we might provisionally describe it as both the least Western offshoot of the West and the most Western of the non-Western alternatives. A comparison with other examples of the same general category would have to deal with many factors: the geopolitical situation, the historical context of the encounter with the West (including the particular aspect or phase of the West that was most actively present), the social forces and actors involved in the civilizational conflict, the traditions that could be perpetuated or reactivated and thus translated into distinctive patterns of modernity, and – last but not least – the varying capacity of non-Western civilizations to draw on alternative currents within the West and adapt them to their own purposes. There is no simple explanation for the emergence of the more original and significant responses to the Western challenge, but it is worth noting that the most effective counter-challenges are not necessarily mounted by those who have the most deep-seated traditional affinities and the most prolonged historical contact with the West (in this respect, a comparison of Islamic civilization with the East Asian region is very instructive). On the other hand, it may be argued that the very peculiar characteristics of the Russian tradition, which combined a peripheral position within the Western world with some attributes of a separate civilization and was shaped by a historical experience that further enhanced both aspects, were conducive to the equally distinctive mixture of a refusal of Western modernity with a claim to outdo it on its own ground and to prefigure its future.

But this particular link between tradition and modernity calls for a more precise description: it is a case of imperial modernization. Among the traditional preconditions that can result in or contribute to distinctive patterns of modernity, imperial formations and imperial traditions stand out as most relevant to our present purpose. As we shall see, both the Russian origins of the Soviet model and some of its later adaptations to other environments can be linked to this context. At this point, however, it becomes more difficult to balance social theory with historical analysis. The most cursory glance at the historical record is enough to convince us of the importance of the imperial background, but the theoretical implications are less obvious and less easily fitted into received frameworks. In general, it must be said that both classical and contemporary approaches to modernization tend to minimize the specificity and significance of imperial formations. This is already characteristic of Max Weber's comparative analysis of civilizations, where the failure to compare different imperial traditions and trajectories is all the more striking because of the results achieved in other regards. In the work of later authors, the contrast between traditional and modern states has mostly overshadowed the more specific features of imperial states. But two recent reformulations of the problem may, despite the fundamental differences between the theoretical projects with which they are associated, help to pinpoint some central issues and relate them to the genealogy of the Soviet model.

Immanuel Wallerstein (1974) contrasts the modern capitalist world-system with pre-modern empires; the latter were, as he sees it, the most comprehensive and therefore most important – although by no means universal – form of social organization in the traditional world. He has not elaborated on the difference between empires and other traditional polities, but the implicit thrust of his argument is clear: it is the imperial form of integration that most effectively transcends the local and tribal contexts of social life, and it therefore exemplifies most clearly both the limits and the extent of the transformative potential of traditional societies. Its expansive dynamic prefigures that of the modern world-system, but on a weaker basis and within a more restricted horizon. Empires cannot, in other words, achieve the level of interdependence and the concentration of economic power that is characteristic of the capitalist world, and the development of the latter renders them irreversibly obsolete. This view of the modern transformation and its antecedents – centred on expansion, mechanisms of global control, and forms of the concentration of power – constitutes a radical revision of the traditional Marxist approach. By contrast, S.N. Eisenstadt's work on the social and political structures of empires (1992) confronts the Weberian legacy and questions some of its basic assumptions, especially with regard to the distinction between traditional and modern forms of domination. Eisenstadt's main concern is with 'historical bureaucratic empires', i.e. those who not only conquered extensive territories, but also had the socio-cultural resources to ensure long-term control over them. As a result of the broader scope of power, its institutional forms became more complex and innovative. The characteristics of traditional, charismatic and legal domination are combined in the imperial centre, and this mixture (which can of course vary from case to case) accentuates its separation from society and enhances its superior status. It also facilitates the growth of bureaucratic institutions. The most significant developments of pre-modern bureaucracy are thus related to the demands and dynamics of imperial rule; Weber's one-sided focus on patrimonialism obscured this connection and led him to underestimate the changes that could occur within a traditional framework. Similarly, the mobilizing capacity of the imperial centre with regard to social forces and resources sets it apart from more traditional states. It is, in other words, more autonomous and innovative, both on the level of symbolism and in the context of strategic action, than the over-generalized notion of the patrimonial state would lead us to expect. All in all, this analysis of imperial formations underlines their historicity and thus relativizes the difference between tradition and modernity: the empires in question are – to a varying extent – the vehicles of changes which in some ways prefigure the more radical trends of the modernizing process, although they remain tied to a traditional basis.

The two lines of argument converge in a far-reaching claim: imperial formations enhance and channel the historicity of traditional societies in a direction that has some affinities with the later breakthrough to modernity, but differs from it in other respects. If we want to take this suggestion further and spell out its implications for the problematic of modernity, it should first of all be linked to the post-functionalist debates and developments mentioned above. The imperial centre can be seen as a concentrated and at the same time transfigured expression of the self-transformative potential of society (Castoriadis, Touraine). Its capacity to transcend the pre-existent forms and boundaries of social life – i.e. its trans-functional dynamic – manifests itself on two interconnected levels: those of power and culture. Empires are born of conquest; they are, in other words, the result of the absorption of more or less developed state systems by a new political centre.[1] But the power that is thus accumulated and concentrated needs a cultural interpretation, and the varying forms of the latter lead – in conjunction with other factors – to the development of different imperial traditions. The most seminal cultural frameworks of imperial power were those that drew, directly or indirectly, on the 'axial revolutions', i.e. the civilizational breakthroughs that gave rise to philosophical traditions and universal religions. It depends on the particular characteristics of both sides – the cultural source and the power formation – how close and effective the connection can become, and the cultural interpretations which help to liberate power from traditional constraints can also impose limitations of another kind. Imperial centres can be more or less expansionist; they can also, in relation to the societies they control, be more or less interventionist; in general, however, their built-in visions of power involve a claim to external hegemony and internal supremacy. This imperial imaginary is a significant part of the imperial legacy and a major factor in its interaction with modernizing processes.

The relationship of imperial configurations of culture and power to the patterns of modernity calls for a comparative analysis: they are more or less compatible with the new forms of accumulation and their cultural context, more or less transferable to a new social and economic basis, and more or less adaptable to the new constellation of social forces and conflicts.

The concept of imperial modernization already presupposes a certain degree of compatibility and continuity. As used below, it refers to four interconnected aspects. In the first place, the structure and symbolism of the imperial centre is modified by the modernizing process; at the same time, the overall framework and direction of change is co-determined by imperial strategies and structures. This combination causes tensions and conflicts which reinforce the more general disintegrative potential of modernity, and it results in crises and collapses that differ from other types of modern revolutions. Finally, the persistence of the imperial syndrome is reflected in post-revolutionary developments as well as in the power structure which grows out of them. Neither the origins nor the later transformations of the totalitarian project can be understood without reference to this background.

A more systematic theory of imperial modernization would have to begin with a comparative analysis of imperial traditions. Such tasks are beyond the scope of this book, but a brief mention of two basic questions is essential to the following argument. On the one hand, the well-known difference between Western and Far Eastern patterns of imperial power has – as we shall see – some bearing on the respective roads to modernity and visions of revolutionary transformation. The fall of the Roman Empire is often contrasted with the survival of its Chinese counterpart; this is, however, only the most conspicuous part of a much more complex picture. It is not simply the exceptional continuity of its imperial tradition that is characteristic of the Far Eastern region. Rather, its history was shaped by the interactions and combination of two imperial traditions: the Chinese and the nomadic (Barfield 1989). The latter was, of course, derivative and more vulnerable to centrifugal trends, but nevertheless capable of playing an important and sometimes decisive role in the history which it shared with the former. As for the West, its imperial tradition did not come to an end with the collapse of the Roman Empire. Aspects of the imperial legacy were retained or reactivated in various ways; its later metamorphoses include the institutions of the Catholic Church and its 'papal monarchy', the intermittent attempts to revive a secular empire, and the rival imperial projects which emerged within the modern European state system. Modern imperialism in the more specific sense (i.e. the historical period marked by the division of the world between Western or Westernized powers and their self-destruction in two world wars) is another symptom of the same trend. Its rise and demise was obviously not unrelated to the development of the capitalist world economy, but neither strategic nor functional rationality is an adequate explanation; rather, the economic transformations opened up a new field for the imperial imaginary and its institutional offshoots. From this point of view we must relativize Wallerstein's distinction between empire and world-system. Within the modern constellation, imperial projects and structures interact with the mechanisms of an increasingly global economy, and their relative strength is subject to change.

On the other hand, the fragmented and intermittent afterlife of the empire in the core regions of the West can be compared with a peripheral zone where it left more lasting traces. Neither the transition from the Roman to the Byzantine Empire nor the relationship of the latter to its Russian and Ottoman successors can be described in terms of one unbroken imperial tradition, but the continuity was strong enough to affect the later history of the region. The rivalry of three Eastern European empires (Russian, Habsburg and Ottoman), their diverse modernizing efforts and their interaction with the European state system, are part of the broader context of Western modernity and deserve more theoretical interest than they have so far received (McNeill 1964). It was the combination of these particularly explosive processes of imperial modernization with the conflicts of the more advanced West which led to the catastrophe of 1914. And recent events have again underlined both contrasts and similarities between the three imperial formations. More specifically, the reappearance of national conflicts within the former Soviet Union has been compared to the aftermath of 1918 in the Habsburg and Ottoman territories. According to Ernest Gellner, who has developed this diagnosis on the basis of a theory of nationalism, both the main problem and the major obstacle to solving it remain the same: the modernizing process strengthens the demand for a national form of integration, and although the imperial centre is – in the long run – incapable of constructing a viable alternative, it could and did create a social environment that – because of its ethnic heterogeneity and underdeveloped political culture – was particularly resistant to the imperatives of the nation-state.

There is no denying the parallels between early and late twentieth-century problems in Eastern Europe. Yet the historical upheavals in between should not be dismissed as a sideshow or an aberration. The empire which was reconstructed after a total collapse and succeeded not only in containing its own centrifugal forces, but also in partly neutralizing the legacy of the other two centres, was not simply resisting history. What most strikingly set it apart from its rivals was, rather, the fact that its crisis gave rise to the most important counter-paradigm of modernity, i.e. the most challenging alternative articulation of the historical horizon that had been opened up by the rise of the West.[2]

Imperial modernization is a secondary but significant aspect of the overall modernizing process; whether it results in distinctive patterns of modernity depends on the historical background and context. In the two outstanding cases, Russia and China, the continuity of the imperial factor was both obscured and enhanced by social revolutions and radical ideologies which drew on oppositional currents within the Western tradition. The diverse sources and changing forms of this constellation will be further analysed in the following chapters. And since the Russian precedent had a decisive impact on the Chinese line of development, the discussion must start with a brief glance at Russian history. In particular, the interplay of empire and revolution must be analysed in connection with the long-term process of state formation and its socio-cultural underpinnings.

As noted above, the question of the Soviet counter-paradigm of modernity is closely linked to the problematic of differentiation and integration. To summarize in advance, the argument is that the most serious problems faced by a modernizing empire were related to new forms and dimensions of differentiation in the global as well as the domestic arena; the post-revolutionary rebuilding of the imperial centre went hand in hand with the development of a new and much more extreme form of integration, but the totalitarian logic of this model could – in the long run – neither absorb nor accommodate the plurality of socio-cultural spheres, and the result was a process of decomposition which ultimately led to the collapse of the centre and the fragmentation of its internal and external periphery. Although this prolonged process of imperial breakdown, reconstruction, fusion and fragmentation obviously limits the autonomy of social actors and the scope of social conflicts, the latter aspect cannot be left out of the picture. It was a social revolution that destroyed the old order and paved the way for the Soviet model. But the forces that mobilized for collective action, their ways of pursuing their goals and articulating their interests, had been shaped by pre-revolutionary developments. The impact of the modernizing imperial order was in this respect double-edged: it both weakened and polarized the main social actors. This explains their self-defeating strategies and mutually destructive conflicts, as well as the rapid transition to a new phase and form of imperial modernization. Once again, the dynamic of power structures prevailed over the dialectic of social actors; the social revolution was absorbed by the imperial context. On the other hand, the terminal crisis of the Soviet regime is to some extent reminiscent of its beginnings. The liberation of society from a repressive state opens up new perspectives for social actors that are badly equipped to take advantage of them. Needless to say, neither the overall contours of the post-Soviet social field nor the nature of its main components can be explained in terms of a return to the pre-revolutionary constellation. But the affinities are obvious enough to call for a more sustained comparison and to cast doubt on the more optimistic visions of the future.

Chapter 2

Sources and components

To locate the Soviet model within the context of modernity – as I tried to do in Chapter 1 – is to emphasize the complexity and heterogeneity of its background. It should, in other words, be viewed as the result of a convergence of different historical processes and a fusion of diverse cultural components. At first sight, it may seem unnecessary to insist on this point; the main sources of the Soviet syndrome are well known and their respective inputs have been examined from various angles. Many authors have stressed the importance of the Russian legacy, distinguished between its imperial and revolutionary aspects, and tried to understand the particular combination of the two traditions that prevailed after the cataclysm of 1917. As for the modernizing role of the Soviet regime, some approaches focus on the general constraints and imperatives of modernization as such, while others draw attention to the particular situation of a latecomer confronted with more advanced Western societies (Trotsky's concept of 'combined development', originally developed in relation to Tsarist Russia but applied to its Soviet sequel by some of his disciples, and Gerschenkron's analysis of the 'advantages of backwardness' are classic examples of this line of argument), or the specific problems of a state simultaneously committed to a strategy of forced industrialization and a quest for global hegemony. Finally, the search for socialist ancestors and antecedents of the Soviet dictatorship has also raised a wide range of questions, some of them related to central themes or constant characteristics of modern revolutionary thought, others more directly to Russian Marxism and its mutation into Bolshevism.

But if it is easy to recognize the variety of historical sources and to identify the main ones, it is more difficult to explain how they interacted and to do so without unduly privileging some factors at the expense of others or collapsing them all into a systemic logic that neutralizes their diversity. Both these tendencies have frequently prevailed in critical analyses of the Soviet Union and other communist regimes. On the one hand, the Soviet model has been treated as the logical continuation or culmination of one dominant component. Its totalitarian features, i.e. its most extreme and distinctive characteristics, have been explained as the result of the development of Russian institutions, rather than any Western or more generally modern ideas (Richard Pipes is perhaps the most representative advocate of this view); as the expression of a pure logic of industrial modernity, separated from its original capitalist context (the decisive development may, in this view, be a generalization of the 'despotism of the factory', as analysed by Marx, or an unrestricted and unmitigated application of functional principles of organization); or, finally, as an inevitable outcome of the revolutionary socialist project, at least in its Leninist version. On the other hand, some of the otherwise most insightful interpretations have assumed that the primary task is to reconstruct a systemic logic which supposedly justifies the description of the Soviet model as a distinctive, coherent and self-reproducing type of modern society. The question of its historical origins and preconditions can then be treated as a separate issue. The emergence of Soviet-type societies in countries with different cultural traditions and social structures made this point of view seem more plausible: as the model spread more widely, its essential features and internal logic could be expected to stand out more clearly in contrast to the more variable conditions and circumstances of the transition. For historical analysis, the original sources mentioned above were still crucially important, but they were – more or less clearly – distinguished from the constituent parts of the system.

If the proliferation of Soviet-type regimes – or at least Soviet techniques of power – during the 1970s lent support to the systemic approach, the crisis and collapse of the Soviet model at the end of the 1980s should raise doubts about it. Earlier assumptions about coherence and reproducibility will now have to be re-examined. By the same token, the diverse and disparate forces that gave rise to the Soviet form of society now seem more relevant to its later history. The following analysis should be read as an attempt to develop a pluralistic genealogy of the Soviet model, and some theoretical implications of this procedure should be noted at the outset. We must, in the first place, reject the idea of a *systemic project*. The Soviet model cannot be analysed in terms of the realization of a pre-existent project; this is not to deny that there was a revolutionary project, but neither its explicit aims nor its latent logic can be regarded as a key to the whole post-revolutionary constellation. Rather, the project interacted with other sources and components, and was transformed in the process. The diversity of the origins is reflected in an internal heterogeneity of the pattern, and for this reason, the relative coherence of the latter cannot be reduced to a self-enclosed *systemic logic*. But if the historical sources re-emerge as structural components, this does not mean that we can no longer distinguish between a historical and a structural analysis. The components were, as we shall see in Chapter 2, refashioned by the new context. The pattern transcends the process which gave birth to it; it is, in other words, distinctive and stable enough to constitute a model. But the diffusion of the latter beyond its original environment does not lead to a *systemic identity* of the societies in question. The built-in tensions and fractures of the Soviet model reappear in new circumstances, and are further compounded by the problematic relationship to other socio-cultural contexts. The main pattern can perhaps be described as an alternation of attempts to reproduce the Soviet model in identical or even more extreme forms and innovative but not *eo ipso* adaptive modifications. Finally, this perspective entails reservations about the applicability of concepts of *systemic crisis*. As I will argue in Chapter 4, the unexpectedly rapid decomposition of the Soviet model is easier to understand if we accept that its systemic unity and rationality were always limited and fragile; more precisely, they were superimposed on a constellation whose disintegrative potential has now been reactivated by new external pressures. From this point of view, the crisis is doubly external to the system (the latter category can only refer to surface structures), rather than primarily internal in the sense of an exhausted developmental potential or a failing ability to contain endogenous conflicts.

In view of the composite character of Soviet-type societies, highly pronounced in the original case and further accentuated in some later versions, the concept of a 'syncretic society' (Casals 1980) seems appropriate, although it was initially used in a more limited sense. If it is more explicitly distinguished from the Marxist notion of a 'transitional society' and thus cleared of evolutionary connotations, we can adapt it to the present frame of reference and use it to describe a new historical constellation: a heterogeneous mixture, concealed behind a systematically enforced but structurally fragile unity. This perspective goes beyond general objections to systemic models of the social field. 'Syncretic society' in the sense suggested above is not simply a manifestation of the irreducible complexity of social life; it involves – as I will try to show – a changing balance of fusion and fragmentation and a mutual intensification of the two aspects. The obverse of its incomplete integration is the built-in possibility of excessive and unbalanced developments which impose the logic of one component upon the others. In the case of the Soviet experience, two ruptures of this kind stand out with particular clarity. In the first phase, the decisive impetus came from a cultural force, more precisely a utopian project which combined traditional and modern, imperial and revolutionary elements. Subsequently, the centre of gravity shifted from culture to power, but the dynamic of the power structure that developed into an extreme form of totalitarianism cannot be understood without reference to the cultural background. The history of the Soviet Union, then, is not simply that of a utopia in power; rather, a utopia with a specific and complex relationship to power is progressively reduced to a more subordinate role within a power apparatus, but not without having a lasting effect on the latter. Finally, the post-Stalinist 'normalized' phase is characterized by the exhaustion of both cultural and political dynamics, but the stabilizing trends and mechanisms have a long-term undermining effect.

To sum up, the genealogical reconstruction should serve to lay the groundwork for a structural analysis without a system-theoretical bias. Our main concern will be with the interaction of the three formative factors mentioned above: the Russian legacy, the challenge from the West, and the revolutionary tradition. This return to the sources is not an attempt to reduce the Soviet model to an episode in Russian history. Rather, the aim is to explain the subsequent global consolidation and diffusion of the model in the light of the original constellation of universal and particular elements. And if the exploration of this background begins with a brief discussion of the Russian state and its trajectory, there is no suggestion of collapsing all other factors into the long-term dynamic of state formation; the point is, on the contrary, that the imperial dimension of a state-building process, together with the universalizing potential of a tradition, became the foundation of the historical synthesis that we are trying to understand.

STATE FORMATION AND STATE TRADITION

There is general agreement on the importance of the Russian tradition as a source of the Soviet model, but no consensus on the details of the connection. We can distinguish several divergent (not always mutually exclusive) views on the most significant parts or phases of the tradition, as well as on the overall character of its relationship to the Soviet experience.

For those who emphasize the Byzantine background to Russian and

Soviet history, the tradition of caesaropapism – or, in more general terms, the fusion of the sacred and the state – is the most obvious symptom of continuity. The concept of caesaropapism would seem to be an oversimplification of the original Byzantine pattern, where there were more tensions between sacred and secular authority than the concept suggests (Ducellier 1988), but it may well be more applicable to the Russian offshoot of Byzantine civilization. The coalescence of secular and sacred power can, however, also be seen as a particular case of a more general trend. Berdyaev (1948) singled out the transfer of religious attitudes and energies to non-religious objects and purposes as a particularly characteristic trait of the culture which Russia had developed on a Byzantine basis; in his view, the Russian revolutionary tradition and the post-revolutionary Bolshevik regime were still drawing on this heritage. The contrast with the Western pattern of a more effective separation of the secular from the sacred and a more far-reaching rationalization of the secular sphere was evident. But the difference between Western and Russian traditions appears much greater when the Mongol conquest is seen as the main landmark in Russian history. Tibor Szamuely's (1974) claim that Russia was conquered twice – by the Mongol army and by the Mongol idea of the state – is perhaps the most extreme version of this thesis: the main implication is that the destruction of Kievan Russia did not mean simply a regression to more primitive conditions, but also a lasting separation from the Occidental world and an assimilation to Oriental patterns of culture and power. The Mongol version of the latter thus became the remote ancestor of post-revolutionary totalitarianism. In this version of Russian history, the Muscovite state figures as the most important transmitter of Mongol influences, but even those who stress its imitative and dependent relationship to the conquerors have to admit that its formation was a more sustained long-term process with more stable results than anything achieved by the Mongols. With or without an Oriental pedigree, the Muscovite regime – described by some historians as an extreme version of the patrimonial state, by others as a garrison state based on forced labour – plays a crucial role in all debates about structural constants and developmental continuities in Russian history. Its successor state is, by contrast, often cast in the role of a pioneer of radical change. Peter the Great's revolution from above has been widely regarded as the source – or at least one of the sources – of images of revolutionary transformation before 1917 as well as the modernizing strategies implemented after 1929. Finally, no genealogy of the Soviet model can ignore the more specific legacy of the Russian revolutionary tradition, which emerged in response to the later events: on the one hand, a populist image of society, on the other, an elitist and potentially despotic conception of revolutionary leadership. Their joint effect was the separation of the revolutionary vision from democratic ideas and institutions.

With regard to the question of the overall relationship between Russian past and Soviet present, we can distinguish at least three different perspectives, and further variations are possible within each of them. The first insists on a *structural continuity* between the Soviet model and the pre-revolutionary Russian state. For example, Richard Pipes argues that the bureaucratic police state, which took shape (on the basis of the Muscovite legacy) in Russia towards the end the nineteenth century, was taken over by the Bolsheviks and became the core of the Soviet system. Richard Hellie's (1977, 1982) account of three successive forms of the 'service state' (Muscovite, Petrine and Stalinist), each marked by a revolutionary transformation of the service class, lays even greater stress on the permanence of the Muscovite pattern. But the structural similarity between imperial and Stalinist Russia can also be seen as the result of a restoration or re-traditionalization. According to Robert Tucker's interpretation of Soviet history, a brief but significant interlude of breakdown and innovation was followed by the resurgence of a traditional pattern that was both more archaic and more revolutionary than the regime which collapsed in 1917: a revolution from above which re-established total control of the state over society. The re-traditionalizing turn is based on an internalization of the past, rather than a controlled and strategic use of its legacy, and in this context, the self-defeating excesses of Stalin's offensive against Soviet society are no less significant than its more realistic goals.

From the second point of view, the connection between the Soviet model and the Russian tradition is primarily *instrumental*. The internal logic of the new regime determines its relationship to the past; more specifically, the needs and problems of the former can lead to a selective revival of some aspects of the past and to the suppression of others. On this assumption, it seems easier to account for the variety of traditional factors: if the problem has to do with reactivated resources, rather than formative influences, it goes without saying that the strategies of reactivation can shift from one epoch to another and lead to artificial combinations. This view is compatible with different opinions on the nature of the Soviet regime. For Alain Besançon (1980: 103–33), post-revolutionary totalitarianism is the embodiment of a radical utopia, immunized against reality and unlimited in its ambitions, and it is precisely the global break with the past that makes the partial and inauthentic returns possible. In particular, institutions and images of absolute power can be absorbed by the totalitarian utopia, whereas other aspects of Russian history have to be minimized or misrepresented. But an analysis which focuses on the social structures of the party-state, rather than its ideology, can lead to similar conclusions with regard to the traditional background. The eclectic and instrumental mobilization of traditions – both official and subversive – then appears as a response to the deepening legitimation crisis of a system which has exhausted its own ideological resources.

There is a third perspective, more sensitive to the complexity of historical processes than the two others; it emphasizes the *synthesizing* relationship of the Soviet model to its traditional sources. More specifically, the decisive development seems to be the fusion of an imperial and a revolutionary tradition. If the Soviet model is the outcome of a genuine synthesis of their contents, the instrumentalist account of their separate and joint roles is obviously misguided; and since the combination must be regarded as an emergent structure, there can be no unbroken continuity with one of its sources. Advocates of this view have mostly seen the victory of Bolshevism as the completion of the synthesis, but agreement on this point is not always based on the same interpretation of the phenomenon in question. For Berdyaev, the main achievement of Bolshevism was to bring together the imperial aspirations of the Russian state and the secularized Messianism of the intelligentsia, whereas Szamuely's more recent variation on the same theme suggests a more material connection: the two traditions converge in the vision of a state-directed and state-centred modernization which excludes the development of democratic institutions.

The following discussion will be in line with the third approach, rather than the first two. Some major qualifications should, however, be noted: the fusion of the two traditions was a more complex and context-bound process than earlier interpretations would lead us to think; it took longer, its course seems less predetermined, and the result is more problematic. But before going on to substantiate these claims, some more general questions about tradition, modernity and their interconnections must be raised. Arguments about the presence of the Russian past within the Soviet model touch upon some central problems of social theory, and a more explicit reference to this context may help to clarify the issues. After a brief detour through basic concepts, I will then try to link the theoretical analysis to the interpretation of Russian history, beginning with the epoch that has gradually come to be regarded as its most formative phase. Although the search for absolute beginnings is as misguided as the construction of unchanging patterns, some starting-points are more revealing and some legacies more enduring than others; in this case, the formation of the Muscovite state throws light on its antecedents as well as on later ruptures, and thus on the whole background to the polarization and synthesis of the two traditions.

The very idea of a constitutive relationship between tradition and modernity runs counter to two widespread preconceptions. It is, in other words, not only alien to those who stress the novelty and universality of modern principles and thus minimize their links to particular traditions; it is also incompatible with the evolutionary interpretation of modernity as the culmination of a global and long-term process determined by transcultural universals. But the emphasis on specific traditions should not be mistaken for a narrowly culturalist approach. We can distinguish two aspects of the relationship in question: the continuity of traditions and their formative influence on modernizing processes has to do with the developmental patterns of both power and culture. Pioneering explorations of both themes are part and parcel of the classical legacy. Tocqueville's analysis of the *ancien régime* and the French Revolution showed that the revolutionaries were continuing a process of state-building that had been initiated by the monarchy; the continuity of power structures and their built-in tendencies was less visible, but arguably more fundamental than the conflict between traditional and modern principles of legitimacy. Max Weber's search for the cultural sources of the capitalist revolution led him to focus on the long-term logic of specific traditions and its impact on the 'fateful force' that had brought about a radical transformation of economic and social life. In both cases, an interpretation which starts with the problematic of power or culture remains sensitive to the other aspect. For Tocqueville, the prehistory of the revolution includes the formation of certain political attitudes and ideas, most importantly those of the eighteenth-century Enlightenment. His account of the latter can, in retrospect, be read as a reconstruction of an emergent political culture. Max Weber became increasingly aware of the rationalization (i.e., first and foremost, bureaucratization) of the state as a major component of the process which paved the way for modern capitalism. But although he went on to explore the interconnections between culture and power in great detail and from many angles, the results fell far short of a systematic integration of the two problematics, and his reductionist definition of the general concept of tradition obscures its two-dimensional context.

There is a strong prima facie case for analysing the continuity of traditions in terms of the interaction of two components. Durable and developable power structures depend on the interpretive contexts which lend meaning, consistency and legitimacy to them. Conversely, power mechanisms are involved in the constitution and transmission of cultural models. If we want to go beyond these general considerations and deal with more concrete patterns of interdependence, it would seem appropriate to begin with the concept of *political culture*. But this highly controversial notion has not always been used or understood as a link between the problematics of culture and power, and much of the debate around it is irrelevant to our present purposes. Methodological disputes – most frequently concerned with the primacy of subjective orientations or observable behaviour – have often overshadowed the more substantive implications for social theory. Even when the theoretical context is taken more seriously, assimilation to pre-existing models may prevail over the innovative connotations of the concept. When the reference to political culture only serves to subsume the political sphere under a global concept of culture, or – from the opposite point of view – to describe cultural inputs into the political system, the analytical yield is strictly limited, and no fundamental questions are raised. The most challenging and promising conception of political culture begins with the analysis of cultural images and interpretations of power; in this view, power structures are co-determined by their cultural contexts, and the general concept of power must be defined in such a way that it is open to cultural variations.[1] The details of the argument depend on the underlying concept of culture. If we reject the reduction of culture to ideological or discursive formations, we can distinguish between two levels of the constitutive relationship between culture and power. Explicit definitions and justifications, more or less adaptable to ideological purposes, are superimposed on implicit and indeterminate perspectives that lend themselves to different and often conflicting interpretations; the latter level corresponds to the 'imaginary significations' which constitute – as Castoriadis has shown – the substratum and horizon of culture.

A distinctive political culture is – by definition – embedded in a tradition, and this connection has proved particularly relevant to the study of Soviet-type societies. Those who introduced the concept of political culture into this area used it to highlight the continuity and diversity of traditions, in contrast to the more uniform ideological and institutional aspects. A more explicit reference to basic concepts would, as suggested above, lend further support to this line of argument. If traditions can be treated as configurations of culture and power, different articulations of the relationship between the two components – in other words: different political cultures – are likely to be a key factor in the overall differentiation of traditions. But our approach has so far stressed the formative role of culture, and the intrinsic dynamics of power must also be taken into account. If we conceptualize power in terms of complex patterns in process, rather than elementary relations of social actors to other actors or to objects of control and transformation, it will be easier to account for its autonomy as well as its openness to cultural determination. The merits of the former strategy are most obvious in analyses of *state formation;* this problematic is, in an important sense, complementary to that of political culture, and both are – as I will try to show – particularly relevant to the Russian background.

Norbert Elias's seminal work on state formation in Western Europe is also the most useful guide to comparative studies and to the problems of a general theory. For our present purposes, two unequally developed aspects of his legacy should be noted. His most pioneering insights and most detailed analyses have to do with the dynamic of a long-term process which involves both the consolidation and the transformation of the state; at the same time, this process is located within a broader context, but Elias's discussion of the latter is more limited in scope and less attentive to some basic questions. In other words: the main emphasis is on the continuity of state formation, rather than its contextuality, and more recent work on this subject shows how difficult it is to balance the two points of view. For example, Anthony Giddens has tried to develop a more complex model of the relationships between the nation-state and other aspects of modernity, but in so doing, he downgrades the other side of state formation, i.e. the more protracted processes that preceded and paved the way for the emergence of the modern state.

For Elias, the process of state formation has a basic structure and an overall direction that remain constant over a long period of time; it can, more specifically, be described as an interplay of three fundamental trends or mechanisms. The first and most elementary is the mechanism of monopolization. The struggle for control over resources, including means of violence as well as the sources of wealth, leads to the formation of monopolies, and thus to the first step towards a separation of state from society. The second mechanism is the gradual transformation of private monopolies into public ones; Elias also describes it as the 'socialization' of the monopoly position. With the growing division of labour and differentiation of society, the monopolies become both more dependent on the social environment and more crucial to its reproduction, and this is reflected in new demands as well as new constraints on the exercise of power. The emergence of representative institutions and the expansion of administrative apparatuses can thus be seen as twin aspects of the same trend. Finally, Elias introduced the concept of the 'royal mechanism' to describe the role of the late medieval and early modern monarchy. On this view, the growing complexity of society and the conflicting interests of social forces strengthen the hand of the rulers; their monopoly on balancing and coordinating functions enables them to increase their power. Although the three mechanisms are interconnected, Elias's model also allows for tensions and changing balances between them. In particular, the massive but temporary predominance of the royal mechanism during the absolutist epoch overshadows the more gradual shift towards a functional democratization of the state.

Helmut Koenigsberger (1977) has reformulated Elias's theory in a way that makes it more sensitive to historical details. His main point is that the relationship between the second and the third mechanism is too variable and too dependent on historical circumstances to be subsumed under a general theory. The royal mechanism dominates the early modern phase of state formation, but it does not triumph everywhere in the same way to the same extent, and although the socializing trend is kept within bounds and in some respects reversed, it is still strong enough to function as a counterweight. The balance between the two aspects of the process, reflected in the relationship between monarchs and parliaments, was not simply determined by the distribution of power within the society in question; it could also be affected by the intervention of external forces or by involvement in more global conflicts, such as the religious struggles that were so characteristic of the epoch. Most importantly, however, Koenigsberger points out that early modern states in Western and Central Europe were in most cases – including the most important ones – composite states: different countries or regions, characterized by different traditions and institutional patterns, were united under the rule of one monarch. Under these circumstances, the 'royal mechanism' could only operate through a series of compromises with social forces, and the variety of such arrangements within each state made it more difficult to follow a coherent strategy of power accumulation.

This adjustment of Elias's original model throws some light on the other side of the problem: the contextual determinants of state formation. But if we want to define the latter in general terms, rather than dissolve them into historical conjunctures and contingencies, we can distinguish two main dimensions: the geopolitical and the socio-cultural one. Elias tends to reduce the former to an unchanging and universal model of interstate competition and thus to neglect the more specific features of the modern context. These include the particular characteristics of the European state system and the globalizing process initiated by (but not reducible to) European expansion as well as the imperial projects and structures which grew out of the interaction between the state system and its global environment. As to the second dimension, Elias links the dynamics of state formation to long-term economic and psychological processes (the commercialization of economic life and the civilization of behaviour), but has much less to say on the broader spectrum of social and cultural developments. A broader perspective would highlight the ambiguity of the whole process – not only the double-edged relationship of the emerging state to cultural currents and social forces that are at best partly adaptable to its imperatives, but also the tensions and conflicts between various interpretations of the socio-cultural background as such. From one point of view, the context of state formation appears as a 'world of nations', increasingly dominated by a new form of collective identity which reinforces some strategies of state-building but undermines others. Alternative accounts can focus on the development of civil society – the arena of self-determining and self-organizing social forces – as a counterweight to the state, on the division of society into classes and the impact of their conflict on the political centre, or on the constitution of a normative order that permits both the legitimation and the contestation of the state. The interpretive models have, in all four cases, grown out of historical constellations, entered into long-term historical processes, and become part of the ongoing self-constitution of society. Because of their close links to Western experiences and traditions, their applicability to other parts of the world cannot be taken for granted, and it is – as we shall see – particularly misleading to identify the general distinction between state and society with the much more specific constellation that sets civil society apart from – and to some extent against – the state.

To stress the importance of state formation is not to suggest that all other transformative processes are reducible or subordinate to it. But it is a key aspect of a more complex pattern, and a better understanding of its part in the transition to modernity has helped to overcome some entrenched misinterpretations. Its particularly decisive role in Russian history is a matter of common knowledge. It is a dominant theme in the work of pre-revolutionary Russian historians (Klyuchevsky, Platonov, Presniakov et al.) whose insights have yet to be integrated into the theory of state formation. Their explanations of the rise and growth of the Russian state differ in many respects, but they agree on some basic preconditions. On the one hand, a long-term colonizing process, involving migrations over a vast territory, had to be brought under control and coordinated with the strategies of the state. On the other hand, state-controlled colonization was in the long run inseparable from military expansion: the stronger the Russian state grew, the more preoccupied it was with war, and its strategic situation made it very difficult to distinguish between defence and conquest. The first thing to note is, in other words, a particularly close and constant connection between state formation and territorial expansion.

In comparison with the West, the state-building process takes off from a less developed basis and goes to more extreme lengths; in Elias's terms, it can perhaps be described as a more comprehensive monopolization of more limited resources. According to Presniakov (1978: 113), 'the political edifice of the tsardom of Muscovy was built on the autocratic rule of all human and material resources of the country'. If we read this as a summary of the grand strategy of the autocratic state, rather than a description of a finished product, there is no reason to disagree. But the goal was harder to achieve than earlier historians tended to think.

Klyuchevsky's well-known recapitulation of Russian history – 'the state swelled up, the people grew lean' – is widely regarded as applicable to both pre- and post-revolutionary stages on the Russian road to modernity. There is much to be said for this view. The successive projects of imperial modernization (from Peter the Great to Witte and Stolypin) transformed the Muscovite legacy, but some essential features of the relationship between state and society were left unchanged or even exacerbated. As for Stalin's revolution from above, it can – at least in part – be explained as an attempt to substitute traditional Russian methods of state control and state intervention for a revolutionary project that had come to a dead end. But the ascendancy of a strong state over a weak society is not the only way in which the past has been perpetuated. The most recent twist in the fortunes of the Soviet superstate should make us more aware of some of the problems it has inherited from its Muscovite and Petrine precursors. Hypertrophic growth has certainly been characteristic of state formation in Russia, but the other side – structural imbalances, cultural heterogeneity, and the fragility of a power structure that related to society through mechanisms of control rather than channels of communication – is no less relevant to the present discussion. Both the revolutionary break and the post-revolutionary realignment with the past reflect this peculiar combination of strengths and weaknesses.

Two essential premises of the following discussion should be noted. On the one hand, it will be taken for granted that historical research – both the work of the Russian pioneers mentioned above and the more recent contributions of Western scholars – has settled the first issue in comparative analysis: the structures of the Russian state, its developmental patterns, and its relationship to society differ significantly from its

Western and Central European counterparts. The Russian experience cannot be subsumed under a generalized model of absolutism. On the other hand, I assume that the implications of the contrast can only be understood in the light of the reinterpretation of the Western trajectory undertaken – but by no means completed – by Elias. More precisely, the analysis of state formation as an autonomous process is a major corrective to Marxist interpretations of the absolutist state as a by-product or surface effect of class struggle and capitalist development. If the state is always endowed with some autonomous power and some ability to control the social forces on which it also depends, and if the consolidation of the modern state is – as we have seen – inseparable from changes in its social context, the difference between Russia and the West cannot be explained in terms of an absolute primacy of either state or society.

The Muscovite epoch (from the early fourteenth to the late seventeenth century) was clearly the most crucial phase in the formation of the Russian state. This does not mean that older traditions and later innovations were of no importance. But the role of the former and the scope of the latter were to a great extent determined by the process which transformed a peripheral principality into the largest empire on earth. The Muscovite state channelled its traditional sources in a specific direction and limited the options of its modernizing successors. Its developmental pattern was, very roughly speaking, made up of four distinctive and interconnected aspects. An unusually sustained and successful strategy of territorial expansion was accompanied by the gradual concentration of power in the hands of an autocratic monarch (as Presniakov (1978) put it, the rise of Muscovy involved both the 'gathering of territories' and the 'gathering of power') and by two major social transformations: on the one hand the absorption of the aristocracy and the creation of a governmental service class whose privileges were more directly dependent on military and administrative functions, on the other hand the enserfment of the peasantry, perhaps more adequately described as the use of the norms of slavery to shape the institution of serfdom (Hellie 1982: 710–13). Elias's distinction between the three mechanisms of state formation is obviously applicable to this process, but their specific forms and combined effects differed from the West.

The Muscovite version of the first mechanism was a particularly extreme and comprehensive one. The service state developed the dual monopoly of taxation and violence into a 'total institution'; its two main requirements were military service and the payment of taxes, and the overall relationship between state and society was adapted to these purposes. This view of the pre-modern Russian state is not inconsistent with the fact that – as many historians have emphasized – its impact on the details and routines of social life was very limited. In more general terms, we can accept Giddens's claim that traditional states were (in contrast to the nation-state) characterized by a low level of administrative power and a strictly limited capability of intervention and surveillance, but this should not obscure the differences within the category of traditional states. As the comparison of Russian and Western trajectories shows, the analysis of state formation as a long-term process is more illuminating on this point than a purely typological approach: the cumulative results of the process may differ in terms of the overall distribution of power between state and society, without the predominance of the former translating into mechanisms of direct control or projects of wholesale transformation (such developments are, as we shall see characteristic of later stages). The disproportionate strength of the state in contrast to society could lead to self-destructive excesses as well as to more constructive interventions, and the ultimate outcome depended on the broader historical context. It seems plausible to describe the policies of Ivan the Terrible and Peter the Great as model cases of the two alternatives, rather than rationalizing the former into an unsuccessful precursor of the latter.

Similar things can be said about the Muscovite autocracy as a distinctive form of the royal mechanism. Attempts to treat it as merely a variant of European absolutism are unconvincing; as more careful analyses have shown, it differed from its Western counterpart in that both the effective and the symbolic concentration of power was much greater. According to Elias, the function of the royal mechanism in the West was to hold the balance between antagonistic forces that were strong enough to block each other's pursuit of power, but lacked both the common ground and the internal unity to arrive at a social compromise on their own. This peculiar constellation strengthened the hand of the monarchs and at the same time limited their scope of action. By contrast, the Muscovite autocracy was much less subject to such limitations (there was no comparable interplay of social forces) and much more strongly rooted in the need to centralize the 'gathering' of territory and power. Moreover, the sovereignty of absolutist rulers in the West was limited by traditions and currents that had no parallel in the Russian context. In a literal sense, the notion of absolutism seems more applicable to the Muscovite model than to the Western regimes with which it is normally associated; as one historian puts it, the former might be described as an 'absolutism from the outset', unaffected by the legacy of Roman law and the struggle against the estates (Torke 1974: 285–6). Such comparisons, however, go beyond the level of power structures and raise questions about political culture; before we move further in that direction, a few words should be said about the second mechanism of state formation – the socialization of the monopolistic centre – and its role in the Russian context.

It seems obvious that the excessive development of the first and the third mechanism, as described above, blocked the development of the second. But if we follow Elias's analysis, the socializing mechanism – i.e. the integration of the power monopoly into a broader and more balanced social figuration – operates on two levels, and the distinctive characteristics of the Muscovite regime affected each of them in a specific way. The socialization of the power centre is, firstly and most obviously, the result of a more complex division of labour. As Elias puts it, the monopoly which grows out of a multi-centred struggle for power resources gradually becomes the 'highest organ of coordination and regulation', and this adaptation to socio-economic imperatives paves the way for later progress towards democratization. In the Muscovite case, this aspect of the socializing process was much less significant than in the West; the formation of the state was a more autonomous process and its internal dynamics overshadowed those of economic development and social differentiation. The other level presents a more complex problem. As Elias shows, the second mechanism functions not only on its own, but also behind and within the third; a socializing effect is, to put it another way, inherent in the very institutionalization of the royal mechanism. The power of the monarchs was limited both by the structures of the bureaucratic apparatus on which they had to rely and those of the court society which grew up around it. The apparent monopolization of power by an absolute centre thus masks its diffusion within a narrowly circumscribed but nevertheless conflict-ridden figuration. In line with this argument (although without reference to it), some recent interpretations of Muscovite Russia have questioned the traditional image of autocracy and sometimes even dismissed it as a 'façade' behind which an aristocratic élite could engage in factional struggle. Given the affinities between pre- and post-revolutionary Russia, it is not surprising that similar questions have been raised about the Stalinist regime. In both cases, legitimate doubts can lead to absurd conclusions (attempts to prove that Ivan the Terrible was a nonentity are about as convincing as the claim that Stalin was not the architect of the great purge), and if the question is to be formulated in a less misleading way, some preliminary clarifications are needed. Discussions about the illusions and realities of autocracy often suffer from a conflation of different issues; there are at least three sets of conceptual distinctions that should be clearly separated.

It is no doubt true that the claims of autocracy cannot be taken at face value (Keenan 1986); we must therefore distinguish between the symbolic representation and the effective exercise of power. This does not mean that the symbolism of autocracy can be reduced to an illusion or a façade. The symbolic transfiguration of the power centre misrepresents its *modus operandi* and obscures its dependence on a broader figuration, but it also becomes a power resource in its own right and helps to control or minimize the inevitable delegation, diffusion and usurpation of power. At the same time, the symbolic status of the ruler makes the difference between the institutional and the individual aspects of autocracy less visible. This second dichotomy corresponds roughly to Elias's distinction between 'dynamics of position' and 'dynamics of individuality'; the main point is that although the institutionalization of the royal mechanism (or, in Elias's terms, the stabilization of the figuration which centres on it) makes it less dependent on individual characteristics and abilities of the rulers, there is no automatic accord between the institution and the individual in which it is embodied, and individual deviations can affect the functioning of the institution in both positive and negative ways. With regard to the institutions of the Muscovite autocracy, even revisionist historians admit its ability to neutralize the forces which Elias associates with the second mechanism. For example, Keenan emphasizes the unusually strict separation of political power and administrative position (or, in Elias's terms, court society and bureaucracy) as well as the organization of intra-aristocratic conflicts around clans and client groups that were in no sense representative of social or political alternatives. If the same authors have nevertheless tried to cast doubt on the traditional view, this seems to reflect their particular interest in the background dynamics that became more visible when the centre was weakened; oligarchic ambitions and factional struggles were always a part of the picture, but although their scope expanded under exceptionally weak rulers or during dynastic crises, such shifts in the balance could still be contained within the institutional limits of autocracy.

A closer examination of the relationship between institutional and individual aspects of autocracy leads to a further distinction on the institutional side: between the functional role of autocracy on one hand and its latent dysfunctionality as well as its transformative potential on the other. The autocratic centre was the core of a power apparatus and the mainstay of state control over society, but at the same time, its disproportionate strength could become a threat to the stability and self-reproduction of the traditional order; it could also be mobilized for the purposes of a revolution from above and a correspondingly radical reconstitution of the power élite. This structural lability, due to the very factors which had most effectively furthered the growth of the Muscovite state, was also a built-in opportunity for individual experiments with the possibilities of autocracy. As suggested above, the contrast between Ivan the Terrible and Peter the Great – i.e. between both their strategies and the results they achieved – exemplifies the different directions which such initiatives could take. But they were also the products of a specific political culture, and this dimension of the Muscovite world may be easier to grasp if we confront the above analysis with some more widespread views.

Elias's theory of state formation has so far not made an appreciable impact on interpretations of Russian history or comparisons with the West. It has implicit – and important – points of contact with some of the most pioneering historical research in this field, but the most influential theoretical approaches have drawn on other sources. Those who rely on the dichotomy of state and civil society tend to see the pre-revolutionary Russian regime as a highly autonomous but primarily coercive state, superimposed on an amorphous and underdeveloped civil society; Miliukov developed this idea partly in answer to and partly as a variation on the Marxian base–superstructure model (the development of the Russian state was not determined by economic structures or interests, but the hypertrophic state and the relatively unstructured economy conditioned each other), and Antonio Gramsci later adapted it to Western Marxism. More recent Western interpretations are often based on the model of the patrimonial state (the work of Richard Pipes is the most obvious case in point). The two perspectives are obviously not incompatible: patrimonial structures can be seen as obstacles to the development of civil society. But the implications and limitations of the latter viewpoint can only be understood in the light of its Weberian background.

To begin with, Weber discusses the patrimonial principle as one of the elementary forms of domination and defines it as a modified version of patriarchal power, characterized – in contrast to primordial patriarchy – by a more extensive delegation of power and distribution of resources. He then analyses in much greater detail the patrimonial organization of political power, i.e. the modelling of control over subjects and territories on the exercise of authority within the household. The move from domination in general to state structures in particular makes the latter appear as an extension of the former and glosses over the long-term processes of state formation. In keeping with this, Weber's analysis of patrimonial regimes is mostly comparative rather than historical. His later work on the origins of the modern state, however, marks a step forward: a far-reaching but temporary strengthening of patrimonial forces now appears as an episode in a much longer and more complex process. If we generalize this point of view and note that the application of patrimonial principles is always linked to state-building processes, the idea of a structural continuity between patriarchy and patrimonialism seems untenable. Rather, the patrimonial phenomenon should be seen as an attempt to impose an image of power, derived from familial and tribal contexts, on more complex structures with a dynamic of their own. It is, in other words, based on a cultural interpretation of power; moreover, the interpretive content is as elementary as it is adaptable, so that the patrimonial interpretation can function as a cultural infrastructure for more specific ones. This explains the broad spectrum of different regimes which Weber tries to subsume under the category of patrimonial domination. Some critics have argued that this sweeping use renders the concept virtually meaningless; if we relate it to the cultural interpretations of power, it can be defended as an incomplete but not irrelevant description. The more concrete formations to which it is applicable range from bureaucratic and paternalistic conceptions of a 'welfare state' to the institutionalization of total dependency, i.e. – in Weber's words – 'the view of the subject as existing for the ruler and the satisfaction of his needs'. Weber coined the concept of the 'leiturgic state' for the most highly developed political structures of the latter kind. The Muscovite service state was not one of his favourite examples, but there can be no doubt that it constitutes one of the most extreme cases within this category.

According to Weber, the developmental potential and direction of patrimonial regimes depends on constellations of power as well as on religious traditions. The above interpretation of patrimonialism links its variations more directly to political cultures, defined as distinctive patterns of the cultural interpretations of power. With regard to the Muscovite state, it can be shown that a very peculiar combination of such patterns was superimposed on the patrimonial model. It is therefore misleading to explain the history of pre-revolutionary Russia simply in terms of the progressive consolidation of the patrimonial state, followed by its 'partial dismantling' (Pipes). In pre-Mongol Russia, especially in the region which later became the core of the Muscovite state, social power was organized along patrimonial lines, but in a way that obstructed rather than favoured state-building. The patrimonial state was not an automatic outgrowth of patrimonial domination; for example, it was only after a long and difficult transition that the principle of 'political primogeniture' was established. For a decisive take-off of the state-building process, more favourable historical conditions and more specific cultural inputs were required.

As indicated above, state formation takes place in a twofold context: a geopolitical and a socio-cultural one. The political culture of the Muscovite state is best understood in terms of a very peculiar relationship between these two dimensions. The primacy of Moscow within the Russian state-system and the subsequent absorption of the latter into the Muscovite empire was the result of a long-drawn-out struggle with other states and proto-states, particularly Novgorod and Lithuania, both of which were closer to the cultural and institutional patterns of the West; but although their initial position was in many ways superior, this did not lead the rulers of Moscow to see them as models to be emulated. The Muscovite road to hegemony and imperial domination was much more directly and lastingly affected by two empires outside the Russian state-system proper, one of which was politically and militarily dominant but culturally too alien to become a consciously accepted model, whereas the other was too weak and distant to exercise any political control, but was still regarded as an indispensable guarantee of cultural identity and legitimacy. The next step should therefore be a brief discussion of Byzantine and Mongol influences on the rising Muscovite state.

The influence of the Byzantine legacy on Russian history – before and after 1917 – has often been overestimated. Toynbee's description of the totalitarian state as a Byzantine invention is perhaps the most extreme example. As Obolensky (1970) has shown, such views reflect a basic misconception: it is true that the entry of Kievan Russia into the Byzantine Commonwealth led to a more complete cultural trans-formation than did any later contacts with other civilizations, but it does not follow that this first encounter established a permanent pattern for all subsequent epochs of Russian history. If we follow Meyendorff's account (1981), the Byzantine connection seems less continuous and one-sided than some earlier historians assumed. During the formative phase of Muscovite history, the relationship to Byzantium was redefined, and this development should be seen against the background of significant changes on both sides. The Byzantine fusion of church and empire was open to different interpretations and compatible with various historical constellations; 'caesaropapism' was one of them, but neither the most natural nor the most legitimate. In the fourteenth century, the imperial component of the Byzantine model was less dominant than before (the empire had been restored on a weaker basis after a temporary collapse), and the authority of the church – enhanced by a vigorous monastic movement – was correspondingly more important for the unity of Byzantine civilization. On the Muscovite side, a highly original pattern of state formation was – as we have seen – creating the preconditions for a more genuinely autocratic rule than the Byzantine emperors had ever achieved. For both these reasons, the systematic use of cultural resources for political purposes was easier than before. Byzantine models of religious life and cultural creation helped to make the Muscovite state more attractive as a civilizational and political centre; at the same time, the symbolic connection with the Byzantine emperor and the partial transfer of his attributes to the Muscovite ruler gave a more distinctive content to the political culture of patrimonialism. This process was obviously double-edged: it can be described as an appropriation of and adaptation to a cultural model. But its limits were no less significant than its results, and they became more visible in connection with the new perspectives opened up by the destruction of the Byzantine empire. Given the record, the ambitions and the ideology of the Muscovite state, it is – as Meyendorff points out – a striking fact that no official *translatio imperii* took place. The heritage of the defunct empire remained a source of strength and legitimacy for the Muscovite rulers, but they did not try to construct an unbroken line of succession. As for the well-known idea of a 'third Rome', its significance was symptomatic rather than strategic; it was, in other words, a representative product of Muscovite political culture, but it should not be mistaken for an official ideology, and the same applies to the less influential attempt to revive Byzantine speculations about the difference between human and divine aspects of imperial authority. In brief, the absorption of the Byzantine imaginary by the Muscovite state was selective and inconclusive. This constellation was, however, more complex and less rationalized than Meyendorff's notion of a 'deliberate ideological self-limitation' suggests. Rather, it was the outcome of the interaction of an imperial and civilizational pattern with a process of state formation which was at the same time affected by another – and very different – pole of attraction.

The impact of the Mongol conquest on Russian history has been exaggerated even more than that of the Byzantine legacy. It was widely believed that the Mongols had cut Russia off from European civilization, disrupted the autonomous development of Russian society, and imposed an alien model of state-building. In the light of more recent historical research, such claims can no longer be taken seriously. The Mongol conquest was neither a terminal catastrophe nor a new beginning. If it still looms unjustifiably large in some readings of the Russian past, the underlying reasons have to do with the search for Oriental ancestors of the Soviet model, rather than with genuine problems of historical interpretation. This is not to deny that the Mongol conquest was a landmark in Russian history, but with regard to the Muscovite state and its development, it was only one of many formative factors, and its influence was limited and channelled by the others. It is now generally acknowledged that the Mongol control over the conquered Russian territories – and therefore also Mongol involvement in the rise of the Muscovite state – was less direct than earlier historians had assumed; in addition, the religious barrier between the two civilizations set limits to cultural influences. 'Because of the Orthodox Christian foundations of Christian society, Muscovite borrowing of Mongol political forms was significant but not wholesale, with profound but not permanent effects on Russian history' (Halperin 1987: 103). Contrary to Szamuely's claim that Russia was conquered by the Mongol idea of the state, selective borrowing of political forms became more important when the Muscovite state became more autonomous, and the institutional framework of the service state was far too stable and distinctive for it to have been modelled on the more ephemeral achievements of the Mongols. The 'political forms' that can be traced back to Mongol sources are of two kinds: they have to do with military and administrative techniques (including, in particular, Mongol methods of taxation) and with political culture. For our present purposes, the latter aspect is more important, and particularly so in relation to the institutionalized image of the ruler. As Cherniavsky (1970) has shown, the use of the term *tsar* (originally applied to the Byzantine emperor) to describe the Mongol overlord was double-edged: together with some other measures, it helped to de-dramatize the fact of conquest and minimize its cultural impact, but in a later phase, it facilitated the fusion of Mongol and Byzantine elements in the Muscovite model of autocracy. Their joint effect was a further strengthening of the autocratic centre with regard to the other mechanisms of state formation.

The double ancestry of Muscovite tsardom exemplifies a more general pattern. Neither the Byzantine nor the Mongol connection can explain the most distinctive forms and trends of Russian history; both sources were important, but only as ingredients of a changing combination within the new context of the Muscovite epoch. As noted above, Muscovite Russia was not a composite state (in Koenigsberger's terms), but it developed a composite political culture, and in a more fundamental sense, it was – or became – a composite civilization. There is, however, another aspect of the Mongol period that should not be overlooked. Halperin uses the concept of an 'ideology of silence' to describe cultural contacts across the ethno-religious frontier of medieval Christendom: ideas and techniques were borrowed from other civilizations, but because they were rooted in or associated with alien traditions, their origin could not be openly acknowledged. In this respect, Russian's relationship with the Mongols was comparable to some other developments on the margins of the Western world. What seems more exceptional is the application of the 'ideology of silence' to the later relationship with the West. As the Muscovite state grew stronger and developed a more ambitious foreign policy, contacts with the West became more important; if later historians have often underestimated this factor, that is largely due to the official self-misrepresentation of Muscovy as more isolated and autarkic than it really was. The 'ideology of silence' thus served to disguise the composite character of Muscovite civilization. The most drastic departure from this pattern began with the Petrine revolution (to be discussed below), but as the Stalinist experience was to show, the 'ideology of silence' could still be reactivated.

Our discussion of the Muscovite state and its place in Russian history would be incomplete without a brief treatment of an episode – more precisely: a sequence of excess, collapse and restoration – which has no parallel in the history of early modern states in the West. The first consolidation of the Muscovite state on an imperial scale was followed by the reign of Ivan the Terrible and then – after a brief intermezzo – by the 'time of troubles'. It can hardly be disputed that the latter was in large part the outcome of Ivan's policies, but the nature of the connection – and hence the evaluation of Ivan as a historical figure – has been one of the most controversial topics in Russian history. Earlier historians were often tempted to rationalize Ivan's behaviour and thus to fit it into a continuous and cumulative historical process. Both the nationalist and the Marxist versions of this argument are unconvincing (not to mention the Stalinist mixture of both). Imperial expansion was clearly one of Ivan's main aims, but there was no coherent project to back it up; and as far as domestic policy is concerned, the terror was too destructive and indiscriminate to be explained in terms of a strategy of state-building or an alliance with one class against another. More recent analyses reflect a growing agreement on this point and a corresponding emphasis on the pathological aspects of Ivan's rule.[2] It goes without saying that no psychological explanation can account for the institutional preconditions of pathological deviation on this scale. Presniakov's attempt to link the two levels is particularly suggestive; as he saw it, Ivan's unbalanced personality reflected the exceptional strains and imbalances inherent in the structure of the Muscovite state as well as in its relationship to society and in the tasks it had set itself in the international arena. In contrast to the more conventional notion of an institutional vacuum or breakdown that gave free rein to a pathological individual, we should, in other words, try to understand the latter as an embodiment of institutional tensions. The structural background was, of course, inseparable from a cultural context: as we have seen, the exorbitant strength – and therefore also the destructive potential – of the autocratic centre was grounded in a political culture which drew on both Byzantine and Mongol images of imperial rule. Moreover, it seems that Western influences on sixteenth-century Muscovy were strong enough to add a third component to its political culture. The description of Ivan the Terrible as a 'Renaissance prince' (Cherniavsky 1968) captures only one aspect of a very complex phenomenon, but there is no doubt that Renaissance rationalizations of tyranny, conquest and transgression had become part of his cultural environment.

This interpretation of Ivan the Terrible leads to a corresponding diagnosis of the crisis at the beginning of the seventeenth century: it was brought about by a self-destructive turn of the process of state formation. This is not to deny the importance of the social conflicts that broke out during the 'time of troubles'. They came close to tearing Muscovite society apart. But in the last instance, their course was determined and their impact limited by the very breakdown which made them possible: the rupture of the relationship between state and society. In Platonov's words, 'the apex of society had been battered by the Wrathful Tsar, while the base was running away by itself, unable to endure its own misfortunes' (1970: 40). The collapse of the political centre left the field to disorganized and disoriented social forces, strong enough to accelerate the process of decomposition but too thoroughly conditioned by the old order and damaged by its crisis to be able to transform it. The rebellion against the service state culminated in a 'shapeless revolt of the have-nots' (Avrich 1972: 45); its destructive force was as remarkable as the total absence of an alternative social project, and the combination of these two features was central to the image of a 'Russian revolt' which grew out of it and became an important but ambivalent part of the Russian tradition. Platonov describes the force which eventually defeated attacks from within and without and put an end to the crisis as an alliance of the middle classes (i.e. gentry and townspeople). In very general terms, this is hardly a matter of dispute, but the fundamental differences in the broader social context – and hence also the relative importance – of class struggles and class alliances in Russia and the West should not be overlooked. In the former case, the initiative of the most strategically situated classes, temporarily left on their own, could only lead to the reconstruction of a social and political order which minimized the chances of collective action. On the other hand, the intervention of social forces had been necessary to restore the autocratic power structure, and this experience was bound to affect the overall balance between state and society. The cause of the change is, however, more obvious than its precise meaning. Platonov's claim that it marked a decisive shift from the patrimonial state to the nation-state is the least convincing part of his analysis of the 'time of troubles', and as we have seen, the search for civil society in Russia (with or without particular reference to seventeenth-century developments) is misguided. To describe the social context of the Muscovite state, we need a concept that is more clearly separated from the Western connotations of autonomy, differentiation and pluralism. H.J. Torke's notion of the 'state-conditioned society', i.e. an institutional framework which reflects the systematic subordination of social life to the imperatives of state formation, would seem to meet this requirement. It also helps to avoid the misconception that the autocratic state as superimposed on an amorphous society. This view is often linked to the over-generalization of the concept of civil society: if a social formation deviated from the implicitly accepted norm, it could only be described in negative terms. But the society that survived the 'time of troubles' was obviously neither unstructured nor incapable of self-regeneration. The question is, rather, what kind of structural pattern prevailed and how it was related to the autocratic and imperial service state.

The re-institutionalization of the relationship between state and society after the 'time of troubles' was a remarkable achievement, but its innovative effects were modest and inconclusive. As the official reference to 'tsar and country' shows, supreme authority was no longer vested as exclusively in the person of the ruler as before, but this qualification of the patrimonial principle did not lead to a sharing of sovereignty with representative institutions. The grip of the service state on society was both more systematic and more fragile than it had been before the crisis: a rigid hierarchy was reinforced through a more elaborate legal framework and at the same time disturbed by more frequent revolts. At the same time, the ambiguous relationship to the West became more pronounced: while the rebuilding of the Muscovite state led to further expansion and more intensive contacts, it also strengthened the ideology of closure and self-sufficiency. Despite its growing involvement in the European world, seventeenth-century Muscovy thus became – or tried to become – more xenophobic and isolationistic than it had been in the fifteenth and sixteenth century. It was – even more than before – an essentially composite civilization, but incapable of recognizing itself as such.

In brief, the restoration of the Muscovite order added new tensions and imbalances to the more traditional ones and thus made the regime doubly vulnerable to a transformation from above. The stage was, in other words, set for the Petrine revolution and the transition from Muscovite to early modern Russia. It might be objected that many historians have questioned the revolutionary character and impact of Peter's reforms. Their case rests partly on the observation that contacts with and influences from the West had played a major role in Russian history long before Peter's reign, and that the development of a more stable and effective bureaucratic administration had been gathering momentum during the seventeenth century. They have also claimed that the scope of Peter's reforms was too narrow (i.e. essentially limited to the building of a stronger war machine) and his initiatives too disjointed to be described as a revolution from above. With regard to the first point, there is no doubt that both the domestic and the foreign policies of the Petrine era had a long prehistory, but it can still be argued that Peter's way of combining the internal and external aspects of his strategy – the rationalization of the Russian state and the opening to the West – amounted to a revolutionary turn. As Wittram (1964) and Raeff (1983) have shown, Peter's restructuring of the Muscovite state was guided by a cultural model imported from the West, more precisely the notion of the 'well-ordered police state', which had been most explicitly formulated and most effectively implemented in Central Europe. Peter's precursors had gone too far for him to be credited with breaking out of cultural autarchy or discovering the dimension of strategic rationality (these claims and other similar ones can be found in the more extreme interpretations of his role), but in his case the intercultural learning process led to a redefinition of the imperatives of state formation. The imperial scale of the state makes this achievement all the more noteworthy (the conventional distinction between Muscovite and imperial Russia is misleading – Muscovy had already absorbed the Russian state-system as well as its former Tatar metropolis, and thus become an empire). No other empire – prior to the twentieth century – ever underwent a transformation that owed so much to external sources. If we describe the Petrine revolution in these terms, we can also dispose of the second objection mentioned above. The external model was essential to Peter's project, but this does not mean that it was systematically applied from the outset. Peter's most intensive and comprehensive legislative work took place during his last years in power; its main motives, however, can be traced back to his first encounter with the West, and a complex learning process, conditioned and disturbed by other factors, was needed before the logic of the model could be mastered in practice. The primacy of the military reforms, due to the war which took up much of Peter's reign, did not ensure that the global strategy was effectively tailored to them. The picture that emerges from the most authoritative accounts is, rather, that of a wide-ranging reformist offensive which in some ways interfered with the conduct of the war, and a military mobilization which in some ways obstructed the course of reform.

If the implementation of a new model of state-building on an imperial scale was the most distinctive feature of Peter's strategy, its long-term consequences – intended and unintended – should be set against the background of the pre-existent service state. As Raeff's analysis shows, the original project of the well-ordered police state was double-edged, and both aspects differ from later connotations of the term; an attempt to expand the role of government in society was combined with a new emphasis on the mobilization of resources and the development of productive capacities. The new interpretation of the state and its tasks was, in other words, inseparable from the modern idea of progress and its impact on the self-understanding of man and society. In drawing on this source, 'Peter attempted to turn the imperial government into an agency for the direction and organization of a dynamic production-oriented society' (Raeff 1983: 204). On the other hand, the Western and Central European version of the early modern state drew support from a whole complex of social forces and institutions which had no parallel in Muscovite Russia. In the absence of backdrops and intermediaries, the intervention of the state in social life had to become much more external and unilateral than it had been in the original context. More importantly, the traditional patterns of Muscovite society were too intractable and the distance between its centre and its periphery too great for an unqualified application of the new model to be possible. The well-ordered police state did not replace the service state; rather, some fundamental principles of the former were grafted onto the most durable structures of the latter, and while this combination was flexible enough to allow for further changes, its built-in tensions and imbalances were reproduced in later phases of the modernizing process. If there was at least a potential conflict between the two fundamental goals of the well-ordered police state (a more interventionist state and a more dynamic society), its adaptation to the Russian environment thus gave rise to much more explosive contradictions.

The expansion and rationalization of the bureaucratic apparatus was the central plank in Peter's strategy. Other mechanisms of the state were adapted to the new role and growing weight of its bureaucratic component. As Klyuchevsky (1965) showed, both Peter's 'Table of Ranks' and his reforms of land tenure and taxation can be explained as attempts to apply the principle of service to the state in a more systematic fashion and thus to regulate the distribution of status, property and power. But if this rationalization of the infrastructures of the service state fitted the short-term purposes of the revolution from above, it had a more problematic effect on its long-term outcome. The adaptable part of the Muscovite legacy was inseparable from a social basis that was to prove a decisive obstacle to further civilizing and rationalizing projects. More specifically, the Petrine version of the modernizing process was accompanied by the expansion and aggravation of serfdom. As far as the *longue durée* of Muscovite history is concerned, there is no doubt that state formation set the course for class formation, rather than the other way round, but the patterns of the former were more amenable to change than those of the latter; although the revolution from above enhanced the autonomy of the state with regard to its strategic and cultural orientations, it was thus forced to perpetuate and consolidate a class structure that bore the stamp of an earlier epoch. The new and more interventionist policies of the state – with reference to Torke's terminology, the change might be described as an attempt to transform the state-conditioned society into a state-regulated one – thus increased the cultural distance between the rulers and the bulk of the population. Later modifications of the Petrine model ultimately led to the abolition of serfdom, but as we shall see, that did not solve the problem of the cultural divide.

The cultural alienation of the state from society explains much of the uncertainty and instability that were so characteristic of Russian politics for several decades after Peter's reign. But there was a more positive side to this development: the less 'organic' relationship of the state to its socio-cultural context made it easier for the former to vary its strategies and shift its priorities. At first sight, the overall result of these changes may seem to amount to little more than a loss of momentum and a drift towards catastrophe: 'What had developed as a dynamically active governmental power in the state-building process proved so strong as a static force later on that it could successfully block its own thorough transformation, as shown by its capacity to withstand the nationwide insurrectionary movement in 1905' (Tucker 1990: 23). While it is no doubt true that the most dynamic and innovative phase of state formation in Russia – the Petrine revolution – was also the prelude to a long-drawn-out process which reduced the capacity of the state to initiate social change and mobilize social forces, some other aspects of the picture should be noted. Even at its most static and repressive, i.e. during the reign of Nicholas I, the Petrine state was still capable of some constructive and modernizing efforts that laid the groundwork for later changes; the following reign began with a set of epoch-making reforms which led to an irreversible and ultimately uncontrollable transformation of Russian society; the subsequent retreat from political reform in the last decades of the nineteenth century did not prevent the bureaucracy from actively and successfully promoting economic modernization. And although the autocracy was in the end reduced to an inert force, the bureaucratic component of the regime could still respond to the challenge of 1905 with a new modernizing strategy, distinctive enough to impress and confound its adversaries, even if the structural obstacles were too massive for it to succeed. In brief, the later history of the Petrine state was characterized by intermittent and unbalanced interventions in a modernizing process which it could neither halt nor master, rather than by a consistent conservative strategy. Moreover, the changing strategies gave rise to images and projections that were also inherited by the post-revolutionary rebuilders of the Russian Empire.

If we follow the most convincing interpretations of Russian history, state formation and state-centred transformation – rather than social conflict – were the dominant aspects of both the Muscovite and the Petrine phases. No class analysis of the Russian state can account for its autonomy and transformative capacity. But the present line of argument also differs from those who try to reduce the whole process to changes in the balance between patrimonial state and civil society. As suggested above, Muscovite patrimonialism was only one component of a more complex picture, and although the concept of civil society is obviously inapplicable, this does not mean that the broader socio-cultural context of state formation was irrelevant, unstructured or immutable. The relationship between state and society was, in other words, too specific to be reduced to an underdeveloped or unbalanced version of the Western model. As for the Petrine epoch, its developmental pattern was far too complex and varied to be described as a 'partial demolition of the patrimonial state' and an incomplete emancipation of civil society (Pipes).[3] On one hand, the modernizing process enhanced the ability of the state to control and transform social life; some traditional mechanisms of control were discarded, but the underlying orientations could now be translated into more flexible instruments (thus, as Raeff et al. have argued, the abolition of the formal obligation to serve the state did not destroy the ethos or the organizational principles of the service state). On the other hand, the mobilization and articulation of social forces was – in the last instance – essential to the modernizing strategy of the state, and when this logic was effectively accepted (as it was, most importantly, after the defeat of Russia by the Western powers in 1855), it could give rise to developments that seemed to foreshadow the constitution of civil society in the Western sense. The failure to complete this mutation was due to structural flaws on both sides: the imperial centre was trying to redefine its relationship to society and at the same time to retain its absolute primacy, while the social actors in question were too marginal, too fragmented or too alienated from the state and its world. Both the defence of autocracy on the part of the rulers and the aspirations to autonomy on the part of society were thus undermined by internal contradictions, and it was this confrontation between two antagonistic but equally disjointed projects (or, more precisely, sets of projects), rather than an incomplete transfer of power from state to society, that set the stage for the subsequent upheaval.

To conclude this discussion of Peter the Great and his legacy, one further aspect should be noted. Rival visions of Russian history have focused on – and disagreed about – Peter's work and personality to such an extent that we can legitimately speak about a Petrine imaginary as their common denominator. As Riasanovsky (1982) shows, Russian representatives of both Enlightenment and Romanticism (including, in particular, the nineteenth-century Westernizers on one hand and the Slavophiles on the other) not only saw the Petrine revolution – for better or worse – as a watershed in Russian history, but also tended to transfigure its real achievements into mythical images of progress or destruction. Even those who otherwise diverged from the main currents of Russian thought remained within this frame of reference (Chaadayev's view of the Petrine reforms as Russia's first step towards civilization is the most obvious case in point). This analysis could be extended to include foreign perceptions and interpretations of Petrine Russia. For example, Marx's views on Russia were based on the belief that Peter had wholly transformed the Muscovite empire and shifted its strategies towards 'the abstract pursuit of power'. The implicit analogy with abstract wealth – a key concept in Marx's critique of capitalism – suggests an over-modernized image of Russia, but the discrepancy between the expansionist momentum of the Petrine empire and its internal fractures could easily give rise to such misconceptions.

According to Riasanovsky, the more rapid progress and more liberal form of Westernization after 1861 enabled Russian historians to take a more critical view of Peter's work, and thus also to relativize his role as a cultural symbol. The same trend prevailed within the revolutionary tradition; Lenin's strikingly limited interest in the Petrine question shows how far the change had gone by the end of the century. But the contrast between earlier and later phases can also serve to highlight the distinction between ideological discourses and their imaginary background: for revolutionary visions of Russian history, the Petrine thematic was no longer as central as before, but they remained dependent on the Petrine imaginary. This connection and its consequences will be discussed in the following section. The main point is, briefly, that the Petrine model of revolution from above prefigured a fusion of the state tradition which it had transformed and the revolutionary aspirations to a more radical change. In the Western context, the substitution of a revolution from above for the revolution from below (in other words, the shift from the revolutionary overthrow of the absolutist state to a social transformation guided by a post-revolutionary dictatorship) was, above all, envisaged by the Jacobin regime and the tradition that grew out of it. But this line of development was blocked by a whole complex of social and cultural forces. By contrast, Russian interpretations of the Jacobin project were reinforced by the Petrine legacy; on the level of political culture (as defined above), the connection between the two poles of the Russian tradition thus became much closer than between absolutism and its adversaries in the West, and it could still affect the underlying assumptions of those who no longer felt the need to define their projects with explicit reference to Peter the Great. This is not to say that the Petrine model was simply internalized by the revolutionary tradition. But the distinctive experience of a revolution from above on an imperial scale was, as we shall see, at the very least a major constraint on the imagination of those who tried to develop an alternative strategy.

REVOLUTIONARY IMAGINATION AND REVOLUTIONARY STRATEGY

The Soviet fusion of imperial and revolutionary projects was preceded by a modernizing process that brought about major changes on both sides. But to understand how the two poles of Russian culture and society interacted and developed during this phase, it is necessary to analyse their historical preconditions. The preceding section dealt with the long-term dynamics of state formation and empire-building. We must now briefly discuss the corresponding internal logic of the revolutionary tradition, its initial crystallization against the background of a particular version of the Petrine state, and its later transformations under the impact of new ideas from the West. A comparison of alternatives within this tradition is beyond the scope of this book; our main concern is with a current that managed to combine far-reaching ideological innovations with a reaffirmation and radicalization of the original cultural premises. That this ambiguity was ultimately to prove a strength rather than a weakness was, of course, the result of complex and contingent historical developments.

The Russian revolutionary tradition was, as is well known, created and transmitted by the intelligentsia, and the latter was originally a by-product of the Petrine revolution. From the social point of view, the history of the intelligentsia begins with the eighteenth-century transformation of the nobility (Raeff 1966); its cultural orientations reflected both the achievements and the imbalances of a revolution from above that had transformed the mentality of the élites more thoroughly than the structures of state and society. The intelligentsia could therefore give voice to demands for a more consistent Westernization as well as to protests against the destruction caused by an autocratic form of Westernization. A very peculiar pattern of socio-cultural differentiation thus took shape: the constitution of a revolutionary counter-culture in opposition to the imperial order was brought about by the abrupt but incomplete adaptation of the imperial centre to a Western model. It is this intercivilizational background that makes it impossible to reduce the Russian phenomenon of the intelligentsia to any general description of modern intellectuals and their relationship to the state. Even the more cautious comparison with later examples of intellectuals in under-developed countries is of very limited value: the Petrine empire was not a precursor of the Third World.

The intelligentsia was too specific to be described as a social stratum among others and too protean to be identified with a cultural model in contrast to others. A definition of the phenomenon should be flexible enough to do justice to the ambiguities, conflicts and conversions that were so characteristic of its history. Those who advocated further Westernization and those who drew on Western sources to defend Russian traditions or a Russian mission belonged to the same universe of discourse (the Slavophile variant of romanticism was, in other words, no less rooted in the experience of the intelligentsia than the Russian versions of Jacobinism). The revolutionary faith was a characteristic but not uncontested product of the intelligentsia; its political culture also included a recurrent critique of revolutionary illusions and a more or less articulate search for alternatives. The populist syndrome, often singled out as particularly significant, was open to conflicting interpretations: it combined 'deification with a marked condescension towards the object of idolatry' (Szamuely 1974: 155–6).

All these currents and countercurrents reflect the structurally ambiguous position of the intelligentsia, torn between Russia and Europe, between an imperial state and an overwhelmingly rural society, between a particularly conflict-ridden civilizing process and a correspondingly radical revolutionary utopia.

This background also explains why the Russian revolutionary tradition was not a self-enclosed subculture. Its links to the broader context of Russian thought made it more sensitive to historical experience and to the problematic of modernity than either the hagiographical or the hypercritical versions of its history would suggest. As for the official Soviet account, it had to serve a double purpose: to minimize the dependence of Bolshevism on the pre-Marxist heritage, so as to emphasize the originality of Lenin's achievement, and to neutralize the more critical legacy that could still pose a threat to the Bolshevik model. The case of Alexander Herzen, perhaps the most exemplary figure of the tradition, is particularly revealing. His belief in an essential affinity between socialism and the Russian people and his rejection of Western modernity became the foundation of a political culture which was – in the long run – enriched rather than transformed by the Marxian input, but the individualistic and democratic aspects of his thought open up other perspectives. Lenin's incorporation of Herzen into the pre-Marxist part of the revolutionary canon was thus both a way of disguising an unacknowledged continuity as progress and an attempt to impose clear boundaries on an ambiguous past.

Herzen's role was crucial from yet another point of view: under the regime of Nicholas I, the model of the well-ordered police state had been reduced to its most rigid and retrograde version (one which unequivocally put control before mobilization), and the response to this situation was built into the foundations of the revolutionary tradition. This is not to suggest that the later direction and final self-destruction of the revolutionary movement were predetermined by an earlier historical constellation. But it can be argued that a formative experience – the extreme alienation of a section of the intelligentsia from a state which had overdeveloped the most repressive aspect of a modernizing project – conditioned later developments. This applies to the reception and reinterpretation of Western ideas as well as to their translation into political strategies. The following discussion will deal briefly with three successive landmarks: the initial and underlying relationship between the Western revolutionary tradition and its Russian counterpart, the encounter with Marxism, and the emergence of Bolshevism as a subculture within the revolutionary tradition.

I will use the concept of a Western revolutionary tradition to refer to a complex of images and ideas which grew out of the French Revolution of 1789 and its aftermath. Its core element is a vision of rapid and radical political change as a privileged or even exclusive vehicle of progress, liberation and reconciliation. This common frame of reference can, however, be developed in different directions. The dissonances between the value-ideas of liberty, equality and fraternity raise questions to which there is no simple or definitive answer. The interaction with other forces generated or strengthened by the revolution, particularly those of nationalism and democracy, affects the content of the revolutionary project. Finally, the revolutionary tradition responds in various ways to the distinctively modern problems of differentiation and integration. For our present purposes, the most significant part of this story is the emergence of the Jacobin current during the most radical phase of the French Revolution. Although the Jacobin regime was too short-lived to develop into a complete paradigm, the logic of its policies was clear enough to constitute a source of inspiration and a set of guidelines for later phases of the tradition (Feher 1987). We can sum up the main trends of the Jacobin syndrome in relation to the three issues mentioned above. There is, first, an attempt to solve the problem of discordant value-ideas by simultaneously radicalizing all three and at the same time immunizing the political centre against their normative implications: a despotic and exclusive exercise of power was presented as a necessary detour on the road towards liberty, equality and fraternity. With regard to rival traditions, the Jacobin turn absolutizes the logic of the revolution, instead of subordinating it to those of the nation-state or democracy, which it claims to override in the name of a more universal goal. As for the third question, the original Jacobin regime was destroyed before it had made any lasting impact, but the de-differentiating thrust of its strategy is undeniable. The primacy of politics set limits to and called for control over the development of other spheres, most obviously the economic one.

The constitution of a Russian revolutionary tradition was, as we have seen, a logical outcome of the early phase of imperial modernization, but the concrete shape that it took can only be understood as a result of the appropriation – more precisely: the selective concretization and radicalization – of Western models. In nineteenth-century Russia, the much more massive presence of the state as an obstacle to the self-articulation and self- organization of society made revolution seem a more urgent task than in the West. There was, in other words, a shorter step from revolutionary imagination to revolutionary strategy. At the same time, those who took this direction could draw on – and had to confront – the experience of a revolution from above that had already been carried out by a modernizing empire-builder (Herzen referred to 'Petrograndism' as an unavoidable temptation for Russian radicals). As suggested above, these circumstances favoured a reception and a further development of Jacobinism: it seemed to offer a way of learning from the imperial precedent while putting it in its proper place and without blurring the vision of a more radical revolution to come. The long-term and logical outcome was the transfiguration of the revolutionary vanguard into a counter-state, programmed to destroy the existing one and carry out the tasks which it had left unfinished or failed to assume. But if the logic of the situation was thus conducive to a radicalization of Jacobinism, it also led to an exacerbation of its inbuilt problems. The revolutionary perspective was both more concrete and more abstract than in the West: it was more plausible to envisage revolution as an imminent and unavoidable rupture, but more difficult to link this expectation to visible and ascendant social forces. A substitute was found in the idea of the people as a collective and an inherently revolutionary subject. The populist turn was thus a complement rather than a counterweight to Russian Jacobinism, and a dialectic of vanguardism and populism, rather than a clear-cut conflict between them, is characteristic of the Russian revolutionary tradition. Both perspectives can be understood as interpretive articulations of the relationship between state and society; as noted above, the underlying structures differed in essential ways from those embodied in the Western notion of civil society, and the introduction of Western principles in some areas had enhanced the contrast in others.

It should be added that each of the two trends was open to internal division: the primary role of the revolutionary vanguard could be either a direct preparation for the seizure of power or a more future-oriented education and organization of the masses, and those who emphasized the autonomous action of the people could be interested in a destructive force to be mobilized against the existing order, or in the more constructive potential of supposedly popular institutions (such as the peasant commune). And it is not being suggested that all branches of this highly diverse tradition can be subsumed under a Jacobin paradigm. The point is, rather, that Jacobinism remained a strong and persistent pole of attraction, even when other options seemed to be gaining the upper hand, and that it played a key role in the genesis of Bolshevism. Recent work in this area has made it clearer than before that Peter Tkachev represents the most authentic expression of Russian Jacobinism. But for this very reason, those who wanted to temper or adjust the Jacobin stance without abandoning its essentials found it difficult to acknowledge their links to him.

The Jacobin legacy was to have a decisive influence on the fate of Russian Marxism. But the incorporation of Marxian elements into the Russian revolutionary tradition was a complex process, and to put it into a proper perspective, we must begin with a glance at the Western sources. What the Russian revolutionaries made of Marx's project can only be understood if we first place it in its own context and spell out the presuppositions that were more difficult to translate into a different theoretical and political language. To start with, the Marxist tradition should be distinguished from both revolutionary and socialist traditions. That the two last-mentioned were not synonymous is well known: for present purposes, the socialist tradition can be defined in the Durkheimian sense, i.e. as the search for ways of reintegrating an anomic economy into social life, and there were reformist versions of socialism as well as non-socialist readings of the revolutionary message. It is less generally understood that Marx's work and the Marxist tradition which grew out of a part of it (other parts remained unknown or unassimilated during the heyday of Marxist movements) cannot be fully subsumed under either of the two larger traditions. The Marxian project is best described as an attempt to rationalize the revolutionary tradition through a synthesis with elements of several other traditions, and the result was a transformation of socialist thought, but not a definitive transition from one type of socialism to another. Among the other traditions, German idealism stands out as the most directly formative; it was a self-critical turn within this current that first brought about the encounter with the revolutionary tradition. But more recent interpretations of Marx have also shown that his relationship to liberalism was more complicated than orthodox disciples or dismissive critics liked to admit. Marx's vision of history and society shares some basic premises with liberal thought, and this affinity has something to do with both the strengths and the weaknesses of his work. It is reflected in the emphasis on individual activity and development that accompanies his critique of more superficial forms of individualism, in the scientism that led him to tone down the philosophical aspects of his own arguments and adapt them to the positivist mainstream of the nineteenth century, and in the economic reductionism which vitiates his attempt to develop a critique of political economy. At the same time, Marx appropriated and reformulated the socialist critique of liberalism. His attitude to all those traditions was explicit and selective enough to make a general distinction between fallacies to be rejected and insights to be developed. With regard to the revolutionary tradition, its critique of power and property was to be separated from its negation of culture (Marx described the latter aspect as 'rude Communism'). The metaphysical illusions of idealism could be discarded without forgetting the results of its interest in the subjective side of social reality. The modern affirmation of human autonomy and creativity, associated with liberalism in the broadest sense (even if Marx did not use the term), became the starting-point for a critique of the restrictive and self-contradictory form which these values had taken in the theory and practice of bourgeois society. And a socialist programme that was supposedly based on a scientific knowledge of the 'laws of motion' of modern society could be opposed to the more particularistic or backward-looking versions of socialist thought.

These four sources and components of Marx's work are easy to distinguish, but some less visible ones could be added to the list. Marx drew heavily on a conception of history which had been developed by the Scottish Enlightenment (Millar, Ferguson et al.); he also owed something to the early modern republican tradition and its reading of antiquity. This is not the place for a more exhaustive reconstruction, and we do not need it for an overall assessment of Marx's role in the prehistory of Communism. His work is located at the crossroads – or one of the crossroads – of modern thought, rather than at the beginning or the end of one of its trajectories. The encounter with different traditions and the effort to bring them into closer contact fell far short of a genuine synthesis. In that sense, Marx's theory of history and modernity was an unfinished project – so thoroughly unfinished that some of his most important texts were abandoned before completion or put aside before publication, and thus did not become part of the official canon of the Marxist tradition. This open-ended and multi-dimensional character of Marx's work, ignored or minimized by his most influential disciples, explains the exceptional importance of his posthumously published writings: they opened up new perspectives, beyond and often against the dominant trends of the Marxist tradition, and thus made Marx's status as one of the major thinkers of the modern world less dependent on the political use of his ideas.

There is, however, another side of Marx's work that is relevant to its impact on Russian thought. If it did not develop into a fully-fledged synthesis of the many sources on which it drew, some latent or provisional linkages were needed to ensure the unity of the project. On the level of underlying images, in contrast to explicit theorizing, the pre-modern background to Marx's critique of capitalism has not gone unnoticed: as many analysts have argued, his elusive conception of the human condition and its future destiny cannot be understood without some reference to pre-capitalist forms of work and social life. Marx's theory was thus, to some extent, rooted in a communitarian imaginary which it could not fully comprehend. And if it was read from a Russian vantage point, the more archaic domestic background was bound to reinforce this connection. On a more visible but less fundamental level, Marx relied on conceptual shortcuts to defuse problems that he was unwilling or unable to tackle in a more systematic fashion. This applies, above all, to the well-known notions (they can hardly be described as concepts) of base and superstructure. They function as substitutes for a properly articulated model and serve to fill the gaps in a fragmentary image of society; their main joint implication is an a priori devaluation of culture and politics. The failure to develop a theory of these dimensions of social life thus becomes less disturbing, and the critical potential of further experience in both areas is neutralized. But in a different setting, where the demand for a complete and systematic theory was stronger, such stopgap notions could easily become guidelines for a more thorough-going reductionism.

The attraction of Marx and Marxism – there was, in this context, no relevant difference between the two – for the Russian revolutionary intelligentsia is easy to explain. Marxist theory opened up new perspectives for the rationalization of the revolutionary project. The interpretation of Russian society and the desire to change it could be linked to a more universal frame of reference. The Westernization of Russian thought took a new turn: a radical critique of Western society served to strengthen and legitimize the opposition to the Tsarist regime. In particular, Marx's critique of the capitalist mode of production and – by implication – the capitalist form of modernity could be invoked against the modernizing efforts and pretensions of the imperial centre. Because of their background, Marx's Russian readers were particularly receptive to an over-systemized image of capitalism, i.e. one that did not take its social embeddedness into account; in Russia, capitalism had from the outset been perceived as an external and at the same time totalizing force.

The reception of Marxism in Russia was based on a limited knowledge and understanding of Marx's work. Some crucial texts remained unknown even in the West, and the broader cultural context was less visible from the Russian angle. On the other hand, the demands and resources of the Russian environment led to further theorizing and thus to a new phase in the history of Marxism. We can, broadly speaking, distinguish two lines of development. One of them involved the incorporation of Marxian ideas into theoretical and political projects which also drew on other sources and tried to come to grips with the preconditions and prospects of Russia's distinctive road to modernity. Both Russian liberalism and the indigenous socialist tradition which came to be represented by the Party of Socialist Revolutionaries were influenced in this way. The liberals played a dominant role in 1905, and the SRs had the broadest support (but not the most strategic position) in 1917; the intellectual and political significance of both these currents has often been underestimated because of the subsequent triumph of Bolshevism. To dismiss the SRs as agrarian is no less unwarranted than to identify the liberals with the bourgeoisie. Their conflicting but partly convergent projects might have seemed likely to shape the future course of Russian history. In retrospect, it can be argued that their defeat was in the last instance due to the lack of a solid social basis and a coherent strategy, and that the apparent success of Lenin's party reflected its ability to turn the same weakness into a strength. The Bolshevik pursuit of power was so single-minded and at the same time flexible because it was relatively unconstrained by the identities and strategies of social actors. But the self-destructive character of the Bolshevik victory (doubly self-destructive in that it led to the liquidation of the revolutionary élite and the perversion of the revolutionary project) showed that in the long run this party was caught up in the same historical constellation as its more vulnerable rivals: the crisis of an imperial order that was too archaic to survive the conversion to modernity but too strongly entrenched to allow the development of a viable alternative.

The political subculture which inspired the Bolshevik response to this predicament was another offshoot of Russian Marxism. In contrast to the liberal or socialist assimilation of Marxian ideas, they could also serve a different purpose: to construct the image of an orthodoxy, i.e. a definitive and comprehensive system of beliefs that would consolidate the autonomy of the revolutionary tradition, reinterpret its history as an irreversible learning process, and ground its aspirations in a global vision of progress. This notion of orthodox Marxism went far beyond the dominant interpretations that were taking shape elsewhere in Europe at the same time, and if later historians have sometimes taken the Marxism of the Second International to be more committed to orthodoxy than it really was, this is largely because later events have made its Russian representatives – Plekhanov above all others – seem more significant than they were at the time. The construction of orthodoxy was, of course, based on a very arbitrary and unauthentic treatment of the raw material: a fragment of an imperfectly understood and intrinsically incomplete work was to be converted into a self-contained *Weltanschauung*, and this could not be done without tacit borrowings from other sources, both nineteenth-century European and more distinctively Russian ones. Notwithstanding its Russian flavour, the initial version of orthodoxy was much closer to classical Marxism and its Western background than was the model that eventually prevailed (Plekhanov was speaking as an orthodox Marxist when he complained that Lenin did not understand the historical role of bourgeois liberalism). But for present purposes, it is the later development that is more significant: an attempt to solve a fundamental and inescapable problem of Marxist orthodoxy in Russia by readjusting the balance between its Russian and Western components in such a way that both sides would become more adaptable to a new historical situation without losing their legitimizing potential.

The problem was the ambiguous impact of Marxian ideas about past, present and future history on the Russian revolutionary project. The Marxian connection gave the coming revolution a more universal content and at the same time seemed to shift it to a more distant future. Its legitimacy was grounded in a general logic of human history, but its possibility was conditional on a process of capitalist development that had yet to run its course. Marx's and Engels's own unorthodox reflections on Russia did not point to a solution – they were only another example of an ongoing study of history that could never be truly integrated into their more restrictive theory. Inasmuch as the Russian Marxists were committed to a particularly rigid version of the theory, they were thus left to their own devices. A comparative analysis of their solutions is not needed here; the only one that is directly relevant to our theme is the strategy formulated by Lenin and embodied in the Bolshevik branch of the revolutionary movement. In this regard, there are two main questions to be discussed: how was Lenin's interpretation of Marx linked to his reactivation of Russian Jacobinism, and to what extent did his early political thought prefigure the fusion of imperial and revolutionary traditions which was later to culminate in the Stalinist regime?

Lukács's well-known interpretation of Lenin can still help to clarify the first question, but only if we turn its main argument upside down. The 'actuality of the revolution' was, as Lukács claimed, the core of Lenin's thought and the fundamental premise which determined his approach to all theoretical and political problems. This does not mean that it was the decisive link between Lenin and Marx or the result of Lenin's having done for his time what Marx did for the capitalist epoch as a whole. Rather, the vision of revolution as an urgent task and an imminent upheaval was the most decisive part of Lenin's Russian inheritance, and together with its less explicit corollaries, it became the key to his understanding of Marx. The 'actuality of the revolution' as a first principle was, in other words, not the logical conclusion of theoretical progress beyond Marx; it was the dominant element in an imaginary substratum to rationalize which an inferior version of Marxism was then used.

Lenin's acknowledged and unacknowledged links to the Russian revolutionary tradition have now been thoroughly documented. He was involved with populist circles before he turned to Marxism for a more systematic revolutionary theory; he was strongly influenced by Chernyshevsky, and this would seem to be the main source of the militant materialism which antedates and underlies his appropriation of Marxist theory; last but not least, a synthesis of Marxist theory and Jacobin strategy had – as several Western historians have shown – been adumbrated by Peter Tkachev. Lenin's project was thus a continuation of older trends by other means rather than a new beginning, and his conversion to Marxism was only a new episode in the cross-cultural flowering of the revolutionary imagination that had begun with Herzen and his contemporaries.

Marx repeatedly revised his theory of capitalism and failed to complete it, but he consistently overestimated the level of capitalist development and its impact on all spheres of social life. For Lenin, however, *Capital* was a comprehensive analysis of modern society and the definitive test of a new science of history. Marx's work could thus be used to construct a more exclusive and exaggerated image of capitalism than he had had in mind. When Lenin applied this model to Russia, the result was double-edged: Russian capitalism seemed more advanced than it really was, but since its very achievements were supposed to bring it closer to a terminal crisis, the economic transformation did not disrupt the continuity of the revolutionary tradition. The maturity of capitalism was a further argument for the actuality of the revolution. There were still some open questions about the relationship between the overdue bourgeois revolution and the approaching proletarian one, but Lenin's frame of reference pre-defined the problem in terms of an overlap, a rapid transition or a fusion. And there was another side to his reading of Marx that was crucial to his revolutionary strategy. Marx's critique of capitalism was multi-dimensional; its three main themes correspond roughly to the Habermasian distinction between cognitive, social and expressive aspects. From the Marxian point of view, capital is an obstacle to the rational organization of production, a structural deformation of the social bond, and a perverse agency of human self-realization. The anarchy of the market, the fetishism of commodities and the alienation of work are distinct but complementary facets of a systemic pattern. In Lenin's version of Marxism, there is a strong emphasis on the first aspect and hardly any understanding of the other two. His main concern is with the organizational irrationality of capitalism, and his version of the socialist alternative is therefore particularly receptive to lessons from the more traditional (i.e. statist and imperial) attempts to cope with this problem.

This point brings us to the second question. The claim that Stalinism was the logical outcome of Lenin's theory and practice is most plausible when it is based on his conception of the revolutionary party formulated for the first time in *What Is To Be Done?* There is no doubt that Lenin used Marxist language to rationalize a Jacobin vision of the vanguard, and that the universalist thrust of his argument takes it far beyond the conjunctural problems of the Russian movement. The reference to Kautsky's conception of scientific socialism as a doctrine brought to the workers by the intellectuals is significant, but it only shows that Lenin was still unaware of the gulf that separated him from the Western branch of the Marxist tradition. In the context of classical Marxism and the Second International, authoritarian implications were checked by theoretical and cultural counterweights that were absent from Lenin's universe of discourse. And if we analyse – with the wisdom of hindsight – the broader connotations of Lenin's model of organization, Castoriadis's description seems apposite: it combines some features of a bureaucratic apparatus with others reminiscent of an army, a factory or a church. The combination as a whole can perhaps be characterized as an imaginary counter-state with an unmistakably totalitarian logic.

But does this mean that the Bolshevik party was 'the elementary institution of totalitarianism' (Agnes Heller)? The direct connection between the pre-revolutionary party and the post-revolutionary state should be briefly considered; the two main objections are that Lenin's later views on revolutionary theory developed beyond the stage represented by *What Is To Be Done?*, and that Bolshevism as a political and cultural current is not reducible to Leninism.

It is true that Lenin was a quick learner and a flexible strategist. As T. Shanin (1986) has shown, his ability to draw crucial lessons from the experience of the 1905 revolution contrasts with the dogmatism of many other participants. This learning process was the background to his effective use of the soviets and his adoption of a populist agrarian programme in 1917. He was also – albeit less frequently and less thoroughly – capable of reconsidering theoretical issues. The notebooks written during World War I show that his philosophical culture did not stagnate at the level of *Materialism and Empiriocriticism*. And some analysts have argued that the utopian dimension of his thought was never fully subordinated to the strategic one; in particular, the relationship of *State and Revolution* to his political actions in 1917 has often seemed unclear. Yet when all this is taken into account, the limits to learning, reflection and imagination stand out all the more clearly. Lenin never wavered in his commitment to a doctrine that was, as he put it, 'omnipotent because it was true', and although this orthodoxy was imaginary in the sense that no such system existed, and Lenin could therefore change his mind on basic issues, it was not wholly indeterminate: its core elements were the idea of an uncompromising materialism, the belief in objective laws of history and the vision of a revolutionary élite that could acquire and apply a scientific knowledge of such laws. These basic orientations remained unquestioned even when Lenin seemed to be exploring new areas or experimenting with new ideas. They were essential to his self-understanding, to his ascendancy within the Bolshevik current, and to his ability to restore that ascendancy after temporary defeat.

It is also true that the real history of the pre-revolutionary Bolshevik movement was very different from the blueprint contained in *What Is To Be Done?* Lenin and his followers had to coexist and contend with various rivals, some of whom were important historical figures in their own right (Bogdanov's role in the crystallization of Bolshevism as an autonomous current during the 1905 revolution may have been as important as Trotsky's contribution to its victory in 1917). There was, in particular, an alternative trend that drew on Western syndicalism and differed from Leninism in its emphasis on direct action, mass participation and collective experience (Williams 1986). And it should be noted that the success of the Bolsheviks in 1917 was, among other things, due to non-Bolshevik elements in the leadership and the strategy: without the tactical adaptation to the agrarian policy of the SR party, the seizure of power would have been impossible, and Trotsky's leading role was inseparable from the idea of permanent revolution which thus became one of the basic premises of Bolshevik strategy (there was an SR connection in this case too: the SR theorist Mikhail Gotz had used the concept of 'permanent revolution' – with explicit reference to Marx – before Parvus and Trotsky). But the other side of the problem should not be overlooked: what made Leninism more resilient than other variants of Bolshevism, more capable of transforming a fluctuating and heterogeneous current into a distinctive tradition, and strong enough to conserve its identity despite substantial borrowings from other sources? The answer seems to be that the imaginary dimension of the revolutionary project was as essential to Lenin as to the other Bolsheviks, but in different ways. If revolutionaries influenced by syndicalism were attracted to Bolshevism, this was because the image of the revolutionary vanguard was still vague enough to serve as an intermediary step towards a broader conception of the revolutionary collective. This redefinition of the Bolshevik project, with a stronger emphasis on its imaginary component, was attuned to the higher level of mobilization during revolutionary crises, but less conducive to a sustained struggle for control over the revolutionary movement and a long-term concentration on revolutionary goals. By contrast, Lenin struck a different balance between imagination and strategy: the phantasm of the enlightened and organized vanguard served to transfigure his own pursuit of power and thus to justify – to himself and to others – the twists and turns of his strategy. And it was flexible enough to allow him to profit from the contributions of the other current.

To sum up, then, the interpretation of Bolshevism as a prefiguration of the totalitarian pattern seems justified. But the connection, although essential, is less straightforward than some analysts have suggested, and biological metaphors are misleading. The development in question is not a case of organic growth. Rather, we need to take into account the imaginary character of the original project, its complex and often paradoxical interaction with the political context, and the decisive role of historical processes which brought some possibilities to fruition and suppressed others.

SOCIAL REVOLUTION AND IMPERIAL MODERNIZATION

As I have tried to show, the cultural premises of the Russian revolutionary tradition – particularly its images of power and its visions of social transformation – channelled its theoretical and practical efforts in a specific direction. This is not to suggest that the mutation of the traditional imperial order into a totalitarian one can be explained in purely culturalist terms. The cultural matrix of the Bolshevik project took shape within a broader historical context and interacted with changing patterns of power; if the cultural factors then became autonomous enough to prefigure – up to a point and in broad outlines – a further transformation of the power structure, this was the outcome of a very peculiar social constellation. As a result of the crisis and decomposition of the imperial state, social actors were set free and allowed to implement their own strategies, but in a situation that was more conducive to mutual destruction than to the institutionalization of conflicts or the stabilization of a new balance of power between state and society. The self-dissolution of society left the field to more elementary forces: a culturally heterogeneous but ideologically unified project was brought to bear on a paralysed but readaptable power centre. Because of the absence of social actors and the fluid state of social structures, the revolutionary élite which engineered this encounter was thrust into an exceptionally strategic position. Its background and its internal dynamics led to a further concentration of power in the hands of individual leaders. But the other side of this process should not be overlooked. It is a commonplace that the paralysis or neutralization of social forces may enable individuals to play a disproportionately dominant role; the 'depersonalizing' effect on the individuals, who thus tend to become embodiments of cultural logics and power dynamics, is more elusive and poses a more challenging problem for the theory of history.

The historical context of these developments was the modernizing process which began with the abolition of serfdom in Russia and came to an end with World War I. If we want to avoid the pitfalls of one-dimensional modernization theory, several aspects of a complex and changing constellation should be distinguished. An earlier phase of imperial modernization – the Petrine revolution – had set the stage for later changes and set Russia apart from both the West which it tried to beat at its own game and the East which it could aspire to conquer. The more radical innovations that began in the second half of the nineteenth century transformed Russian society and its patterns of conflict, while at the same time the Russian state became more deeply involved in a global struggle for power. The joint effect of internal tensions and external pressures was a social revolution of extraordinary depth and complexity, irreducible to any general formula. But despite the unequalled scope and intensity of the revolutionary crisis, the infrastructural imperatives of the old order were strong enough to leave their mark on the regime which succeeded it.

The relationship between pre-revolutionary trends and post-revolutionary structures remains controversial. For those who emphasize continuity, the decisive factor is either the legacy of a past history of state- and empire-building (Richard Pipes) or the unchanging imperatives of international competition and modernization as a 'revolution from without' (Laue 1966). The case for discontinuity is based either on the claim that the party which seized power in 1917 developed into a new ruling class (variously defined as bureaucracy, nomenklatura or intelligentsia) or on the assumption that the totalitarian project represents a break-out from history and a new beginning, rather than a cumulative result of historical processes. As I will try to show, a closer look at the interplay of imperial modernization and social revolution suggests a more balanced view. The changes in Russian imperial society after 1861 did not add up to a coherent pattern that could be described and evaluated as a more or less successful strategy of development; rather, the tensions between conflicting forces and contradictory imperatives grew in such a way that they were bound to culminate in a systemic crisis, even if its course and outcome depended on historical circumstances. A new pattern was then needed to put together the fragments left behind by the defunct regime. Bolshevik Russia inherited problems, resources and premises from its imperial predecessor, but they now became part of another interpretive and strategic framework. The picture would, however, be incomplete without a final point: a revolutionary élite that assumed the task of rebuilding a ruined empire was inevitably set on a self-destructive course.

Further discussion of these issues should be linked to the theoretical questions raised above, especially those related to the distinction between economic, political and cultural structures as well as to the integrative patterns superimposed on them. Muscovite and Petrine Russia was a political society in the specific sense that it was dominated by the imperatives of state formation and imperial expansion. But it seems clear that some earlier notions about the scope of state power will have to be revised in the light of recent historical research: important aspects of economic and cultural life were beyond the direct reach of the political centre, although the latter was strong enough to contain this residual autonomy. The political closure of social space blocked the constitution and interaction of social forces. As suggested above, the concept of a state-conditioned – rather than fully state-controlled – society seems appropriate. To put it another way, the impact of the state on society was double-edged: centralization was accompanied by segmentation. This applies most obviously to rural society. Moshe Lewin uses the concept of the 'rural nexus' to describe a key feature of the *longue durée* of Russian history, but it might be suggested that there was also a rural hiatus: if the enserfed peasantry was the economic basis of the service state and its imperial dynamic, it also constituted a society unto itself and a sub-civilization where cultural distance from cities and rulers could, if enhanced by other factors, undermine the whole regime. More generally speaking, the caste-like divisions which the autocratic state imposed on society (the '*soslovie* paradigm', as some historians have described them) functioned both as obstacles to social integration (neither an urban society nor a unified middle class could develop under such circumstances) and as incentives to subcultural fragmentation.

This dialectic of centralization and fragmentation was already built into the Muscovite pattern of state formation, but the problem became more acute after the transition to the Petrine state and in the course of further modernization. The main impetus to change was external: the imperial Russian state was involved in an unending struggle to defend and strengthen its position with regard to the European state system. On this level there could be no equivalent to the final solution that the Muscovite rulers had imposed on the Russian state system. When a hegemonic position seemed to have been achieved (after 1815), so that the 'revolution from without' could now be brought under control, the result was that Russia fell further behind the Western powers and finally suffered a defeat which abruptly changed her international position. The Crimean War threw the empire into a crisis and thus launched a new phase of imperial modernization. For present purposes, the main point to be noted is that this fresh start accentuated the trends and aggravated the problems that had already been prefigured by the Petrine model. The Russian economy was drawn into a global context of capitalist develop- ment and forced to adapt to its dynamics; as the recurrent 'industrialization debates' showed, this process was a permanent challenge to the imperial order, and the problem of coordinating it with the political strategies of the centre was never solved. At the same time, no further modernization of Russian state and society was possible without intensified cultural contacts with the West and the inevitable strengthening of a countercurrent which turned its own images and projections of the West against a semi-Westernized state.

In brief, the imperial Russian state was now – in the second half of the nineteenth century – exposed to economic and cultural forces on which it became more and more dependent and by which it was at the same time irresistibly undermined. This predicament was not simply that of a traditional state in a rapidly modernizing world. Rather, the modernizing and self-strengthening strategy of the state brought it into conflict with developments in other spheres. The first and most fundamental reform, the abolition of serfdom, was neither due to economic causes nor geared to economic projects. Its main aim was to restructure the social basis of the state in such a way that it could more effectively mobilize its resources against external threats and rivals. In that sense, the rationale for liberation was the same as it had been for the introduction of serfdom. When the state later took a more positive and interventionist approach to industrialization, the reformed version of the rural nexus (including, in particular, a strengthened peasant commune) had become a major obstacle. In any case, changing policies did not alter the fact that all modernizing projects from above aimed at keeping a strong imperial centre intact, and could therefore envisage only limited concessions to social and political forces. In this broad sense, Weber's description of political reforms in Russia as 'pseudo-constitutional' was undoubtedly correct. But the very consistency of this strategy gave rise to further problems. The Petrine revolution was both the culmination of autocracy and a decisive boost to the bureaucratic component of the state; further modernization was bound to increase the relative weight of the bureaucracy, but the autocracy remained strong enough to block the development of a coherent bureaucratic apparatus and undercut the bureaucratic projects of reform.

This background – a changing and increasingly unbalanced constellation of economic, political and cultural factors – was reflected in exceptionally polarized patterns of social conflict. Trotsky's analysis of the 'uneven and combined development' which fused the contradictions of a pre-capitalist state with those of a rapidly growing capitalist economy can still help to clarify the problem, but only if we separate it from his ideological and strategic frame of reference. As Trotsky saw it, capitalist and pre-capitalist structures interacted in such a way that the internal contradictions of the former matured more rapidly and led more directly to a proletarian revolution than in the more advanced countries. In retrospect, the emphasis on two mutually reinforcing sources of conflict – traditional and modern – seems more justified than the claim that their joint effect pointed the way to a world revolution. The relevant part of Trotsky's argument has now been incorporated into a much more complex and realistic analysis of pre-revolutionary Russia. Tim McDaniel's thesis is that the explosive mixture of autocracy and capitalism 'gave rise to the closest approximation in history to a proletarian revolution' (McDaniel 1988: 407), but the overall explanatory framework and the broader historical perspective differ sharply from the conventional Marxist accounts of capitalist development and worker radicalism in Russia. I will first recapitulate the most salient points of McDaniel's analysis and then go on to argue that some of its implications become clearer if they are linked to the problematic of imperial modernization.[4]

McDaniel's claim is that a 'whole complex of contradictory institutions, paralysed élites and a revolutionary social movement decisively shaped the 1917 revolution' (ibid.: 14). The contradictory institutions were, first and foremost, those of autocracy and capitalism. They were structurally dependent on each other: the modernization which the autocratic state needed to strengthen its international position was impossible without the development of a capitalist economy, and the state played a key role in promoting industrialization. But the symbiosis also weakened both sides. The political logic of the state and its interest in retaining overall control led it to pursue policies which undermined the social basis of capitalism. Neither the integration nor the innovative capacity of the industrial élite could make much progress under an autocratic regime. Conversely, the economic logic of capitalist institutions created new problems and imposed new constraints on the state. It gave rise to a more divisive class structure, incompatible with the traditional social context of autocracy, and it drew the government into conflicts which it could not avoid because of its commitment to capitalist industrialization nor regulate because of its refusal to accept a genuine constitutional reform. Last but not least, the expansion and inter-nationalization of the capitalist economy undermined the rural nexus. But in addition to these political and economic cross-currents, there was also a conflict between the respective cultural premises of autocracy and capitalism. Within the traditional Russian frame of reference, the legitimacy of private property and entrepreneurial authority was at best conditional. As for the culture of capitalism, even in its dependent and truncated Russian version, it eroded traditions and stimulated new demands which the autocracy was ill equipped to meet. On top of this, nineteenth- and early twentieth-century Russia was exposed to cultural influences from the West, and the liberal current that fed on them undermined the autocracy without integrating the social forces linked to capitalist industrialization into an alternative historical bloc.

But as we have seen, the European connection was also reflected in a socialist tradition. Following McDaniel, its development can be seen as the other side of the relationship between autocracy and capitalism: the contradictory institutions and the paralysed élites were in the end swept away by a revolutionary movement based on a unique conjunction of radical ideas and radicalized masses. The labour movement that took shape together with the capitalist economy could not be integrated into the institutional framework of the regime, and the two dominant components of the latter obstructed each other's attempts to cope with it. A growing and strategically situated social force was thus excluded from the social order. At the same time, the established order was solid enough to block the self-organization of the urban working class and to prevent it from articulating its interests along the same lines as in more advanced industrial societies. The social movement which developed under these conditions had some very distinctive characteristics. Contrary to what has often been suggested, the urban workers of pre-revolutionary Russia were not simply a semi-urbanized offshoot of the peasantry. Although they inevitably drew on peasant traditions, their collective experience found expression in attitudes and modes of action that set them apart from the rest of Russian society. In the absence of institutional outlets, they developed their own tradition of extreme but intermittent radicalism; an active minority, made up of 'conscious workers', ensured the continuity of the movement and became the focus of a class solidarity in times of unrest. The fusion of autocracy and capitalism facilitated a similar fusion of political and economic radicalism on the side of those who were most directly exposed to their joint rule. In this way, the structural logic of the workers' movement converged with the political culture of the revolutionary intelligentsia, and the radicalization of the masses went hand in hand with the growing influence of the socialist parties. There is no denying that this line of development – a radicalizing process which made the industrial workers increasingly receptive to the idea of a total rupture with the established order – bears some resemblance to the Marxian scenario of the proletarian revolution, and that the revolutionary potential of working-class solidarity went far beyond the limits of the 'trade-unionist' mentality as defined by Lenin. But there were limitations of another kind. The road from class struggle to revolutionary strategy did not take the universalist turn envisaged by classical Marxism; it led, rather, to the self-confinement of the movement within a political counter-culture that was in many ways a mirror image of the old regime. Moreover, the contradictions of autocratic capitalism were reflected in a similar predicament of its adversaries: just as the Tsarist state and the industrialists joined hands in a way that was to prove fatal to both, the revolutionary intelligentsia helped to consolidate working-class identity in a way that maximized its destructive potential but limited its historical life-span, while worker radicalism exhausted itself in an upheaval that put a fraction of the intelligentsia in possession of the state and then left it with a monopoly of power but without a social basis.

The merits of this interpretation are obvious. It throws light on the role of the class factor in the Russian revolution and does so without any concessions to the mythology of the 'betrayed revolution'. The growth and radicalization of the labour movement before 1914 – all the more remarkable in that 'economic expansion and labour militance went hand in hand' (Bonnell 1983: 352) – appears as an essential part of the revolutionary process. McDaniel's approach also highlights the continuity of the urban revolution of 1917: the prior experience and radical tradition of the workers enabled them to play a key role in the February revolution and made it possible for the soviets to develop into an alternative power structure alongside the Provisional Government. The soviets were, of course, from the outset controlled by the socialist parties to a much greater extent than they had been in 1905. But if the Bolsheviks could defeat their rivals in the contest for this power base and use it to take over the remnants of the Tsarist state, this was largely due to their ability to take advantage of the radicalization of the class struggle during 1917. According to conventional explanations, the Bolsheviks drew their strength from a mass revolt against war and deprivation; what is missing from this picture is the more specific connection between Bolshevik strategy and an escalating class struggle in the urban centres where the fate of the revolution was decided. Between February and October, class conflict developed further in the direction that had been prefigured by the structural contradictions of autocratic capitalism, although the autocratic part of the regime had now been destroyed and the capitalist one irreparably weakened.

The analysis recapitulated above is thus a decisive step beyond the traditional terms of debate about the Russian revolution. For one school of thought, it was a proletarian revolution, continued or betrayed by the post-revolutionary regime, whereas others saw it as a seizure of power by a marginal fraction of the intelligentsia, backed by a peasant revolution or an elemental rebellion of the masses. Neither side could explain the interaction between a structurally distorted but dynamic pattern of capitalist development and the more traditional factors that made Russian society prone to revolutionary crises. This conjunction determined and limited the role of the workers' movement. The focus on autocratic capitalism and its contradictions helps to understand the class structure of pre-revolutionary Russian society and the role of class struggle in the revolutionary process, without postulating a class identity of the political project which prevailed or a class character of the regime that grew out of the revolution.

The concept of imperial modernization may, as I will now try to show, serve to clarify some further implications of McDaniel's argument as well as possible links to other perspectives. There is, to begin with, a structural connection between empire and autocracy. Autocracy is often seen as the most extreme form of patrimonial authority, where the constraints of law and tradition are reduced to a minimum. But it acquires a more specific content and a more solid basis when it is linked to an imperial order. The sovereignty of autocratic rule and the supremacy of the imperial centre reinforce each other. As suggested in the introductory discussion of empires, the concrete characteristics of this fusion vary widely; the imperial project may be oriented towards global conquest or the maintenance of a cultural model of cosmic order (the twin imperial traditions of the Far Eastern region gave rise to classic examples of both types), and it can be linked to a religious mission or a civilizational model. Some peculiarities of the Russian imperial constellation will be noted later; for the time being, suffice it to say that the imperial dimension of autocracy is the key to its role in the modernizing process. From this point of view, the notion of autocratic capitalism seems somewhat misleading: it places a one-sided emphasis on the second component, rather than underlining the conjunction of autocracy and capitalism as inter-dependent but mutually erosive agencies of modernization.

It is only in the light of imperial ambitions that the commitment of the autocratic state to capitalist industrialization becomes fully under-standable. The situation of Russia after the Crimean War was that of a great power which had suddenly lost its dominant position within the European state system and faced the threat of further regression to a peripheral status. In the domain of international politics, the long-term results of the Petrine revolution had been even more spectacular than at home: Russia had – partly because of favourable historical conjunctures – risen to disproportionate prominence despite the fragility of its internal power structure, and this imbalance made the impact of an unexpected defeat all the more momentous. At the same time, the Petrine precedent made it easier to envisage further mobilization of social and natural resources. The problem was thus not simply one of 'disparity between Russian ambition and Russian resources, between pretension and realities' (Laue 1966: 50). The ambition was an attempt to regain an earlier position of strength, and it could take advantage of the fact that the European image of Russian power was still influenced by past experience; as for the resources, the underused potential of the Russian empire was obvious enough to justify the belief that its decline could be reversed. For all these reasons, the strategy of imperial modernization was much more than a pretension undermined by backwardness.

Neither industrialization as such nor the later steps towards a more active involvement of the state were obvious choices for the autocracy. But for an imperial power involved in global competition with more advanced states, there was no other way out. The result was, as we have seen, an explosive mixture of structural tensions and social conflicts. The modernizing process culminated in an uncontrollable dynamic of economic, political and cultural forces and an uncontainable escalation of both the class struggle and the conflict between state and society. It was, however, an international crisis that finally brought these trends to a head and brought about the collapse of the regime. As long as the world war is seen as a catastrophe which overtook Tsarist Russia from the outside, it can still be argued that its domestic problems were not obviously insoluble, and that further economic and political modernization might have staved off a revolution. If we want to claim that it was the same driving force – the imperial pursuit of power in a rapidly changing environment – which pushed the autocracy further along the road of capitalist development and deeper into the maelstrom of a global struggle for hegemony, and that the internal and external roots of revolution were thus closely interconnected, more must be said about the specific characteristics of Russian imperialism. Against attempts to blame an incompetent government for both the conflict with Japan and the decision to go to war in 1914, some historians have argued that the course of events was more or less predetermined by the international constellation: neither the growth of Japanese power in the Far East nor the German bid for hegemony in Europe could be treated with indifference by a Eurasian empire bent on further expansion. This view seems plausible, but a closer examination of Russian initiatives and responses is needed.

The autocratic connection affected the pattern of capitalist development in Russia, but did not alter its immanent logic. Rather, the end result was an exacerbation of its inbuilt conflicts. Similarly, the growing involvement in a capitalist world economy forced the Russian imperial formation to confront new challenges and enabled it to draw on new resources without changing its rationale. In the long run, the reinvigorated imperial project was on collision course with other historical forces. The rivalry with the two other empires of the 'steppe frontier' (McNeill 1964), the Habsburg and the Ottoman, had played a decisive role in its earlier history; it was an incentive to develop bureaucratic and military forms of control, but it was also the matrix of an imperial imaginary that placed a disproportionate emphasis on involvement in Eastern and Southeastern European affairs. On the other hand, Russia differed from its rivals in that it could still expand towards the East. As we have seen, the Petrine revolution laid the foundation for further advances in both the Western and the Eastern arenas. In a sense, the renewed expansion and the reassertion of Russian power in the last decades of the nineteenth century brought about a return to the Petrine constellation: a Russian empire whose size, location and single-minded pursuit of external power enabled it to claim a more dominant role in world affairs than its level of development would otherwise have warranted, but also led it to overreach itself and become involved in a global contest with other states whose economies and societies had been much more thoroughly transformed by capitalist modernization. Although the more ambitious economic strategists of late imperial Russia (especially Witte) wanted to coordinate the expansionist drive with the demands of industrialization, it seems clear that the outcome of their efforts was rather the opposite: capitalist industrialization did not transform or reorient Russian imperialism, but it helped to rationalize and justify the continuation of a much older and more traditional bureaucratic-military version of imperialism (Geyer 1987). This trend culminated in an all-out conflict with the strongest European power, an aspiring empire which could – in contrast to Russia – draw on the resources of a solidly integrated nation-state and an incomparably more advanced capitalist economy.

Neither the history nor the legacy of Russian imperialism can be understood without some reference to its cultural context. It was made up of more heterogeneous elements and underwent more radical changes than the traditions of the other empires with which Russia was confronted. As noted above, the political culture of Muscovite Russia borrowed extensively from two imperial neighbours; the resultant mixture was adapted to the organizational principles of a state which later had to be restructured along the lines of a different model. With Peter the Great the imperial centre took a cosmopolitan turn. If its direct impact was momentous, the unintended consequences were even more far-reaching. The revolution from above brought Russia into closer contact with the West and thus opened up a cultural space within which a revolutionary tradition could develop; at the same time, it strained the cultural bond between state and society and thus reduced the integrative capacity of the centre. The well-known formula of 'autocracy, orthodoxy and nationality' could never develop into a viable imperial ideology. In the course of the transition from Muscovite to Petrine Russia, the religious component had been irreparably weakened both by the subordination of the church to direct state control and by the schism of the Old Believers. As for nationalism, its symbiosis with the imperial state was at best unstable and ambiguous. The last decades of Tsarism saw its most sustained attempt to harness nationalism as a legitimizing and mobilizing ideology, but this new strategy was undermined by several factors: the legacy of Westernization from above, the alienation of the intelligentsia from the imperial centre and the inability of the autocratic state to commit itself unreservedly to a policy of social and cultural mobilization. When the last autocrat took a more nationalistic turn, this went hand in hand with a regression to more archaic political attitudes that made it impossible for him to cooperate with the reformist wing of the bureaucracy.

The imperial centre thus lacked the cultural resources that might have made it more capable of managing economic and political conflicts. This does not mean that the imperial idea – or, more precisely, the imperial imaginary – had no impact on Russian society on the eve of the revolution. Its influence was diffuse but not negligible; for example, some representatives of the liberal movement had internalized it to such an extent that it became a major liability during the revolutionary crisis of 1917. The most striking aspect, though, is the absence of a dominant and definitive version of the imperial ideology. Interpretations of Russian imperialism ranged from nationalistic or Pan-Slavic doctrines to those who saw the empire as a vehicle of Westernization and civilization or – at the other extreme – those who dreamt of an Eurasian alternative to Western domination. This confusion made the imperial order more vulnerable to crisis, but also easier to restore in a new form: the imperial imaginary could be adapted to new strategies and structures.

If the contribution of Russian nationalism to the imperial project was thus both limited and problematic, the growth of nationalism among the non-Russian peoples was a potentially important but by no means guaranteed asset for the revolutionary movement. In this regard, there were some fundamental similarities between Russia and the two other Eastern European empires: in all three cases the centre was challenged by nationalist movements on the periphery, and there was no imperial ideology that could have aspired to neutralize them through a new strategy of integration. In Russia the dominant nation was stronger and the anti-imperial nationalist forces – in most cases – less entrenched than in the Habsburg and Ottoman domains, and this may in retrospect help to explain why it was the only imperial constellation to survive the revolutionary crisis at the end of World War I. On the other hand, because of the explosive combination of autocracy and capitalism, the conflicts within the central structures were much more destructive than elsewhere. Only an acute crisis could bring the two sets of disintegrative factors into closer contact, and the pattern of their interaction depended on historical circumstances. In 1905, the combination of national and social unrest led to a higher level of revolutionary mobilization in some parts of the periphery than in Russia itself, but the national factor could also be divisive, and some regions were only marginally affected by the crisis. When, by contrast, the crisis began with a collapse of the centre (because its imperial ambitions had been exposed to a much more severe test than in 1905), national conflicts could easily escalate out of control and lead to a dismemberment of the empire. But it was one thing for national and social conflicts to coincide in such a way that the revolutionary potential was maximized, and – as we shall see – another for the revolutionary leadership to develop a strategy that would allow it both to treat nationalist movements as allies in the struggle against the imperial regime and to manipulate or outmanoeuvre them so as to construct a new imperial order.

Finally, the interaction between the 'rural nexus' and the revolutionary process should be analysed in the context of imperial modernization. The development of serfdom had been a key part of the long-term process of state formation on an increasingly imperial scale; the emancipation of the peasants in 1861 – it would be better described as the substitution of a new system of control for the old one – was similarly linked to a new turn of the imperial trajectory. The architects of the reform were primarily concerned with the social basis and the military potential of the state, but the strategy which they adopted was bound to come into conflict with other decisions taken for the same reasons. There is some dispute about mitigating factors and regional variations, but is seems clear that the general crisis of peasant economy and society in late imperial Russia – at least in the heartland of the empire – was caused by the joint impact of three major changes. Capitalist development and the industrial policies of the government had a double-edged effect on the rural sector, imposing new constraints and at the same time opening up new outlets. Because of the long-standing links between the state and the landowning nobility, the reform had been a compromise in that it reduced the power and undermined the authority of the landowners, but gave disproportionate weight to their interests. The survival of a privileged class, deprived of its traditional strength and legitimacy, aggravated the conflicts that had always been built into the rural basis of the imperial order. Finally, the new combination of state control with communal property and self-administration was both a step towards autonomy and an obstacle to development. The post-reform structure of rural society proved conducive to more independent collective action of the peasantry, but channelled it in a direction opposed to the 'revolution from without' that was implemented – and translated into differing strategies – by the urban centres and élites.

If the communal institutions had always been part and parcel of the long-term process of state formation, rather than an external substratum, their relationship to the other parts had now changed in such a way that it could – under the influence of other disintegrative factors – lead to a frontal collision. Peasant society in early twentieth-century Russia may, in other words, be described as a fragment of the imperial order that had, as a result of challenges, concessions and pressures from the more central actors, acquired a defensive dynamic of its own and a more clearly articulated collective identity. The peasantry was 'a social system with its own specific culture' and 'a world in its own right, not really from our time' (Lewin 1985: 13). In more specific terms, it developed into a separate constellation of economic, political and cultural patterns, unadaptable to the autocratic-capitalist modernizing process and unintelligible to those who tried to fit it into the class structure of urban society. The peasant world had its distinctive forms of property, its administrative institutions and customary law, and its cultural traditions (Lewin refers to their version of Orthodoxy as 'rural Christianity'). The revolutionary potential of this sub-society, enhanced by the collapse of the imperial mystique which had previously helped to keep it under control, was clearly revealed for the first time in 1905. But no observers or participants drew adequate lessons from this experience. It can be said with some justification that Lenin responded more effectively to the challenge than his socialist rivals did (Shanin 1986); however, the limits to his 'learning from history' are all too clear. It went far enough to enable him to develop a more flexible tactic for future crises, but did not change his basic misconceptions about class divisions within the peasantry and its supposedly irreversible transformation through capitalist development. He learnt enough to take temporary advantage of forces whose mainsprings remained as hidden to him as before, and to enlist their services for a strategy that fell apart at the very moment of success.

As I have tried to show, the context of imperial modernization helps to understand the connection between internal and external causes of the revolutionary crisis, and to grasp the broad spectrum of structural and social conflicts which converged against the autocratic regime. The question of possible alternatives to the revolution should also be related to this background. It is still very much a matter of debate among historians whether the collapse of the Tsarist state and the radical social revolution that followed were more or less inevitable, or whether Russian society could have transformed itself in a less catastrophic way. The reference to imperial modernization does not settle this dispute, and it should certainly not be taken as an attempt to eliminate contingency from the revolutionary process. But it may help to reformulate the question and to specify the issue of contingency. If we take all the above-mentioned aspects of the imperial context into account, its destructive potential seems to have made the disintegration of state and society overwhelmingly probable and the seizure of power by a radical minority at least a plausible expectation. It is much less obvious that there were no alternatives to the consolidation of the Bolshevik regime and its successful efforts to reconstruct the empire. The contingent factors that come into play at this level include more or less calculated choices as well as unforeseen circumstances, and in the present context there is no need for a more detailed description. The following remarks will, rather, focus on one of the factors, the Leninist strategy, and its function as a bridge between pre- and post-revolutionary versions of the imperial constellation. To stress this connection is not to suggest that it was inevitable; Lenin's project should be analysed as the articulation of a historical possibility, not as a mere reflection of the force of circumstances.

As the Russian state became more deeply involved in the global state system and its conflicts, a similar internationalization of the frame of reference took place within the Russian revolutionary movement. But on the whole, the results did not go beyond the projection of Russian perspectives onto the international arena and the translation of Russian models into a more universal language. The Russian revolutionary tradition had developed in the wake of a Westernizing revolution from above, and the pioneers of its Marxist phase saw themselves as radical Westernizers, but the underlying significance of Marxist orthodoxy turned out to be the very opposite: it helped to consolidate the independence and the hegemonic aspirations of a revolutionary movement which had now become capable of subordinating its original sources of inspiration to its own strategic principles. Lenin's belief in the 'actuality of the revolution' should, as suggested above, be interpreted from this point of view: the appropriation of Marxist categories enabled him to rationalize the Russian vision of an imminent revolution. The same applies to the notion of the revolutionary vanguard; in *What Is To Be Done?*, Lenin claims international relevance and a universal-historical mission for a specifically Russian variant of Jacobinism. Lenin's ideological experiments during the world war can be seen as a further step in this direction. His 'theory' of imperialism was an unorganized mixture of unoriginal ideas, but it served a strategic purpose in that it helped to link the revolutionary perspective to a visible rather than an expected crisis. The tensions of the expanding European state system had taken a destructive turn, and this seemed to open up new opportunities for revolutionary action. Lenin adapted to the situation without accepting the challenge to his theoretical premises; rather than acknowledging that the dynamics of state ·formation, interstate competition and imperial expansion had prevailed over those of class formation and class struggle, he reduced the new constellation to a by-product of capitalist development and read it as further evidence for the connection he had already made between the actuality of the revolution and the contradictions of capitalism. At the same time, his new interest in the state and his attempt to reactivate the half-baked and half-forgotten notion of the 'dictatorship of the proletariat' brought the revolutionary imagination into closer contact with history. If the original model of the vanguard can be described as an imaginary counter-state, the blueprint for a dictatorial post-revolutionary state was the logical first step towards concretization. Lenin's reference to the withering away of the state was a self-deceiving evasion: a latent but radical statism was built into his vision of the revolutionary party. The later history of Leninism was, as we shall see, to a large extent shaped by the state-building and state-centred implications of its core idea; its original background as well as its most important embodiment was a state of imperial dimensions.

Lenin's projects and expectations underwent major changes between 1914 and 1918. Although there is some disagreement about the details, it seems clear that three successive stages can be distinguished. At first Lenin saw Germany, the strongest state and the most dynamic capitalist economy in Europe, as the most likely setting for a revolutionary breakthrough, and it is probably true that this imaginary German connection was essential to the first formulation of a strategic goal that could later be pursued to much greater effect in Russia. Even after the revolution, Lenin saw the war economy of imperial Germany as a model that could now be adapted to a new political context and integrated into the socialist project that had won its first political victory in Russia. The second stage was the rise to power in 1917, made possible by the urban revolution and justified as the opening move of a European revolution. It is hard to imagine Lenin taking this course and even harder to imagine the Bolsheviks following him without the conviction that a revolutionary crisis was developing in the West; those who advocated a more cautious policy did so because they doubted this premise. Finally, the extreme weakness and isolation of the Bolshevik government during its first year in power forced it, first, to accept the status of a de facto German protectorate, and then – at the beginning of the civil war – to envisage far-reaching concessions to the victorious Western powers. In the event, the threat from the West proved easier to avert than the Bolsheviks had expected. But the Brest-Litovsk treaty had been more than a tactical manoeuvre: it marked the insertion of the Soviet regime into the European state system. A new strategy was in the making, based on the assumption that the Soviet state would have to coexist with a capitalist world for an indefinite span of time, and that its survival was more important than any other concerns. Although it took a few years to construct the ideological groundwork for this new course, some contemporary observers saw it as an ominous turn: in the summer of 1918, Rosa Luxemburg denounced the alliance of Bolshevism and imperial Germany as a danger to international socialism. She overestimated this particular threat, but she foresaw the mutation of the Bolshevik imaginary into a new *raison d'état*.

Lenin's idea of the party and its historical mission had far-reaching implications, and the collapse of the imperial order made it possible to translate them into practical terms. With the separation of the revolutionary vanguard from the revolutionary class, it became easier to develop and justify alliances with other social groups; the Leninist devaluation of 'spontaneity' reduced the labour movement to one of the many forces which the vanguard could mobilize, theoretically privileged but in practice not invariably the most important. It was only in 1917 that the tactical potential of this ideological innovation was fully realized. It enabled the Bolsheviks to draw support from diverse sources without giving up the imaginary identification with objective interests of the working class that was still essential to their self-understanding. After the revolution, the sovereignty of the vanguard could be invoked to justify the repression of working-class protest and the unlimited authority of a party-state that had – as Lenin occasionally acknowledged – lost its class basis. Most importantly, Lenin's party-centred frame of reference was flexible enough to allow him, as he put it, to take allies seriously on the tactical level without making any concessions to them on the strategic level, and thus to take advantage of the rural and national revolutions without letting them interfere with the Bolshevik conquest of the imperial centre. His well-known reinterpretation of the idea of national self-determination and his appropriation of the SR programme of land reform were, in this sense, tactical operations, but they were crucial parts of a grand strategy.

But the very success of that strategy was to cause further trouble. The rural revolution of 1917 destroyed the traditional basis of the imperial regime and thus paved the way for the Bolshevik offensive against its urban remnants; although the first attempts to bring rural society under control backfired, the Bolsheviks won the civil war because their policies were more successful in neutralizing the peasantry than those of their opponents; finally, the new regime survived because the local peasant revolt that followed in the wake of the civil war did not develop into a nation-wide *jacquerie*. To take the dynamic of the peasant factor into account was, however, not the same thing as to control it: the obverse of the Bolsheviks' success was their inability to check or channel a peasant revolution that reversed pre-war trends and reconsolidated communal institutions. The consequences of this transformation were far-reaching and double-edged. On the one hand, rural society underwent some internal changes as it became more autonomous. Redistributive measures were to some extent accompanied by a democratization of its institutions. On the other hand, the joint effect of rural autarchy and urban disintegration was, as Lewin puts it, a massive archaization of Russian society. The victorious Bolsheviks were thus confronted with the problematic of the rural nexus in a multiply aggravated form; the relative weight of rural society had increased, its institutions had broken away from the traditional system of control, and the urban centres were weakened by economic and cultural regression.

The consequences of the national revolution were, in the short and middle run, more controllable. Most of the former empire was reconquered by the Bolsheviks, and the fragments that remained independent posed no threat to their rule. But here, too, the course of events revealed the underlying ambiguity of Lenin's strategy and the danger that it might release forces which he and his successors could neither control nor comprehend. In the aftermath of the revolution the Bolshevik regime benefited from the action of nationalist movements: they dealt the final blow to the imperial order and paralysed the conservative attempts to restore it. More direct support came from movements that had, at least for a while, managed to unite national and social radicalism (a well-known example is the role of the Latvian Bolsheviks in the revolution and the first phase of post-revolutionary consolidation). On the other hand, victory in the civil war led directly to the emergence of national Communism in the Muslim regions of the empire – a phenomenon long neglected by analysts of the Soviet experience – and an open conflict between the aspirations of centre and periphery. A new solution to the national problem was essential to the survival of the regime, and there was no blueprint for such a solution in the Leninist canon.

The Bolsheviks thus inherited the two perennial problems of the old order that they had most effectively taken advantage of in 1917: a refractory rural society and an unevenly developed multinational polity. In the light of the subsequent fate of the Soviet Union, some parallels and contrasts between their responses to those two challenges can now be noted. The national factor was more manageable than the rural one, but also more revivable: national movements and nation-state projects were to play an active role in the demise of the Soviet Union, whereas its underdeveloped and overexploited rural sector sapped the strength of the regime but did not give birth to any oppositional forces. On the other hand, the restoration of the rural nexus and the recolonization of peasant society during Stalin's second revolution was only achieved at the price of a catastrophe which – in retrospect – seems to be the most decisive turning-point of a self-destructive trajectory. In that sense, the head-on collision between the post-revolutionary state and the peasantry was more significant than the sustained but ultimately unsuccessful effort to absorb nationalism.

But the unsolved problems were only one aspect of the imperial legacy. The continuity of the geopolitical, social and historical context within which they had to be solved was no less important. At first there seemed to be only an indirect connection. As Martin Malia (1980) has emphasized, the year 1918 – rather than 1917 – was decisive for the survival of the Bolshevik regime: its hold on power in Petrograd had been very precarious, and it was only during the following year that the new power structure of the party-state began to take shape. The subordination of the soviets to the emerging dictatorship and the exclusion of other socialist parties from political power were the first decisive steps. This development could only take place in the extraordinary social and political vacuum which the collapsed empire had left behind, and which now enabled the Bolsheviks to entrench themselves in the traditional heartland of the Muscovite state while fragmentation continued in the outlying regions. As the new regime extended its territorial basis, the imperial background re-emerged in a more constructive mode: the Bolsheviks had inherited the remnants of a bureaucratic and military apparatus, and the reintegration of the imperial fragments went hand in hand with the reconstruction of these mechanisms of control. Finally, the underlying affinities between the imperial and revolutionary traditions became more manifest when the new regime moved to implement its transformative strategy, and the 'construction of socialism' drew on the legacy of imperial revolutions from above. This reappropriation of the past will be discussed in Chapter 3.

To conclude, the analysis of continuities and discontinuities in the relationship between imperial and Soviet Russia should be related to the question of modernity and its alternative versions. It would seem justified to describe the Petrine state as an early counter-paradigm of modernity: although it was grafted onto the traditional infrastructures of the service state, its innovative dynamic was strong enough to move Russia from a marginal to a prominent position within the European state system, and to create a framework for an ongoing and intensive assimilation of Western civilizational patterns. But the very success of this model destroyed its foundations. Late imperial Russia was, as we have seen, no longer capable of integrating its multiple modernizing dynamics into a coherent pattern. The tensions and contradictions that were escalating out of control are best understood as joint effects of traditional and modern forces. The urban class conflict, intrinsic to the modern capitalist economy, became explosive because of the additional polarizing effect of the autocratic state. As for the political sphere, conflicts between the imperatives of state formation and the interests of social forces are an integral part of the modernizing process, but the historical background and the global reach of the Russian empire aggravated this problem to an extreme degree. The fusion of a dogmatic interpretation of modern science with an authoritarian conception of the self-constituting society is a recurrent trend in modern culture, but the alienation of the Russian intellectuals from both state and society made them receptive to its most radical version. Russian society was, in short, exposed to the divergent dynamics of modernity and at the same time burdened with a legacy which exacerbated them and blocked the growth of balancing and integrative forces. Under these circumstances, there was little chance of a democratic transformation. The claim that liberal democracy would have been the logical outcome of the semi-constitutional reforms after 1905 is no more convincing than the attempts to present Soviet democracy as an alternative to Bolshevik dictatorship. If we can speak about a logic of modern democracy and distinguish between more and less adequate forms of its institutionalization, one of the key criteria concerns the relationship between its representative and participatory aspects: models of democracy must be judged in terms of their ability to keep this question open and to allow for a broad and changing spectrum of conditional answers to it. In the Russian case, an authoritarian political culture – developed in different but interdependent ways by the imperial and the revolutionary traditions – barred the way in both directions; breakthroughs were only possible in the context of revolutionary crises which at the same time polarized social forces beyond the limits of democratic mediation; last but not least, the two visions of democracy were – in 1917 – separated from and pitted against each other, with fatal consequences for both. This turn of events reflected the more fundamental self-destructive dynamic of the whole imperial complex.

Imperial Russia had proved capable of assimilating or initiating modernizing processes in various areas, but incapable of moulding them into a viable version of modernity. The regime which inherited its fragments had to develop a new pattern of integration. More specifically, its main task was to restructure and unify the economic, political and cultural patterns of social life; each of the three factors had, as stated above, had its share in the terminal crisis of the imperial order. The result was undeniably a new counter-paradigm of modernity, arguably the most important of its kind. But if it brought the imperial order back to life in a new shape, it also – as we now know – reactivated its self-destructive dynamic. The analysis of its basic structures and its adaptive transformations will have to take both aspects into account.

Chapter 3

The model and its variants

The demise of the Soviet model has thrown new light on some of the most protracted debates about it. It would, in particular, be hard to deny that recent events have strengthened the case for the concept of totalitarianism, but in a rather paradoxical way. In view of the systemic features which became more visible when the regime was put to the test of reform, as well as with regard to the legacy it left behind, those who stressed its extreme, historically novel and socially destructive character were clearly right, and those who tried to subsume the phenomena in question under more conventional categories were just as obviously wrong. But if the notion of totalitarian domination can still serve to highlight the structural logic and the global impact of the Soviet model, the process of decomposition which led to its extinction will now also have to be taken into account. One of the standard objections to theories of totalitarianism has been that they mistake the fiction of total control for historical reality and thus ignore the real changes that have taken place as well as the possibility of future transformations. This is not equally true of all of them; some models of totalitarianism allow for successive phases and alternative versions, and some analysts have noted the close connection between strengths and weaknesses of the regimes in question.[1] A revised and updated version would, however, have to go further than the most flexible interpretations could go before the collapse of 1989–91: the task is now to link the long-term self-destructive logic of the model to its ambitions and achievements. If it is true that Soviet-type societies proved less resistant to radical change than most observers had expected, it is no less true that this change took the form of decomposition rather than self-transformation; an adequate theory of totalitarianism would – among other things – have to clarify the causes of the former without losing sight of the obstacles to the latter.

We cannot redefine the concept of totalitarianism without reopening the debate with other interpretive constructs. Their basic assumptions may have proved untenable, but there are – at least in some cases – insights to be acknowledged and open questions to be integrated into a new theoretical framework. To begin with one of the least plausible alternatives: the notion of 'transitional society' was rightly rejected by those who saw the Soviet type of modern society as distinctive, coherent and capable of self-reproduction, but it is now easier to accept that it contained a grain of truth. The extreme fragility of the Soviet model sets it apart from more durable patterns of modernity. And the idea of a conflict between two developmental logics should be taken seriously, even if it has to be disconnected from the traditional dichotomy of capitalism and socialism. There is an obvious difference between the trends which culminated in the full-blown totalitarianism of the late Stalin era and later attempts to rationalize the system in response to the demands of modernization and global competition; the reform that turned out to be only a brief prelude to self-destruction may be seen as the last episode of the second phase. The contrasts and connections between these two parts of the Soviet trajectory must be one of the central themes for any theoretical interpretation.

Some Marxist critics of the Soviet system saw it as a deviant or extreme version of capitalism, based on bureaucratic control instead of private property. It is now beyond dispute that the Soviet economy did not obey a capitalist logic – if it had, its history would have taken a very different course. But on the other hand, its final breakdown highlighted its dependent relationship to the capitalist world. Not only was it always more closely linked to the world market than the official visions of autarky and global antagonism would suggest; more importantly, its performance could not but be confronted with the model of economic rationality established by modern capitalism, and it was thus confined within the historical universe of the latter. It is not on the basis of its economic institutions as such that the Soviet model can be described as a counter-paradigm of modernity. In this sphere, it deviated from the capitalist pattern but failed to transcend it. But the economic structures were, as we shall see, embedded in a broader institutional complex and subordinated to its distinctive organizational principles. The concept of totalitarian domination can be applied – and must be adapted – to this overall framework.

The Soviet model has often been interpreted as a new class structure, and the new ruling class has been described – in more or less Marxian ways – as a state bourgeoisie, a managerial élite, a monopolistic bureaucracy, or a conquering intelligentsia. It was never easy to apply the concepts of class and class conflict to a power structure that differed so markedly from their original Western background, but its collapse is even harder to explain in terms of class theory than its rise and reproduction ever were. The events that led to the 'Leninist extinction' (Jowitt 1992) bear no resemblance to the traditional picture of a dominant class defeated by an ascendant one; they have much more to do with the implosion of an overstretched apparatus and the loss of control over a social space that has yet to be occupied and structured by autonomous social forces. This does not mean that the questions raised by class theorists are of no importance. Patterns of economic and political inequality were an important aspect of Soviet-type societies, and the totalitarian regime should be seen as the context within which they emerged and evolved, rather than as the sole and exclusive repository of social power. More specifically, the theory of totalitarianism must deal with two contrasting but complementary aspects of the phenomenon: its levelling tendencies and its stratified social structure. The Soviet model has been associated with redistributive strategies as well as with new patterns of inequality and privilege; the relative weight of those two trends can vary over time and from country to country, and some variants involve a more systematic combination than others. Earlier theories of totalitarianism often tended to focus on one role at the expense of the other. From an Eastern European perspective, especially during the declining years of the local regimes, the levelling dynamic was more visible and could give rise to the idea of a 'totalitarian-egalitarian syndrome', whereas some Western analysts have been more sensitive to the hierarchical aspects of totalitarian domination.

Finally, the downfall of the Soviet model has conclusively disproved some earlier claims of modernization theory. It is no longer possible to rationalize the Soviet record, at home and abroad, in terms of substitutes or shortcuts within a universal project of modernity. But these developments have at the same time underlined the connection between the theory of totalitarianism and the problematic of modernity; the totalitarian regime articulated and imposed its own interpretation of modernity, and it was the confrontation with other patterns that brought to light its developmental potential as well as its built-in tensions and imbalances. This viewpoint will be central to the following discussion.

The agenda sketched above is too extensive to be fully covered in this book. Our task is, rather, a preliminary one: to re-examine and redefine the concept of totalitarianism in such a way that it would become more responsive to new evidence and alternative perspectives. This cannot be done without reference to the historical context of the phenomena in question. The societal model which first emerged in post-revolutionary Russia was later – sometimes under direct Soviet pressure or predominance, sometimes as a result of more autonomous decisions – imposed on countries as different from each other as Cuba and Czechoslovakia, South Yemen and East Germany. In the course of this global expansion, it had to be adapted to different traditions and constellations; its structural principles were implemented in a more or less selective way, and the overall result could be an attenuated or a more extreme version of the original pattern. If the concept of totalitarian domination is to be used to refer to common and distinctive characteristics of Soviet-type societies, it must therefore be compatible with a wide range of variations. And we cannot simply treat the original version of the model as the standard one, in contrast to the more or less unorthodox variants developed in later phases and other places. The Stalinist stage of Soviet history has been aptly described as 'disequilibrium incarnate' (Lewin 1985: 45); there can be no doubt about its totalitarian character, but it took certain tendencies inherent in the general pattern to such extremes that they became a direct threat to its stability and survival. On the other hand, the post-Stalinist readjustment did not simply mean a return to normality. Rather, the regime redefined its goals and redirected its efforts towards a strategy that was also to prove self-defeating, albeit in a more gradual and less visible way.

The Soviet model was, in other words, subject to major variations not only when it was exported to other countries, but also within its original boundaries, and these transformations were brought about by its internal logic in conjunction with the changing historical circumstances to which it had to adapt. A structural analysis must therefore be linked to a genealogical one, beginning with the interpretation of the totalitarian project as a restructuring of the imperial legacy. At this point, however, a brief statement of basic assumptions may help to clarify the line of argument. For present purposes, the totalitarian paradigm can be reduced to a few basic, omnipresent and interconnected features of Soviet-type societies. They are, first and foremost, characterized by a fusion of diverse forms of social power; more precisely, economic, political and cultural practices and processes are subordinated to a common centre. The institutional embodiment of this unity is the party-state (as we shall see, it is also – in an important sense – an imaginary institution). Its dual character is significant: it is true that the party bureaucracy controlled the state apparatus, but it is no less true that the party exercised its power through the state, and that it was only the fusion with the state that transformed a party with totalitarian visions into a machine with a totalitarian grip on social life. The aspiration to total power was grounded in an ideology with equally totalizing claims, accepted as a scientific world-view by its adherents and condemned as a secular religion by its critics. This ideological framework also served to legitimize the systematic exclusion of alternatives and the rejection of any constitutional limitations to party-state sovereignty.

Within this general framework, we can distinguish various types and levels of totalitarian domination. The exercise of power may involve mass terror or selective repression combined with more regular forms of control. Autocratic rule can be replaced with a more oligarchic regime. The official ideology can lose its quasi-religious character and shrink to a routinized but non-contestable frame of reference; in the more extreme cases, its aim is to control the individual mind from within, but its role can also be limited to determining the boundaries of legitimate public discourse. Although an excessive emphasis on control is, by definition, characteristic of all totalitarian systems, the problem of combining control with mobilization and development is not always solved in the same way. During the Stalinist phase, the regime strove to maximize both control and mobilization in the interest of rapid but one-sided development. A more or less clearly perceived need to rationalize the mechanisms of control and adapt them to a more complex mode of development was at the root of later reform projects. By contrast, some variants of the model came to pursue a strategy of total control at the expense of development (the Albanian regime opted for this alternative when it withdrew from the Soviet bloc, and a similar shift of priorities seems to have occurred in Cuba after the failure of an ultra-developmentalist strategy in the early 1960s; but as the contrast between these two examples shows, it depended on circumstances whether the change was accompanied by an isolationist or an interventionist turn in foreign policy). On the other hand, control and mobilization can – albeit only temporarily – serve the purpose of destroying an existing model of development, so as to clear the ground for an imaginary alternative, but with the result that the whole system is thrown into chaos and has to be readapted to its internal and external environment. The Chinese cultural revolution is the most obvious case in point.

Now that the Soviet model has run its course, it is easier to compare with other cases of totalitarian domination. In contrast to Fascist Italy or Nazi Germany, it lasted much longer, underwent more significant changes and proved more capable of global expansion. For all these reasons, its developmental pattern and potential stands out in clearer relief and can throw light on the more inchoate or more condensed history of the other regimes. A detailed comparison is beyond our scope, but one fundamental point should be noted. According to Hannah Arendt, fully developed totalitarian regimes could only emerge in states that were large enough to survive the destructive impact and sustain the expansive dynamic of this new form of power. Later experience has, however, shown that totalitarianism could be taken to its extreme limits in relatively small states, such as Albania, North Korea or Cambodia. But with regard to the original background and basis of the totalitarian phenomenon, Arendt's thesis points to an important aspect that can now be described in more precise terms: the imperial dimensions of the pioneering totalitarian projects. In the Italian case, this connection was less pronounced than in the other two; the Fascist regime can, nevertheless, be analysed as a foredoomed attempt to compensate for an earlier failure to realize imperial ambitions, and its imaginary identification with a past empire as a substitute for a genuine imperial tradition. With regard to the Nazi regime in Germany, 1933 was – as various authors have argued – the continuation of 1914 by other means; the totalitarian regime was, in other words, inseparable from the renewal of an imperial project, much more solidly based and temporarily more successful than the Italian one. And as the whole analysis above has stressed, the Soviet model grew out of the post-revolutionary reconstruction of the Russian empire. These parallels suggest an underlying affinity between imperial and totalitarian patterns of power: if imperial structures are, as argued above, based on the accumulation and absolutization of power beyond the limits of more self-contained social formations, they prefigure – up to a point – the logic of modern totalitarianism.

THE TOTALITARIAN PROJECT

The history of Soviet-type societies cannot be reduced to an unfolding totalitarian logic, and we should therefore talk about a totalitarian project confronted with both internal and external obstacles, rather than a fully-fledged totalitarian system. On the other hand, we can only describe a power structure as totalitarian if it imposes – with some degree of success – a comprehensive pattern of social and cultural life. The project was, to put it another way, less than a programming code, but more than one component among others. A brief glance at Castoriadis's interpretation of the Soviet model may help to clarify this point. He sees the totalitarian invention of the party-state as one of three factors that shaped the development of post-revolutionary Russian society; the other two were the world-historical context of modern capitalism, with its rationality geared to the accumulation of wealth and power, and the imperial legacy which had reasserted itself after a period of partial Westernization. What this analysis misses is the capacity of the totalitarian project to absorb and restructure the two other components. It is true that the emergence of totalitarianism depended on historical preconditions, modern as well as traditional, and external as well as internal. But the totalitarian regime reintegrated the imperial fragments into a new institutional framework that could at the same time claim to represent an alternative pattern of modernity and a counter-challenge to the West. As we now know, both the reappropriation of the Russian past and the redefinition of modernity were essentially incomplete and only temporarily successful, but they went far enough and lasted long enough to have an unprecedented global impact.

As Robert Tucker has shown, Stalin's 'second revolution' was the most decisive turn in the history of the Soviet model. This 'state-initiated, state-directed and state-enforced process, which radically reconstituted the Soviet order as it had existed in the 1920s' (Tucker 1990: xiv), began with forced collectivization in 1929 and culminated in the great purge of 1936–8. It was not guided by a pre-existent blueprint for a new order; rather, the totalitarian project took shape in and through the process, and earlier experiments in theory and practice did not amount to more than partial prefigurations. The totalitarian potential inherent in Lenin's vision of the vanguard, discussed above, could only be realized when the party had taken exclusive control of and entered into a symbiosis with a state apparatus. Within the pre-revolutionary tradition of Bolshevism, the pretensions to privileged insight and universal leadership were at odds with the habits of a party functioning in a pluralistic environment, and the claim that it already constituted a totalitarian subculture is therefore unjustified. It is also misleading to treat the first phase of the post-revolutionary dictatorship – the policies of War Communism – as a premature attempt to implement a totalitarian design. Although it is true that War Communism predated the civil war, went far beyond emergency measures and outlasted the counter-revolutionary threat, it never developed into a coherent and comprehensive strategy. There was, as yet, no firmly established ideological framework. Political life within the party was still characterized by residual pluralism; in the economic sphere, state control was – after the retreat from an initial attempt to intervene more directly in rural affairs – limited to the rapidly shrinking urban sector and even there it fell far short of an effective command economy. This is not to suggest that War Communism was an insignificant episode. For a variety of reasons (including, in particular, the class conflict that continued after the Bolshevik seizure of power), the emerging party-state found itself compelled to subject the economy to much stricter controls than it had envisaged. In doing so, it could draw on the experience of the Russian war economy as well as the example of the vastly superior but overidealized German one, and link these historical innovations to the ideological vision of a demonetarized macro-*oikos*. Both connections were important: the need to retain and expand a war economy led the Bolsheviks – in contrast to classical Marxism – to think of the abolition of commodity production as a short-term goal, and the revised Marxist image of a post-capitalist economy inspired a more extreme response to the crisis than a mere struggle for control would have done. The most significant legacy of War Communism was, then, the incipient fusion of revolutionary utopia and imperial strategy, and in this sense it paved the way for a later totalitarian breakthrough. It should be noted that the whole party, irrespective of other differences, accepted War Communism as a strategic frame of reference, and the shift to other policies after 1921 could only be seen as a retreat. Conflicting interpretations of the NEP strategy during the 1920s never changed this underlying attitude. Moreover, political developments during the NEP interlude – the growth of the bureaucratic apparatus of the party-state and the suppression of oppositional currents within the party – ran counter to the liberalization of the economy and reinforced the trends that were to culminate in Stalin's 'second revolution'.

There is another side to this historical background. The second revolution took place after a triple failure of Bolshevik strategy: the seizure of power in Russia had not been followed by revolution in the West, the outcome of the revolutionary crises and conflicts was a massive regression of Russian society, and Lenin's belated turn towards a gradualist approach had not developed into a political alternative. In short, some foundational premises of pre- and post-revolutionary Bolshevism had been refuted, and the situation was ripe for a new political project which could legitimize itself as a substitute for the original programme and claim to revive the revolutionary process. In retrospect, it seems clear that Stalin was preparing the ground for such a turn long before he took the offensive, but his opponents can hardly be blamed for misjudging him: the goals which he was pursuing were beyond the horizon of mainstream Bolshevism. Tucker (1987: 70, 116) describes his position as 'a Bolshevism of the radical right', and his revolution from above as 'a reversion to a developmental mode that had existed in earlier Russian history'; there is no reason to disagree, but the syncretic character of Stalin's traditionalism should also be noted. There is – as Tucker shows – ample evidence for his identification with both Ivan the Terrible and Peter the Great. Since the real legacies of these two role models were, as we have seen, very different, Stalin's adoption of them resulted in an original and explosive combination. In particular, it helped to justify an a priori equation of terror and mobilization. Moreover, Stalin combined the policy of opening to the West, characteristic of both Ivan and Peter, with the isolationism that had been stronger during the more stagnant phases of Muscovite history. The Westernizing thrust of his strategy was evident not only in the technological transfer that was essential to Soviet industrialization, but also in the construction of a universalist state ideology which drew on Western sources and tried to turn the Western idea of progress against Western hegemony. At the same time, this ideology was adapted to the Russian context in such a way that it could justify cultural isolation from the contemporary West and a far-reaching rehabilitation of the imperial past.

Contrary to what some theorists of totalitarianism have suggested, the second revolution does not fit into a cycle of offensives and retreats on the part of a state which strove to absorb society but could not survive without periodic concessions to it. There was no comparable attempt before 1929, and the performance was never repeated. The unique and decisive role of the second revolution becomes more obvious if we see it as an economic, political and cultural upheaval that lasted for a whole decade and ended with the liquidation of a large section of its original leadership. In retrospect, it is of course much easier to make sense of the first half of the decade: the overall direction of the process and the interconnections between its various aspects are relatively clear. The industrializing drive and the abrupt stepping up of state intervention, somewhat euphemistically described as 'central planning', were closely linked to the militarization of the economy, in the double sense of orienting it towards a military build-up and adopting a military approach to economic problems. As for the forced collectivization of agriculture, there is no doubt that those who launched the operation had both a political and an economic rationale: Stalin's strategy of state-building and mobilization could not be implemented without more effective control over the rural majority of the population, and the transfer of resources from the agricultural sector was seen as essential to rapid industrialization. Both aims were to some extent achieved, but the adverse long-term consequences are well known, and even the apparent short-term success is open to doubt: some recent research suggests that the chaos and confusion brought about by the collectivization disaster may have more than offset any contribution to economic growth and dislocated the political system of control, thus provoking extreme counter-measures and a slide of the party-state into autocracy. In any case, the strengthening of the Soviet state, which was the primary goal of the second revolution, led to further concentration of power at its core and further consolidation of its ideological monopoly. It was during this phase that Marxism-Leninism developed into a closed and definitive world-view.

The opening moves of the second revolution had some unexpected effects, and its strategists had to adapt to a situation that was in many ways beyond their control and understanding. But if there is nevertheless a visible structural logic to the first phase of this process, the same can hardly be said about the second one. It is difficult to contextualize the great purge – the most fateful and least intelligible episode in Soviet history – without running the risk of overrationalizing an obviously pathological phenomenon. For our present purposes it is enough to note a few points that now seem reasonably clear. Most importantly, the purge completed the transition from the oligarchic to the autocratic form of the party-state. The institutional base of a new autocracy had been in the making for some time. Although the role of Stalin's 'special apparatus' is and will probably – for lack of information – remain controversial, there is no doubt that its power had grown at the expense of more official institutions (Rosenfeldt 1978; Tucker (1990: 124) describes it as 'an unofficial government subordinate directly and exclusively to Stalin'). In the aftermath of the civil war, the apparatus had taken control of the party, and a secret apparatus was now taking control of the formal one. The tension between an incipient autocracy and a destabilized oligarchy (another version of 'dual power') added to the overall disequilibrium, characteristic of the first phase of the second revolution; the abortive political manoeuvres that took place in connection with the 1934 party congress may have aimed at blocking the road to autocracy, but Stalin's counter-offensive showed that the trend was already irreversible. The general strategy of restructuring the apparatus could, of course, incor-porate a variety of more specific goals. Remnants of the intraparty opposition had to be liquidated, not because they represented a real threat, but because their very existence was an obstacle to the reinterpretation of history and therefore to the legitimation of the new regime. Large sections of the party-state élite had supported the economic strategy of the second revolution but were – or seemed – less committed to its political project as defined by the autocratic centre; they were destroyed in the purge and replaced with a new and more adaptable generation of functionaries. The recruitment of new cadres went hand in hand with the creation of a new system of privileges (this was the other side of the 'social mobility' overemphasized by some historians of Stalinism). Last but not least, the cultural and political élites of the non-Russian republics were decimated. A policy of imperial centralization and Russification had been an integral part of the second revolution from the outset, and the great purge reinforced this trend. As the totalitarian regime entered its most extreme phase, the identification with imperial models and traditions also became more explicit.

On the other hand, it can be argued that the institutional imbalance of a regime thrown into crisis and threatened with chaos converged with the paranoid personality of the ruler (Lewin 1985: 279), and that the result was a wave of dysfunctional terror. There was, in other words, an explosion of irrationality that went far beyond the above-mentioned structural and strategic pressures. In addition, the great purge may – within the limits set by a triumphant autocracy – have become an outlet for conflicts and rivalries on the lower level of the apparatus.[2] But if this increasingly uncontrolled terror was a symptom of a more fundamental inability to control the whole society, the initial strategic rationale for the purge was irrational in another sense: state terror helped to consolidate the developmental pattern which the Stalinist leadership had imposed on Soviet society, but it was bound to cause massive disruptions on all levels of the modernizing process on which the strength of the state depended.

It was Stalin's second revolution, rather than the Bolshevik takeover of the 1917 revolution, that completed the fusion of imperial and revolutionary traditions, and his reactivation of Muscovite and Petrine models was accompanied by a massive reorientation – but not a liquidation – of the Bolshevik legacy. The Trotskyist critics and conservative sympathizers who took 'socialism in one country' to mean a retreat from revolutionary to nationalist perspectives were profoundly wrong. The new strategy was imperial, rather than nationalist, and could therefore more easily accommodate a revolutionary ideology and retain control over revolutionary movements while confining them to a subaltern role. And it was a breakthrough, rather than a retreat; far from being a mediocrity, Stalin thus proved to be one of the most disastrously effective innovators of this century. This may help to understand his charismatic appeal, often wrongly explained as an artificial product of the apparatus. But with regard to his achievements, we must distinguish the short-term results of the second revolution from the long-term ones. The pioneering theorists of totalitarianism tended to focus too strongly on 'High Stalinism', i.e. the relatively short phase of Soviet history (1938–53) that was characterized by autocratic rule, permanent purge, and the complete subordination of culture and science to an obscurantist ideology. This acute version of the totalitarian syndrome has been imitated by some other Soviet-type regimes, sometimes with even more extreme methods and more lasting results, but always with some significant deviations from the original model. In the present context, however, we are mainly concerned with the more basic and permanent structures that took shape during the second revolution, remained in place during the post-Stalinist era and began to decompose in the second half of the 1980s. If the post-autocratic phase of the party-state differed markedly from the pre-autocratic one, the main reason was that the autocratic regime had functioned as a crucible of institutional patterns that now proved capable of surviving it. It is the relative stability of these reproducible and transferable patterns that justifies the notion of a Soviet model. Its core structures remained intact despite the changes brought about by the urbanization and industrialization of Soviet society, and they could be imposed on other countries with very different traditions and levels of development. Dissatisfaction with oversimplified theories led some historians to stress the micro- and macro-social adaptations of the model, rather than its unifying logic; such variations are certainly not irrelevant, but they should not lead us to forget the framework within which they were contained. Our main task is to account for the relative coherence of the model without losing sight of its underlying fractures and ultimate limits.

For the reasons indicated above, it seems most appropriate to analyse the model as a configuration of economic, political and cultural patterns, and the political component is obviously the dominant one. Economic transformation and ideological adaptation served the purposes of state- and empire-building. In that sense, it is undoubtedly correct to describe the Soviet Union as a political society. But at the same time, the strategies that were applied and institutionalized in the economic and cultural domains had a retroactive impact on the political centre: they forced it to face challenges that in turn enhanced its ambitions beyond measure. With the attempt to construct from above an economic machine that would not only ensure more effective mobilization of resources, but also sustain competition with the more advanced West and beat it at its own game, the Soviet regime took an ultra-interventionistic turn; the statist and imperial tradition and the centralist bias of pre- and post-revolutionary Bolshevism combined to push the leadership in this direction, rather than towards more balanced economic policies. Analogously, the construction of an official, exhaustive and exclusive world-view, endowed with legislative power over all areas of social life, was both an incentive and a rationale for uninhibited state intervention.

All three spheres were drawn into the modernizing process, but it can nevertheless be argued that each of them was particularly strongly influenced by one of the separate sources of the Soviet model. The continuity with the Russian part was, as we have seen, most pronounced on the political level: the second revolution was also a definitive return to the imperial sources. The imperative of modernization, more precisely the demand for imitative or alternative strategies of catching up with the West, was most urgent in the economic sphere. The cultural framework, i.e. the ideological edifice of Marxism-Leninism, drew on a revolutionary and utopian tradition, imported from the West but adapted to indigenous premises in such a way that it could serve to synthesize conflicting strands of the Russian tradition. This cultural background co-determined the course of economic and political development. On the one hand, the economic reductionism of Marxist-Leninist orthodoxy, which went far beyond that of classical Marxism and lacked the counterweights of the latter, gave the necessary ideological support to a strategy of competition with the capitalist economies on their own ground and according to their own standards. This combination of policy and doctrine was as plausible during the formative phase of the Soviet model (which coincided with the most serious crisis of capitalist development in the West) as it was to prove disastrous at a later stage. On the other hand, the adaptation of a universalist ideology and a utopian vision of the future to an imperial power structure should not be mistaken for a pure and simple instrumentalization: the new cultural horizon raised the imperial project to a higher level, with regard to both ambitions and resources. To what extent individual Soviet leaders were motivated by utopian or imperial concerns is a question we need not discuss here (the evidence suggests that this varied from case to case, and that there was a gradual shift towards more traditionally imperial attitudes); the main point is that the Stalinist synthesis renewed the imperial pursuit of power in a more global and extreme fashion, irrespective of the particular interests and rationalizations that could from time to time be incorporated into it.

But in order to clarify the logic of the totalitarian project, we must also look at its specific contents within the three spheres. In each case, an absolutizing and totalizing logic was put into practice, but its institutional façade must be distinguished from its operative mechanisms as well as from the unacknowledged adjustments that are essential to the self-reproduction of the pattern as a whole. The following analysis will, in other words, focus on three interconnected levels within each sphere. There is, to begin with, an explicit self-definition that might also be described as a constitutive myth; since it is not only essential to the legitimation of the regime, but also – even if more intermittently – conducive to both self-defeating excesses and incipient challenges from within, it cannot be dismissed as a mere mask or misrepresentation of underlying realities. But it should not be confused with the next level, that of a functioning logic which draws on the imaginary core of the myth and translates it into strategies and structures. Both the transformative impact and the internal contradictions of the totalitarian project are most directly related to this context. Finally, the tensions and imbalances generated by the totalitarian drive give rise to complementary patterns that are in principle incompatible with the logic of the project, but in practice indispensable for its survival. As we shall see, the interconnections between the three levels develop in specific ways within the economic, political and cultural dimensions of the model.

Economy

Although it is now well known that 'central planning' was a highly idealized description of Soviet economic mechanisms, the 'cult of the plan', as some reformist critics called it, was an integral part of the Soviet model. The visions of a centrally controlled economy and a future state of abundance, the latter to be reached through organized progress, were of course not indigenous to the Russian tradition. If the orientation towards an 'infinite expansion of rational mastery' (Castoriadis) was one of the most basic cultural premises of modernity, the idea of a planned economy can be seen as one of various attempts to rationalize this imaginary goal. As for the idea of abundance, it is best understood as a utopian response to the experience of capitalist development: the accumulation of abstract wealth was to be replaced with an equally unlimited satisfaction of human needs. The self-interpretation of the Soviet model was thus closely linked to the most central trends and conflicts of Western modernity. But does this mean that the Soviet experience was 'a practical test of the limits of Enlightenment utopia' (Bauman et al. 1984: 176), as well as those of its socialist offshoots? As I have been trying to show, the constitution of the Soviet model involved a long-drawn-out process of selective appropriation and adaptation, rather than a straightforward transfer of the modern imaginary. The phantasms of total control and unlimited wealth were separated from the more complex traditions of Western radicalism and fused with the strategy of an imperial state, engaged in a project of economic transformation that was essential to its legitimacy as well as to its survival as a great power.

In this context, the myth of the plan played a double-edged role: it seemed to hold out the prospect of complete control over the economic sphere, and it claimed to represent a higher level of economic rationality. Both aspects were – in varying combinations – important for the international appeal of the Soviet model. Their relationship to domestic policies is somewhat more complex. On the one hand, it seems clear that illusions about planning as a perfect instrument of state control led to self-defeating excesses and aggravated the built-in tensions of the regime. This trend was most pronounced during the second revolution (Lewin (1973) describes it as 'the disappearance of planning in the plan'). But the main long-term consequence – the refusal to recognize uncertainty and innovation as essential aspects of economic life – was paralysing rather than disruptive. On the other hand, utopian versions of a less politicized and therefore more rational planning mechanism could become part of reformist strategies. This was to some extent the case with Khrushchev's policies (his plan to restructure the whole party apparatus in connection with a reorganization of the economy was probably the decisive cause of his downfall), and the same approach is reflected in later (and more academic) ideas of an economic reform that would use the most advanced technology of information to rationalize the plan and thus avoid concessions to the market.

But as many analysts have shown, the real functioning of the supposedly planned economy has always been characterized by a massive waste of resources and at the same time by the systematic creation of shortage. The concept of the command economy is now widely used to underline the irrational consequences of state intervention, but in view of the comprehensive and dynamic character of the Soviet model, it seems more appropriate to talk about a 'mobilized economy' (Sapir 1990). For our present purposes, two major implications of this concept should be noted. In the first place, the mobilized economy can be seen as an extension and radicalization of pre-revolutionary experiments with a militarized economy. But it is a much more thoroughgoing attempt to subordinate economic growth to an indefinite accumulation of power. In this sense, it is a new expression of the modern mirage of rational mastery and a particularly extreme example of the overextension of a restrictive model of rationality. Inasmuch as the mobilized economy was thus geared to an indefinite (and in the long run incoherent) goal, it can also be described as a de-functionalized one. In the historical context, however, this meant that it served the purposes of state- and empire-building. Since the logic of the economic sphere is thus subordinated to political imperatives, the search for a Soviet economic system or a 'Soviet mode of production' is misguided; if the Soviet model is to be compared with other patterns of modernity, the focus should be on a specific relationship between the political and the economic, and on the restricted autonomy of the latter. It should, however, also be noted that a politicized economy is not simply a 'war economy sui generis' (Lange 1970: 101). The overall military orientation of Soviet economic institutions is indisputable, but its relative strength varies from case to case; more specifically, the Khrushchev era was characterized by an attempt to redirect the mobilized economy towards economic competition with the West, and it was the failure of this strategy that led to the reconsolidation of the military-industrial complex.

But on the other hand, the mobilized economy is still a form of economic life, and as such, it could never dispense with the elementary structures that have become consubstantial to economic life in the modern world. The strategies of control have always been implemented in part through market transactions and monetary forms. 'Far from the Soviet economy functioning as one giant enterprise, the traces of commercial relations are omnipresent within the state economy' (Sapir 1990: 17). This finding can hardly be disputed, and it has some obvious implications. The mobilized economy deviated from the pattern of modern capitalism, but did not transcend it; there was, rather, a twofold continuity: the limited militarization of capitalist economies served as an indispensable precedent for a much more ambitious project, and some basic mechanisms of capitalist development survived in a fragmented form. It is the relationship between the project and the mechanisms that explains both the distinctive features and the fundamental problems of Soviet-type economies. In contrast to the phantasm of total planning, the mobilized economy remains in a state of constant tension between the political centre and the less powerful but never fully controllable economic units. This unbalanced power structure gives rise to a perverted form of economic rationality: 'a logic of systematic preference for the present against the future' (ibid.: 51), reflected in the well-known behavioural patterns of Soviet enterprises (such as the hoarding of resources, the negative attitude to innovation, and the 'quantity drive').

The mobilized economy thus presupposes a limited and fragmented autonomy of economic actors as well as a highly asymmetric but inescapable dialectic of control between them and the centre. This constellation is also the key to a further development: the emergence of counterweights and correctives to the imbalances of the mobilized economy. The concept of a 'second economy' has often been used to describe the most striking phenomena of this kind, but from the present point of view, they constitute a third level of economic life (in contrast to the institutionalized but unrealizable myth of the plan and the effective but incomplete project of mobilization). It is not limited to the private sector, and it is not – as some definitions of the 'second economy' suggest – uniformly illegal. If we use the distinction between vertical and horizontal economic mechanisms (Katsenelinboigen 1990: 244–53), this third level is made up of the more or less market-like horizontal mechanisms of coordination that develop alongside – rather than inside – the framework of the mobilized economy. It is a complementary economy, but not an alternative one: as experience has shown, it does not develop into a counter-model that could in due course absorb or replace the state-controlled economy.

The relationship between the three layers of Soviet economic institutions should be seen in historical perspective. Although the myth of the plan could never be translated into a really existing economy, it made more apparent sense and contributed more effectively to the legitimacy of the regime during a phase of radical transformation and rapid if unbalanced growth than in the later stages of development. The operative mechanisms of the mobilized economy were, as we have seen, best suited to the tasks of rapid industrialization for military purposes, and their permanently dominant role was reflected in a growing gap between developmental levels and capacities of the military and the civil sector. Finally, the growing significance of the 'second economy' was due to both economic and political causes: it was not only indispensable to the reproduction of an increasingly complex society, but it could also expand into new areas as a result of economic policies designed – together with other concessions – to reduce tensions between state and society. In this context, the 'second economy' could to some extent function as a 'spontaneous surrogate economic reform' (Grossman 1977: 40). The effect was, of course, double-edged: an essentially unbalanced economy became more viable, but the discrepancy between official and unofficial rules undermined both the rationality and the legitimacy of the whole system.

Political factors

On the political level, the constitutive myth is the 'leading role of the party'. The fiction of an enlightened vanguard, entrusted with the task of programming and controlling social development, has the same ancestry as the myth of the plan. It is, on the one hand, rooted in modern visions of the fusion and joint growth of knowledge and power, but it also plays a key role in the self-representation of an imperial state bent on upgrading both its resources and its strategies. The adapted and institutionalized image of the party gives rise to a new pattern of legitimation, based on the claim to scientific knowledge of objective interests and historical laws, and irreducible to other traditional or modern types of legitimate domination. One of its advantages is that the definition of the party as the only authentic representative of the people relativizes the principle of popular sovereignty without openly rejecting it. In a formal sense, the Leninist inversion of the relationship between party and class was thus radicalized and generalized beyond its original context; but in a substantive sense, it was given a new meaning through the totalitarian reconstruction of an imperial centre. In addition to its legitimizing function, the myth of the party also had a more limited and intermittent mobilizing effect: it seems likely that the aim of recreating the party in a more genuinely monolithic form was part of Stalin's strategy for the second revolution, and at the other end of the spectrum, reformist projects could sometimes start with an effort to reactivate party life against the apparatus which had paralysed it.

It was, of course, the supremacy of the party-state apparatus that was most characteristic of the political organization of Soviet-type societies and as central to the political sphere as the vertical mechanisms of mobilization were to the economic one. As the party-state developed, the power centre shifted from the nominally sovereign institutions of the party to the apparatus which at the same time absorbed and transformed the pre-existent state structures. The apparatus remains at the core of the totalitarian project, even if its *modus operandi* can change: during the autocratic phase, power was to a significant extent exercised through informal, improvised and secret channels, whereas oligarchic rule was based on a more formal and stable hierarchy.

The novelty and complexity of the apparatus as a power structure has been most effectively highlighted by unconvincing attempts to analyse it in terms of traditional categories. As many critics have pointed out, it is not simply a new and more extreme form of bureaucratic domination. On the one hand, the arbitrary rule of the apparatus falls behind modern bureaucratic standards of division of labour, regulation of authority, and reliance on expert knowledge; on the other hand, its methods of control and its mobilizing capacity go far beyond the classical (i.e. Weberian) model of the bureaucratic machine. It is equally misleading to treat the party-state as merely a further step towards the '*étatisation*' of society and to describe totalitarian rule as a 'tendential property of the modern state' (Giddens 1985: 295). As we have seen, the process of state formation involves the development of monopolies of resources and mechanisms of control. Its scope and impact vary from case to case, and the countertrends which accompany it can be more or less effective; but the monopolies and mechanisms in question are limited and specific, whereas the totalitarian regime is based on a project of total control and comprehensive monopolization. It is an imaginary institution, never capable of functioning as a coherent system, but permanently striving for embodiment in effective mechanisms. The institutionalization of the party as a separate and superior level of the apparatus serves to safeguard the totalizing logic of the project against the more limited strategies through which it has to be implemented. This characteristic of Soviet-type societies – the construction of an integral system of controls and the creation of a specific institutional framework to enforce the principle of unity against processes of differentiation – has led some analysts to describe them as mono-organizational (Rigby 1990) or monocratic (Strmiska 1983). But the organizational pattern which is thus singled out is inseparable from a broader and more dynamic context. The monocratic concentration of power is also a regime of accumulation; its mainspring is, in other words, a power-maximizing drive, sustained by the same cultural sources and confined within the same cultural horizon as the mobilized economy.

The party-state builds on the results of earlier processes of state formation, but differs from its precursors in both scale and scope. Its power structure differs from class domination in more basic ways. This is not simply due to the subordination of all forms of power to a political centre. More importantly, the apparatus is, as G. Markus has put it, 'constituted in a way that is in principle different from a class' (Feher et al. 1983: 118). Classes in the original and paradigmatic sense emerged within a very specific social constellation. Its most important feature was a limited but significant differentiation of state and society which opened up the social and political space for a new type of conflictual action. Classes are – to cut a long and intricate story short – conflicting social forces that on the whole and in the long run tend to act towards each other in accordance with their differential positions within the social structure; the relative importance of economic, political and cultural determinants of the latter is one of the main points of debate between rival theories of class. The concept of class thus refers to a specific and complex relationship between structure, action and conflict. By contrast, the supremacy of the centralized and totalizing apparatus brings about a radical change in this relationship. Instead of the external correlation characteristic of class societies, the organizational principles of the apparatus guarantee and codify the subordination of social action to the imperatives of the power structure. This does not apply only to the internal functioning of the apparatus; over and above that, the assimilation of society to its logic is – although never completed and periodically thwarted by various countertendencies – a systemic goal. Open contestation is excluded, and the conflictual aspect that is essential to the concept of class is thus eliminated.

If the power structure that is at the centre of the Soviet model differs from traditional class- and state-centred patterns, it is nevertheless true that these antecedent mechanisms continue to play a residual role. The apparatus emerges and develops through the transformation of state institutions as well as the redistribution of power and privilege. More importantly, the political *modus operandi* of the apparatus resembles the command economy in that it generates countertrends which are both alien to the logic of the model and indispensable to its functioning. There is, to begin with, a proliferation of local and regional sub-apparatuses; the concentration of power at the top is reproduced on a lesser scale by subordinate authorities striving to reduce their dependence on the centre, expand their sphere of influence and outdistance their rivals. Since the twin tasks of control and mobilization call for a minimum of local autonomy, this fragmenting process is an inevitable side-effect, and there is no definitive way of containing it – the differences between the autocratic and the oligarchic form of the party-state are, to a very significant extent, the result of different solutions to this problem. But if the oligarchic regime imposes more balanced and regular forms of control, it also opens up new spaces for the centrifugal tendencies. During the post-Stalinist era, analysts of the latter development disagreed on its implications: some saw the emergence of rival power blocs and conflicting interests within the apparatus as the first step towards a genuinely pluralistic and in that sense more modern political system, whereas others read the same phenomena as signs of a return to more traditional patterns and used notions like neo-patrimonialism and clientelism to draw parallels with other societies that resisted political modernization. Jowitt (1992) coined the concept of neo-traditionalism to describe the overall retreat of the Soviet regime from its earlier, more ambitious and innovative principles of organization. Both hypotheses contained some grains of truth, but their more far-reaching versions have now been refuted. The Soviet model succumbed to history, but neither through gradual pluralization nor through creeping patrimonialization. The trends that could be taken to point in these two directions were blocked by a set of mechanisms which in the end proved conducive to implosion rather than adaptation. The unofficial aspects of political life were significant enough to constitute a third level in the sense defined above, but not strong enough to coalesce into an alternative pattern.

The question of conflicting trends and perspectives within the political sphere cannot be discussed without some reference to the corresponding forms of legitimation; we must therefore briefly consider the relationship between the three levels from this point of view. Although Weber's analysis and typology of legitimation is the most convenient frame of reference, it should not be regarded as an exhaustive inventory. In particular, the myth of the vanguard-party represents a new mode of legitimation that has some affinity with each of Weber's three types, but also some distinctive characteristics of its own. The link to the revolutionary tradition can be seen as a source of traditional legitimacy *sui generis*; its main function, however, was the historical grounding of a transformative project, not – as in the Weberian model – the sacralization of an inherited order. There is no doubt that the image of the revolutionary party has something in common with that of the charismatic leader, but this is not a sufficient reason for defining the Soviet pattern of legitimacy as collective or impersonal charisma (Jowitt 1992: 127–39). The crucial difference is that the role of the party is justified in terms of a rational knowledge of the laws of history and a translation of this knowledge into rational principles of organization; the charismatic element is, in other words, rationalized a priori rather than a posteriori. But this does not mean that the Soviet model can be subsumed under a suitably expanded Weberian concept of rational legitimacy. The claim that the focus of legitimacy shifts from formal-legal rationality to goal rationality (Rigby 1982) does not do full justice to the originality of Soviet-type regimes: their ideological framework involves a comprehensive redefinition of rationality which aspires – among other things – to transcend the Weberian dichotomy of goal- and value-rationality, and this alternative model of rationality is in turn based on a reinterpretation of cultural premises that are – as suggested above – common to modern societies but compatible with different projects of modernity.

In short, the Soviet mode of legitimation incorporates some aspects of all the types identified by Weber but, taken as a whole, it constitutes a new and original phenomenon. There is, however, another side to Weber's argument that may help to understand both the significance and the limits of the innovation. The legitimizing process must, as Weber sees it, be analysed on two levels: with regard to the 'administrative staff' as well as to the subjects of the rulers that are laying claim to legitimacy. It is, in other words, related to the core power structure as well as the broader social context, and on both levels, the legitimizing effect can range from mere acceptance of the regime in question to a more active identification with it: legitimacy can be more or less conducive to mobilization. It was characteristic of the Soviet model during its formative phase that its legitimizing myth had a strong grip on a highly mobilized minority, directly involved in the exercise of power, but a much more limited and problematic impact on other sections of society.

This imbalance between internal and external effects is a structural weakness of the Soviet mode of legitimation, and it has therefore from the outset been forced to draw on supplementary sources. Agnes Heller's distinction between dominant and auxiliary forms of legitimation (Feher et al. 1983: 143ff) is relevant to this issue, even if her account of the relationship between them is questionable; in particular, it would seem that the reference to 'substantive rationality' – if we use this controversial concept to denote the vision of history and progress embodied in the myth of the vanguard – remained dominant throughout, at least in the sense that it continued to shape the official self-representation of the regime. On the other hand, the exercise of power by the apparatus has always been dependent on a whole set of auxiliary sources, and there is no doubt that in the course of time they became more important to the stability of the model. But on the level of explicit claims and principles, they remained subordinate in the sense that they had to be filtered through and adapted to the framework of the founding myth. The declining appeal of the latter can, of course, lead to redefinitions which shift its focus from the historical mission of the party to more modest and specific tasks: the emphasis may be on an overall managerial function in the modernizing process or – as now seems increasingly to be the case in China – on the maintenance of national unity.

The auxiliary patterns of legitimation include the three Weberian types (as separate modes, not to be confused with the partially analogous aspects of the dominant mode) and some additional factors that were not integrated into Weber's theory of legitimation, but can – as later critics have shown – be analysed from a Weberian perspective. Each of them is inherently ambiguous and open to divergent interpretations, related to the more general contrast between autocratic and oligarchic power structures, but all of them can be kept under control as long as more fundamental structural problems do not give rise to a legitimation crisis.

The second revolution and the rise of the Stalinist autocracy was, as we have seen, accompanied by an explicit reactivation of the Russian tradition and its models of imperial power. With the transition from autocracy to oligarchy, this quest for traditional legitimacy took a rather different turn: a more diffuse reference to the Russian tradition could now be combined with the construction of a 'Soviet way of life' (V. Zaslavsky) as a tradition in its own right. To the extent that this reconstructed tradition functioned as a medium of consensus-building and conflict management, it helped to consolidate an oligarchic regime and grant some legitimacy to interest groups within the apparatus, without endangering the overall system of control. After the disintegration of the model, a more emphatic reference to the Russian tradition may serve to de-legitimize the Soviet interlude (although it is too early to judge the political impact of this trend), but traditionalism as such did not play an active role in the destruction of the regime. Similar conclusions can be drawn with regard to rational-legal forms of legitimation. In the context of the Stalinist autocracy, they were a subordinate but by no means wholly insignificant device; for both international and domestic purposes, the 'Stalin constitution' was an indispensable part of the power structure that grew out of the second revolution. It provided the party-state with a formal and detailed legal framework. The stronger emphasis on 'social legality' during the oligarchic phase was double-edged in that it led on the one hand to a more explicit constitutionalization of the 'leading role of the party' (it was more strongly affirmed in Brezhnev's constitution than in Stalin's) and on the other hand to the rejection of mass terror as a mode of government. When legal norms are superimposed on patterns of command and obedience and accepted as a normal frame of reference, rather than an instrument that can be discarded at will, they serve to stabilize a balance of power between diverse sections of the apparatus. Once legal-constitutional procedures had got out of control, the drive for further extension was hard to resist. In that sense, the Soviet elections of 1989 were clearly a major landmark. But the move from a purely auxiliary to a partly constitutive status must be explained in terms of prior crises and conflicts within the apparatus, rather than any general logic of legality.

Charismatic legitimacy was essential to the Stalinist autocracy, and it was systematically built up during the second revolution. For all its prominence, however, it had to be grounded in the specific framework imposed by the state doctrine and linked to other auxiliary forms. Stalin's notorious *Short Course*, published at the end of the great purge, can be read as an attempt to codify these connections. It confirmed Stalin's status as a charismatic leader and Lenin's sole legitimate heir, but it also laid down the definitive and comprehensive version of the Marxist-Leninist world-view. In addition, it gave the charismatic leadership a traditional basis through a mythical account of party history, and it stressed Stalin's achievements as law-maker and state-builder. After the war, Stalin claimed authorship of this canonical text; in conjunction with other moves, this may be seen as part of an abortive attempt to make charismatic legitimacy less dependent on the ideological and institutional framework of the party-state. Such trends were, in any case, cut short by Stalin's death and the subsequent transition to oligarchy. But that was not the end of charismatic legitimacy. Rather, the post-Stalinist phase saw a revival of the Lenin cult which aimed at providing the regime with a source of charismatic legitimacy while preventing its appropriation by a living leader. The slogan 'Lenin lives!' sums up this peculiar strategy: the model of charismatic leadership was to be kept alive for ideological use but kept out of the routinized politics of the party-state. While this new combination protected the apparatus against a return to autocratic rule, it also weakened the position of reformist leaders who had to operate within the obligatory framework of a return to Leninist norms and were thus prevented from claiming a charismatic legitimacy of their own. The emerging pattern of post-Soviet Russian politics suggests that charismatic status was rather easily acquired by a leader who challenged the apparatus from the outside; but for this to be possible, the power structure and its patterns of legitimacy had first to reach a stage of advanced crisis.

The suggestion that a more fully developed Weberian theory should include imperialism and nationalism as sources of legitimacy (Collins 1986) is clearly relevant to the Soviet experience. Imperial legitimacy was never insignificant and never self-sufficient, but its relative weight varied. It was more important under the conditions of fully-fledged autocracy (1938–53) and consolidated oligarchy (after 1964) than during the formative or transitional phases. In the Russian context, the legitimizing role of nationalism was inseparable from the imperial tradition which drew on it but at the same time went beyond it and therefore had to reconcile its claims with those of other forces. The role of separate national legitimacy in some other variants of the Soviet model will be discussed later. As for Russian nationalism, it was only in a situation of acute crisis that it could take a partial and probably temporary anti-imperial turn: the bankrupt empire was condemned as a betrayal of more authentic national values.

The shift from autocracy to oligarchy changed the political parameters of the Soviet model in a way that has no parallel in the two other spheres. It was mainly because of this internal and official transformation that the more unorthodox patterns of political life (in Jowitt's (1992: 121) terms: the 'informal practices' that threaten to become 'corrupt practices') could be contained within more effective limits than those associated with the 'second economy'. This is another symptom of the primacy of politics in

Soviet-type societies: their self-transformative capacity was more pronounced in this sphere than in the others, but the change which it brought about became an obstacle to major economic and cultural reforms. The core structures of the mobilized economy had to remain intact because the power and privileges of the oligarchy – both official and unofficial – depended on them. Similarly, the ideology that had established ground rules for cultural and scientific development as well as for public discourse was an indispensable instrument of control, and adjustments had to be confined within the limits set by the primacy of this function. With regard to the modes of legitimation, the view argued above is that the oligarchic regime was based on the same principles as the autocratic one, but combined and balanced them in a different way. Although the result was a highly composite pattern of legitimacy, its disintegrative potential was kept under control: the crisis which ultimately engulfed the regime was, among other things, a legitimation crisis, but it was brought about by the broader context within which the regime operated, rather than by any internal logic of or tensions between its own legitimizing principles.

In this view, the post-Stalinist regimes did not invent any new modes of legitimation. It may be recalled that some observers of Brezhnev's Russia and its satellites had come to the opposite conclusion. Two arguments of this kind should be briefly considered: Castoriadis's theory of 'stratocracy' as the historical successor of the party-state and Ferenc Feher's analysis of state paternalism as a new and effective principle of legitimacy. For Castoriadis (1981), the rise of stratocracy was the result of a progressive erosion of party sovereignty and a concomitant shift of power towards the military establishment. In the present context, however, it is only the impact of this process on the patterns of legitimacy that concerns us. It is true that Castoriadis does not describe the stratocratic regime in such terms: its cultural novelty consists, as he sees it, in the absolutization of brute force for its own sake, both as the sole constitutive principle of social life and as the only criterion of success in local or global competition. But this conversion to the cult of brute force can be seen as a new and paradoxical form of legitimation in that it validates the absence of legitimacy. The absence of justification becomes a mark of authenticity, and the previous decline of legitimacy is thus turned into a gain rather than a loss. For Castoriadis, this negative mode of legitimation is more effective within the power élite than in relation to society at large; in conjunction with the national-imperial imaginary which it tends to absorb, it is more congenial to the army than to the party and thus reinforces the general trend towards stratocracy. By contrast,

Feher (1982) refers to paternalism as a 'powerful new mode of legitimation' and stresses its mass appeal. As he sees it, the self-representation
of the post-Stalinist state as an 'authoritarian community', offering
protection in exchange for submission, is based on some real and
significant changes. Arbitrary terror has been abolished, and the
authorities now demand passive conformity rather than active commitment; at the same time, the mechanisms of the mobilized economy
have been adjusted so as to allow for a gradual increase in living
standards. These developments made the paternalistic claim to legitimacy
more than a mere slogan. But the structure of paternalism – as described
by Feher – bears some resemblance to Castoriadis's analysis of
stratocracy; inasmuch as it is based on a vaguely generalized image of
paternal authority, it represents a regression to a more elementary level
and an attempt to dispense with elaborate procedures of legitimation. It is
– in contrast to stratocracy – not an outright affirmation of illegitimacy,
but it is moving towards what might be called the zero degree of
legitimacy.

There is no doubt that both these diagnoses were to some extent
founded on fact, but it is now equally clear that militarism and
paternalism were less effective stabilizing factors than they may have
seemed around 1980. In retrospect, it seems that the trends noted by
Castoriadis and Feher were residual rather than innovative. In other
words, they reflect the convergence of an atrophied version of the original
myth with other similarly impoverished sources, and their capacity to
stave off a legitimation crisis was correspondingly limited. A militaristic
strain had always been integral to Bolshevism. Lenin's proposal to
transform world war into civil war, the key to the strategy which brought
him to power in 1917, was – as Victor Chernov (1924) observed – rooted
in a way of thinking that had turned both Marx and Clausewitz upside
down: civil war became the model for the class struggle, and politics
became the continuation of war by other means. As the ideological
sublimations of this attitude lost their power to motivate and mobilize, the
legacy that remained became harder to distinguish from other incentives
to militarism. In addition to the time-honoured militarism of the Russian
tradition, there was the fact that the most spectacular success of the Soviet
regime – achieved under an autocratic leadership – had been victory in a
total war, and that it was still finding it easier to compete with the West
on the military level than in any other context. But the drift towards a
more purely militaristic conception of Soviet power and its rivalry with
the West had some further implications. Since military power was
dependent on other forms and sources of power, an attempt to ignore this

connection was bound to backfire: when the leadership finally had to acknowledge the need for a more balanced strategy, the apparatus was ill equipped to cope with the task. A narrow but for some time effective approach to global competition left the regime disarmed in the face of a new constellation.

The retreat into paternalism was similarly short-sighted and self-defeating. It represented another face of residual Leninism: the myth of the vanguard, with its emphasis on guiding and protecting the masses, contained a strong paternalistic ingredient that could outlast its more elaborate and fragile versions. This could be linked to the paternalistic pretensions of the Russian state tradition and the cultural legacy of autocratic rule. But for the paternalistic turn to be possible at all, the party-state had to readjust its relationship to society – as it had done with the transition to oligarchic rule – and settle for much more modest levels of control and mobilization. In that regard, paternalistic policies set limits to the militaristic turn that was taken at the same time. There was, in other words, a built-in tension between the two last-ditch claims to legitimacy, and it became more acute as economic development slowed down and failed to meet their respective requirements.

To sum up, we can draw a rough parallel between the patterns of legitimacy and the three levels (institutionalized myth, party-state apparatus and unofficial mechanisms) of the political structure. Inherent in the official myth is the claim that the whole question of legitimacy has been shifted to a new and more advanced level where a scientific answer becomes possible. While this phantasm is integral to the public self-image of the regimes in question, it is not a solution to their real legitimation problems, and they must therefore – at a second level – operate with a composite mode of legitimation that includes some well-known and widespread mechanisms as well as a more distinctive framework to which they are linked and adapted. But in a more historical perspective (and at a third level of analysis), it seems clear that each of the auxiliary modes has to some extent functioned on its own, although none of them has of its own accord transgressed the boundaries of the Soviet model, and that during the final phase the different modes tended to shrink to a lower common denominator.

The cultural framework

The legitimation problems of Soviet-type regimes are linked to their overall cultural framework and its weaknesses. If the primary sources of legitimacy have proved insufficient, this reflects a more general interpretive fracture that can be analysed along the same lines as the disunities within the economic and political dimensions.

The constitutive myth is in this case that of Marxism-Leninism as a definitive, exhaustive and exclusive world-view. Lenin's interpretation of classical Marxism as a critical synthesis of the most progressive currents of bourgeois thought is combined with the claim that Lenin's own work represents the adaptation of Marxism to a more advanced state of capitalist development and a more acute phase of the class struggle; as for the further 'creative development' of Leninism, its forms and contents vary in connection with other changes to the model, and specific innovations are less essential to the party-state than the supreme authority to introduce or revoke them. Some fundamental premises are, however, built into the very notion of Marxism-Leninism and thus immunized against revision. Most importantly, Leninism is equated with the defence and systematic elaboration of materialism as a general philosophical perspective; in conjunction with the interpretation of dialectics as a theory of the most fundamental laws of nature and society, this opens the way for the construction of a pseudo-scientific cosmology, officially described as 'dialectical materialism', the conversion of Marx's theory of history into 'historical materialism', and the subsumption of the latter under the general axioms of the former. Leninism is further defined as a simultaneous commitment to objective truth and a party standpoint. The dogmatic assumption of an a priori harmony between these two principles serves to reconcile the claim to scientific legitimacy with the fulfilment of an ideological function. If we use the concept of ideology in a broad sense, i.e. to describe the adaptation of cultural orientations to the imperatives of power structures, it is obviously applicable to Soviet Marxism and its self-representation as a scientific world-view, preserved and applied by a revolutionary vanguard. Whether this ideological formation should be described as a secular religion is a more difficult question. As far as the explicit aims and claims are concerned, it seems more appropriate to speak about a partial functional equivalence between Marxism-Leninism and traditional theological systems: it resembles them in its efforts to achieve an uncontestable and all-encompassing fusion of cognitive and normative authority, but differs from them in its basic assumptions about the human condition and its answers to the recurrent questions of the Western tradition. Those who try to establish a closer connection with Gnostic sources tend to rely on a caricatural view of the latter.

A critical analysis of Soviet Marxism must distinguish between its official self-understanding and its historical constitution. The doctrine that interpreted itself as the result of a logical and progressive development of Marxist theory was in reality the joint product of diverse cultural currents, some of them stronger and more formative than others, but none of them fully absorbed by the Soviet synthesis. Fragments of the Marxian legacy were appropriated and transformed in a way that had to some extent been prefigured by developments within the pre-Bolshevik Marxist tradition. In particular, two apparently divergent but in fact complementary trends should be noted. On the one hand, Soviet Marxism continued the scientistic turn which the dominant branch of the Marxist tradition had taken during the era of the Second International. On the other hand, it also drew on the redemptive visions which revolutionary Marxism shared with other forms of socialist thought. It is a matter of debate whether we can identify a 'redemptive paradigm' of modern politics (Feher 1985), but there is no doubt that more or less explicitly redemptive images have been essential to the revolutionary tradition and proved adaptable to different theoretical languages. In the Bolshevik context, the result was a simultaneous scientization and sacralization of the revolutionary project as well as of the vanguard to which it was entrusted, and both aspects were reinforced by the Russian background. It is on this level – i.e. with regard to latent connections and connotations, rather than articulated beliefs – that the notion of a secular religion becomes more appropriate, if we use it to refer to an ideology which excludes the thematization of the sacred but continues to rely on an implicit reference to it. Stalin's second revolution led to further changes in this direction, although they were less spectacular than in the economic and political domains. A systematic attempt was now made to translate the myth of the scientific world-view into a detailed and binding doctrine, and as the phantasm of orthodoxy thus acquired a more practical content, it was also subjected to more direct political control. It would, however, be misleading to describe this operation as an unqualified subordination of culture to power: the ideology that was developed to match the strategy of the political centre became at the same time more receptive to an imperial imaginary which had previously found expression in the Russian tradition, but remained open to new interpretations and adaptable to new power structures. The Stalinist synthesis made it possible to identify the imperial ambitions of the party-state with the meaning of history and the laws of progress.

With regard to the ideological framework and cultural context of the Soviet model, we can thus distinguish the historical content from the official self-representation in roughly the same way as in the economic and political dimensions. It remains to give a brief account of a third level:

the patterns of coexistence with unofficial ideologies and cultural models. They vary from case to case and reflect the different legacies which the model has had to accommodate. For our present purposes, it is enough to note two recurrent and – in retrospect – particularly significant trends. They might be described as political counter-cultures that could be neutralized for some time, but never eradicated, and were bound to gain strength as Soviet-type regimes moved towards a terminal crisis. On the one hand, the ambiguous relationship to the West, characterized by a changing mixture of dependence and antagonism, has been reflected in a latent Westernism, more openly expressed in times of transition or crisis than during the ascendant phases of the Soviet model, but never fully absorbed by the orthodox view. The vision of the West – and more particularly America – as a symbol and standard of progress was a permanent challenge, and none of the successive responses proved equal to it. The reference to America in Stalin's 1924 definition of Leninism (a combination of 'Russian revolutionary sweep' and 'American efficiency') was typical of post-revolutionary Bolshevik culture: the symptoms range from Lenin's enthusiastic acceptance of Taylorism to less significant speculations about the new man as a 'Russian American'. A very different line was taken during the autocratic phase. But the insistence on Soviet superiority and the glorification of the Russian past can be seen as an attempt to exorcize the problem that had been more openly recognized during the formative years of the party-state. Khrushchev's new strategy of competition with the West in general and America in particular gave a more rational turn to the rivalry; when it failed, the search for compensatory policies was accompanied by a less visible but in the long run more effective conversion to Westernism. The image of the more advanced West was, of course, open to different interpretations. Dissident subcultures could identify with democracy and pluralism, whereas technocratic and consumerist versions were easier to reconcile with remnants of the official ideology, and in the aftermath of the collapse, the cult of the market overshadowed all other concerns. The final stage of this development can only be understood in the context of the crisis that will be discussed in Chapter 4.

On the other hand, the Soviet model had to contend and come to terms with various forms of nationalism. This was not the only link between the cultural patterns of Soviet-type societies and their more indigenous traditions, but it was the most resilient and dynamic one (by contrast, the impact of religious traditions has been much more limited and largely dependent on their relationship to ethnic or national factors). Nationalism has – in different circumstances – been both a source of and an obstacle to legitimacy, but this is only one aspect of its cultural significance; above and beyond that, it involves definitions of collective identity and visions of history which pose a potential and sometimes explicit threat to the official doctrine. Because of the resurgence of nationalism in the post-Communist world, there is now a general tendency to regard it as a victorious adversary of the Soviet model and to forget the much more complex interconnections that were characteristic of the recent past. At this point, a brief typological digression may be useful, even if some of the phenomena in question are closely related to the subject matter of later sections. As I will try to show, the changing relationship between nationalism and Communism must be seen against the background of imperial constellations. From this point of view, we can distinguish four main patterns, but further nuances within each of them should also be noted.

There was, first of all, a nationalist aspect to the imperial versions of the Soviet model. In the original case, the reconstitution of the imperial centre was accompanied by a revival of Russian nationalism, but the multi-ethnic character and the universalist ambitions of the empire made a complete fusion with nationalism impossible, and the tensions between the two foci of identity created problems not altogether unlike those of the old regime. Under these circumstances, nationalism could take a dissident turn. In China, a much older imperial tradition had achieved a much higher level of ethnic and cultural homogeneity, and it was there-fore easier for the post-revolutionary regime to identify with the imperial heritage as well as with the cause of Chinese nationalism; some of the problems which it nevertheless had to face will be discussed below. The second type, national Communism in a broad sense, is best defined as a deviation from or reaction against the imperial models. Its first but largely forgotten version took shape within the Soviet Union and before the second revolution, most visibly among Islamic nationalities and in the Ukraine. Those who wanted to develop the connection between social revolution and national self-determination into something more than a tactical alliance found themselves on collision course with the imperial centre and its strategy of reabsorption. The victory of the latter was a foregone conclusion, and when national Communism reappeared within a global context that had already been transformed by the Stalinist autocracy, its motives and perspectives had also changed in response to historical experience. Yugoslavia is often regarded as a pioneer and paradigm case, but this view must now be revised in the light of later events. What caused the rift between Stalin and Tito was – as we shall see – the emergence of a separate power centre with some imperial pretensions of its own; at a later stage, the Yugoslav regime tried to strengthen its position by claiming a national identity as well as a distinctive social character. In the long run, both attempts failed, but their indirect effects should not be underestimated. The symbolic resurrection of national Communism opened up new political horizons that became more relevant when the relaxation of imperial control over Eastern Europe left the whole region in a state of latent crisis. In this context, the national Communist perspective could be adapted to two very different lines of development. On the one hand, it served to strengthen established regimes which sought more independence from the Soviet centre but did not envisage major changes to the Soviet model and could even try to conserve the archaic patterns that had been discarded by the post-Stalinist Soviet regime. Albania and Romania are the prime examples. On the other hand, national demands became an integral part of more complex reformist projects directed against local offshoots of Stalinism and towards a restructured version of the Soviet model. This applies to the short but not insignificant episode of reform Communism in Hungary in the mid-1950s as well as to the much stronger movement which developed in Czechoslovakia during the following decade.

The demise of the Soviet model has thrown new light on another pattern of its interaction with nationalism. It seemed less significant as long as the regimes in question were in control of their respective societies, but there can be no doubt about its long-term destabilizing impact. This type differs from the two above-mentioned in that national identities and aspirations are treated as external factors that must be kept under control but can to a certain extent be adapted to the imperatives of the model. In Soviet-dominated Eastern Europe, the local power élites – i.e. those that wanted neither reform nor autonomy – tried to mask their subaltern status by posing as heirs to national traditions and defenders of national statehood but keeping such claims within the limits set by the imperial order. All the Eastern European party-states made some use of this selective and instrumental nationalism; it was perhaps easiest to handle in Bulgaria, where it was least likely to take an anti-Russian turn; at the other end of the spectrum, the East German regime, though most directly dependent on the Soviet centre, also tried to acquire some national credentials. In retrospect, it seems clear that this was a self-undermining strategy: it helped to ensure the survival of forms of collective identity and frameworks of collective action that remained alien to the Soviet model and could be turned against it when other disintegrative factors became strong enough to bring about a crisis. The seemingly advantageous compromise with nationalism thus turned out to be an irreversible concession to extra-systemic forces. Something similar can be said about developments within the Soviet Union. Although the real content of national autonomy varied from phase to phase and depended on the strategies of the centre, the national-territorial principle of organization became an integral part of the new imperial order and at the same time a potential basis for challenges to it. The imperial use of national institutions and élites was effective as long as the centre could rely on other mechanisms to back it up, but it proved conducive to a reconstitution of national identities and divisions that reasserted themselves when the centralized power structure began to fall apart. It is worth noting that this unintended consequence of imperial rule involved the conversion of artificial boundaries into more genuinely national ones (Uzbek nationalism seems to be a case in point) as well as the strengthening of older national formations.

If anti-imperial nationalism was to play a major role in the destruction of the Soviet model, it had in another context and in an earlier phase been one of its most promising outlets. On its Eastern front, the Soviet regime had from the outset sought an alliance with nationalist forces against both direct and indirect forms of Western hegemony. This strategy did not work where it seemed most likely to succeed (when Communism triumphed in China, anti-Western nationalism was of course one of the currents that converged in its victory, but it quickly became clear that this element was subordinated to imperial aspirations which ultimately brought China into sharper conflict with the Soviet Union than with the West); its most impressive results were achieved much later and in a more unexpected way. During the 1960s and 1970s, the adoption of more or less adjusted versions of the Soviet model by anti-Western and developmentalist regimes in the Third World was widely mistaken for a global trend towards Soviet hegemony. As is now well-known, this belated proliferation was accompanied by a less visible structural decline. The connection between the two processes will be examined more closely in Chapter 4. But if this fourth and last configuration of nationalism and Communism has come to an end with the general crisis of the latter, it should be noted that the outcome is by no means an unequivocal victory of nationalism. Rather, the demise of semi- or pseudo-Communist experiments in developing countries can often – especially in the case of the defunct 'Afro-Marxist' regimes, but also, albeit in a different context, in Afghanistan – be seen as a failure of both nationalism and the Soviet model. Improvised combinations of these two integrative principles have proved incapable of overcoming ethnic and tribal divisions. On the other hand, the most resilient Soviet-type regimes in this category – such as

Cuba and Vietnam – were those that most successfully incorporated nationalism in their own strategies.

The above analysis of nationalism as a key part of the broader context of the Soviet model may help to highlight a more general point that will need further discussion below. It is on the level of culture and its interaction with politics that the variations of the Soviet model are most visible, and this shows that it cannot be reduced to a strategy of development and mobilization. If the latter function had been its sole or main rationale, we would expect its structural modifications to centre on adapting the developmental project to different conditions, and such efforts would first of all affect the economic sphere. But the historical record suggests that changes in the economic institutions of 'real socialism' have on the whole been dependent on cultural and political preconditions.

EXPANSION, REPRODUCTION AND REFORM

The above outline of basic and recurrent characteristics of the Soviet model should now be linked to the more general theoretical questions raised in the introduction. The core structures of Soviet-type societies must, in other words, be located in the context of a multidimensional and multilinear modernity, and this background will help to clarify the problems inherent in their reproduction and expansion.

As suggested above, differentiation and integration are complementary aspects of modernizing processes, and diverse patterns of modernity must be defined in terms of the direction they give to those twin developments as well as their way of combining them. More precisely, the dynamics of differentiation have to do with the autonomy and rationalization of the economic, political and cultural spheres, and patterns of integration can be seen as more or less coherent frameworks for their conflictual interaction. As I will try to show, the constitution of the Soviet model involves the restructuring of all three spheres along similar lines: certain aspects of the pre-existent Western paradigm of modernity are radicalized while others are excluded, and this selective differentiation – grounded in a project that is meant to transcend and supplant its Western rival – paves the way for a restrictive form of integration which in turn becomes an obstacle to further development.

Contrary to what is now widely believed, the most distinctive characteristic – and the most fundamental flaw – of Soviet-style economies was not their emphasis on the redistribution rather than the creation of wealth. They were based on productivist premises that in the long run turned out to be self-defeating; as a result of this internal limit to growth, redistributive strategies (both those linked to empire-building and those aimed at defusing social conflict) became increasingly difficult to sustain, and this symptom could be mistaken for the main problem. But the original and underlying economic rationale of the model was production-oriented. It was, more precisely, a bid to emulate and outdo capitalism with regard to the mobilization of productive forces. The specific Soviet contribution to this line of development was an attempt to link the general goal of mobilization to the particular strategy of mobilization that had first taken shape in response to the demands of global warfare. The result was, as we have seen, the subordination of economic development to a system of administrative control which became a structural obstacle to innovation. On the level of economic modernization, the logic of the Soviet model was thus double-edged: it was conducive to mobilization but resistant to innovation. Its ability to compete with the West was correspondingly limited. It could 'manage and even expand output using incrementally improved pre-1917 heavy industry technologies' (Rostow 1991: 63), but it was increasingly incapable of adapting to later technological breakthroughs. The 'gigantomania' and 'quantity drive' noted by many observers should be seen against this background: the mobilized economy was driven by a growth imperative, but in such a way that it led to pathological excesses within a pre-given technological paradigm, rather than the exploration of new technological frontiers. As the Soviet experience shows, this was a recipe for an ecological catastrophe of unprecedented dimensions.

There was a similar flaw in the Soviet version of political modernization. In the course of the original breakthrough to modernity, the political sphere had undergone a differentiating process that made the state more clearly separate from society and at the same time enhanced its capacity to control and transform its social environment. The Soviet model was, among other things, an attempt to push this twofold trend to its extreme limits. But as shown above, the systemic strategy developed for this purpose was essentially unbalanced in that it maximized some aspects of political modernity and was incompatible with others. It was based on a comprehensive monopolization of social power, undisturbed by the democratic countercurrents which had accompanied and modified the processes of state formation in the West. The logic of the Soviet model exaggerated the role of the modern state as a centre of control and intervention, but disregarded its complementary functions as a focus for the articulation and institutionalization of social conflict. This led to a self-perpetuating rupture between state and society and ensured the prevalence of paternalism over citizenship. Later attempts to 'normalize' Soviet rule left this authoritarian pattern untouched. In particular, the more egalitarian income policies and the rising living standards of the post-Stalinist era – due to and circumscribed by strategic considerations, rather than any fundamental choice, and never allowed to interfere with more essential priorities – can be seen as a paternalistic substitute for structural reforms that would have altered the balance of power between state and society.

Finally, the ideological mainstay of the Soviet model was a cultural image of modern science, indebted to Western sources but taken to much more extreme lengths and immunized against countercurrents. According to this view, scientific progress consists in the discovery, systematization and application of laws, and its logical outcome is the construction of a scientific world-view which can replace traditional belief-systems and fulfil their legitimate functions in a more rational way. What this interpretation excludes is the more distinctively modern side of the scientific enterprise, i.e. the institutionalization of permanent critique and revision as well as – in the long run – the relativization of all interpretive frameworks. A one-sided and immature conception of scientific rationality was thus transformed into an exhaustive and exclusive cultural model; at the same time, over-generalization deprived it of all specific content and made it more adaptable to the demands of the power structure which it served to consolidate. Both its overt assumptions and its ideological effects stood in the way of further cultural modernization. It legitimized the more or less direct supervision of all spheres of cultural production and scientific inquiry by the party-state. The oligarchic version of the latter was, on the whole, characterized by less arbitrary intervention and more flexible forms of control than the autocratic one, but these changes – unavoidable after the counterproductive excesses of the earlier phase – were contained within the limits of an ideology that retained its claims to universal authority and its reserve powers to intervene.

In comparison with Western models, the Soviet counter-paradigm of modernity was thus extreme and immature at the same time. Its 'mono-organizational' character led some analysts to regard it as a particularly clear-cut embodiment of functional principles. The above summary, however, suggests that the overall framework should rather be described as essentially dysfunctional. As I argued in the introduction, the modernizing processes of differentiation and integration follow a trans-functional logic that can in part be subsumed under but never fully absorbed by functional principles of organization. In the case of the

Soviet model, the tensions built into these basic determinants of modernity took a more explosive turn. As a result of the developmental patterns described above, the three spheres are – in a sense – overdifferentiated: each of them is made to obey a logic which absolutizes some aspects of a complex pattern at the expense of others and unbalances the relationship with the other spheres. This is, of course, most obvious in relation to the political sphere. The imperatives of the party-state apparatus always took precedence over other demands and never ceased to interfere with economic and cultural developments. But the two last-mentioned spheres also had a disruptive dynamic of their own, although its effects were more limited and intermittent. There are some reasons to believe that the economic policies of the second revolution, based on aberrant notions of an instant breakthrough, overstrained the political centre and reinforced the trend towards autocracy. At a later stage and in a very different context, it appears that the failure of the reformist interlude between 1956 and 1964 was partly due to an economistic strategy which not only led Khrushchev and his associates to disregard the need for political and ideological changes, but also brought them into conflict with the apparatus when they tried to harness it to their projects of economic reform. As for the cultural factor, the absolutized claims of Marxism-Leninism as a scientific world-view led to the invention of pseudo-sciences as well as the rejection of some major but unassimilable scientific innovations, and the results were in both cases bound to affect the overall developmental potential of the model; in a more general though less spectacular way, the dogmatic character of the state ideology had a paralysing effect that was never fully offset by its adaptation to political priorities. But if all three spheres are thus – albeit not to the same extent – characterized by and separated from each other by a self-absolutizing logic, they are also underdifferentiated in the sense that the structure of the model blocks some of the developmental paths and closes some of the horizons initially opened up by the modern transformation.

These restrictions were, as we have seen, integral to the economic, political and cultural institutions of Soviet-type societies, and they were maintained by the party-state mechanisms of control. Inasmuch as this pattern limits the autonomy of the different spheres, deforms their development and subsumes them under a unified power structure, we can describe the entire complex as overintegrated. On the other hand and in the long run, however, it is also underintegrated in that the very hypertrophy of the centre prevents the development of more flexible and inclusive forms of integration. This weakness was to prove fatal when the centre was paralysed. Soviet-type regimes had no second line of defence, and it was only a short step from crisis to collapse.

The power structure that barred the way to more balanced development was also an obstacle to self-thematization. But some central problems of the Soviet model were, however briefly and obliquely, brought to light in connection with the most sustained attempts to reform it from within. As the project of reform Communism became more articulate, it gave rise to distinctive – but also distorted – perspectives on each of the three spheres. In the economic context, the most significant debate developed around the twin notions of the 'scientific and technological revolution' as a prerequisite for completing the socialist project and the combination of plan and market as the only adequate mode of regulation for a complex economy. Such ideas ran counter to orthodoxy in that they questioned the identification of the established pattern of growth with the 'construction of socialism' and highlighted the need for major changes to the technological basis as well as the organizational principles of the Soviet model. Their critical potential was, however, limited by an overrationalized vision of the command economy: its really existing version was regarded as an initially adequate but now obsolete strategy of extensive growth, and its idealized self-image – the phantasm of central planning – was accepted as a guarantee of further progress. But what the reformists mistook for an emergent model of economic rationality – superior in principle, if not yet in practice, to that of the market – was in reality a system of controls with a political rather than an economic rationale. Central planning was, in other words, only one of several masks of a centralized power structure which in the long run limited the scope of economic reforms and retarded the pace of technological progress.

The conflation of power and rationality is no less evident in the plans for political reform. Their starting-point was a partial recognition of pluralism. In contrast to the orthodox image of a homogeneous and harmonious society, the articulation of diverse interests was to become a legitimate part of the political process. At its most ambitious, this developed into a project that is best described as 'globalistic democratization' (Strmiska 1989); its aim was to restructure the Soviet model in a way that would ensure more autonomy for social organizations and associations, more freedom for public debate, and more legal protection for individual liberties, and at the same time to contain these changes within a restrictive paradigm of democracy which would involve a redefinition rather than a rejection of the 'leading role of the party'. By subordinating the logic of democracy to a substantive goal – the cooperative pursuit of collective interests – and retaining the basic ideological premise that the 'socialist transformation' had in principle paved the way for a higher form of conflict management, the reformers tried to stave off more radical challenges. The existing institutions of the party-state were treated as imperfect but rationalizable mechanisms of mediation and synthesis, not as an entrenched power structure with its own imperatives of survival and sovereignty. The combination of democratic reforms with a defence of party prerogatives was, of course, an attempt to square the circle, but its real outcome depended on the broader context (the Prague Spring and Gorbachev's perestroika are the two prime examples).

A similar inconsistency was characteristic of the 'revisionist' proposals for ideological reform. On the one hand, the discovery or rehabilitation of sciences that had been excluded from the Marxist-Leninist synthesis helped to undermine the orthodox modes of thought and images of society. Cybernetics and sociology are the most obvious cases in point. Analogously, the revolt against the aesthetic canon of socialist realism contributed to a more general emancipation of culture from ideology. On the other hand, the doctrinal *aggiornamento* carried out in response to such challenges left some basic principles un-questioned. The idea of a totalizing and legislating world-view remained in force, but it was now to be developed in a less dogmatic and reductionist way. This led, among other things, to a significant revival of Hegelian Marxism: it was a plausible alternative to the more primitive approach of dialectical materialism, and at the same time it gave the myth of the dialectic – a supposedly privileged and universally applicable mode of thought – a new lease of life. Its supporters could denounce the over-simplifications of Soviet orthodoxy ('institutional Marxism', as it was sometimes called) as instruments of Soviet power, but their philosophical premises were still tailored to the legitimation of political control through privileged knowledge.

In the history of Soviet-type societies, clear-cut and far-reaching reformist projects were of course very much the exception rather than the rule. The ideas summarized above were most forcefully articulated in connection with the Czechoslovak reform movement of the 1960s, but some of them emerged elsewhere under less critical conditions. For our present purposes, their symptomatic content is more important than their historical effects: they reflect the structural problems and limits of the Soviet model, seen from within but in a particularly revealing constellation. If we want to place them in their proper historical context, they must first of all be distinguished from a much broader and more diffuse current of aspirations to reform that could also be channelled in other directions. If the needs and pressures for reforms became too obvious to be ignored by the rulers, they could try to devise a strategy that would at least make the model more efficient in some areas while avoiding democratic concessions. A less rational response was the reorganization mania with which Soviet-type regimes have been periodically afflicted. On a more elementary level, the ideological readjustment which accompanied the stabilization of oligarchic rule in the Soviet Union and within its imperial domain can be seen as an attempt to defuse this problem: the new emphasis on socialism as a specific social formation and historical epoch with its own laws, rather than a mere transitional phase between capitalism and communism, made it easier to accommodate the idea of reforms within a stable framework. If socialism was a society in long-term progress towards more advanced forms, this principle could – according to circumstances – be invoked either to justify reformist programmes or to cut them down to size. The glorification of 'really existing socialism' as a fully developed way of life was the most conservative variation on this theme.

The structure of Soviet-type societies excluded open contestation, but could not suppress all awareness of the gap between pretensions and performance; hence the recurrent theme of reform and the permanent uncertainty about its practical limits. It was, however, only in the post-Stalinist phase that notions of reform and strategies of controlled reform became a legitimate part of political life. This qualified opening to change was the obverse of oligarchic stabilization, and both aspects must be set against the background of a historical conjuncture which had made the most spectacular global breakthrough of the Soviet model appear as a triumph of its most extreme version and thus delayed the reaction against its excesses.

The Soviet counter-paradigm of modernity was, as we have seen, a complex and intrinsically fragile combination which could only emerge in a very specific context: that of the Russian tradition and its interaction with the West. Its claim to a more universal historical mission proved unsustainable in its original forms. After the partial reinsertion of the Soviet regime into the Eurasian state system, it was still committed to the strategy of expansion in the name of revolution in East and West, even if the tactics and the ideological framework were subject to some variations, but the first quarter of a century after the Bolshevik victory in Russia was marked by a series of defeats on both fronts. It proved impossible to export revolution from Russia to Europe; the strongest and most strategically situated branch of the Communist movement in the West was destroyed in 1933, partly as a result of self-defeating Soviet policies; finally, the attempt to bring the European Communist parties out of isolation through the popular front strategy had failed by the end of the thirties, also in large measure because it was undermined by developments in the Soviet Union. Similarly, there were three major failures on the Eastern front, but a conclusive defeat came earlier there than in the West. In the aftermath of the revolution, the Soviet leadership had high hopes for an alliance with – and radicalization of – Islamic reformism against the West; this strategy found its most official expression in the Baku congress of 1920, but it self-destructed soon after that. Expectations of a revolutionary wave in India, which had figured prominently on Lenin's agenda, proved equally misguided. And finally, the most important and promising development, the incipient Chinese revolution of the 1920s, ended in a disaster for both Soviet foreign policy and the Chinese Communist movement.

The situation changed rapidly and radically after 1945. The Soviet regime acquired a new imperial domain in Eastern Europe, and the Soviet model was adopted (with qualifications and unexpected effects, as we shall see) by a new imperial centre in China. Both those breakthroughs were primarily due to changes in the international balance of power. It was the defeat of Nazi Germany that paved the way for the Sovietization of Eastern Europe, and the victory of the Chinese Communists would not have been possible without the Japanese invasion, its destructive impact on the Guomindang regime, and the new opportunities opened up by the subsequent collapse of the Japanese empire. On both fronts, then, the Soviet model expanded into a vacuum left behind by failed bids for hegemony. But the way in which it responded to the new constellation and was in turn affected by it can only be understood in the light of the changes it had undergone in the meantime.

The failure abroad had been accompanied by a mutation at home; as we have seen, the totalitarian synthesis of imperial and revolutionary projects was finalized during the decade that also saw the mirage of world revolution recede further than ever. The connection between these two developments was not as close as it seemed to some contemporary observers. If the global strategy of Leninism missed its mark, this was mainly because of its intrinsic incoherence rather than betrayal or manipulation by the Soviet apparatus, and the push towards a fully-fledged totalitarian regime had more to do with Russia's internal dynamics than with its international situation. But there is no doubt that isolation made it easier for Stalin's archaic version of Bolshevism to prevail over its more Westernized rivals. Conversely, the retraditionalization and Russification of the Soviet regime in the course of the second revolution gave a more openly imperial twist to its international strategy. The damage this did to international Communism was to some extent offset by the fact that the second revolution coincided with the great depression in the West. But by the end of the decade, the great purge and the alliance with Germany had brought the international prestige of the Soviet Union to its lowest point. In brief, the second revolution completed the construction of the Soviet model and at the same time undermined its universalist claims. Moreover, the autocratic regime that presided over the building of Soviet institutions also had a destabilizing impact on them, both through its unbalanced strategy of development and through the massive terror it used to strengthen its grip on society. Its double-edged effect on the Soviet war machine was particularly striking: the prime aim of Stalin's industrial revolution was a military build-up, but his purges decimated the military establishment and thus greatly weakened the international position of the Soviet Union. At the end of the 1930s, it was an open question whether the mobilizing or the self-destructive dynamic would prove more decisive.

The war with Nazi Germany settled this issue. While it is probably true that the Soviet model was better suited to the conditions of total war than to the long-term tasks of development, the benefits of victory were both deceptive and disproportionate. On the one hand, several external factors (Hitler's strategic errors, the alliance with the Western powers, and the lack of coordination between the global strategies of Germany and Japan) had helped the Soviet Union to win the war, but since its own efforts were the most visible factor, the regime could claim more credit than it deserved and thus re-legitimize the model *en bloc*. On the other hand, the new global constellation enabled the Soviet Union to expand its sphere of influence and to act as one of two hegemonic powers. As a result, the regime slid into an imperial overstrain, reminiscent of some earlier episodes in Russian history, and a permanent confrontation with a more advanced and adaptable rival. The discrepancy between internal conditions and international ambitions provided a prima-facie rationale for renewed mobilization; given the apparent success of the original strategy, the easiest way out for those in power was to continue it on a larger scale. The Stalinist autocracy, which during the war had not only lost control of large territories, but also been forced to make concessions that seemed to hold out the promise of more radical changes, thus rebuilt its power structure and its economic basis in line with the model of the second revolution (Werth 1990). A new great purge, linking up with the post-war purges in Eastern Europe, would have been the logical conclusion of this repeat performance, but it was cut short by Stalin's death. Prior to that, the autocratic centre had been subverting party institutions more openly than before; although it is unclear how far this process could have gone, there is no doubt that a major upheaval was in the making.

To say that the re-legitimizing effect of the 'Great Patriotic War' aided the reconsolidation of Stalinism is not to suggest that there was broad popular support for the policies in question. Rather, the regime had to reassert its power over a society where further relaxation was widely expected to follow victory. But the newly-found strength and prestige helped Stalin and his associates to reintroduce tighter controls, suppress dissent within the apparatus, and avoid an otherwise likely backlash. The triumphant return to pre-war principles was no less evident in Soviet conceptions of empire. As the examples of Finland and Afghanistan before 1978 show, the Soviet regime occasionally resorted to the more traditional and flexible methods of imperial control, and there is no reason to believe that it could not in principle have used them more widely; if the imposition of a uniform model and the integration into a homogeneous bloc seemed the most adequate way of securing Soviet power over Eastern Europe, this must in part have been due to the illusions about the original Soviet achievement. In the post-war context, it was easy to overrate the merits of the Soviet model as a strategy of control and transformation. There was, in other words, a strong element of hubris and delusion in the new imperial design. And the illusions which influenced the attitude of Soviet leaders to Eastern Europe also led them to underestimate the long-term significance of the very different breakthrough that had occurred in China: as they saw it, the assimilative capacity of the model was, even in the absence of direct control, strong enough to guarantee a gradual absorption into the bloc.

There is no reason to disagree with Brzezinski's (1967: ix) description of postwar Communism as an interstate system: the Stalinist leadership saw the new Soviet bloc simply 'as a slightly more expanded Soviet system'. But it should be added that there were two sides to the expansion; they might be described as globalization and miniaturization of the Soviet model, and each of them was to create specific problems for the Soviet centre that strove to retain control. On the one hand, the claim to represent a global alternative to the West became more serious and sustainable than it had been during the phase of 'socialism in one country'. Both the imperial and the modernizing dynamics of the Soviet model could now operate on a broader international basis, but for that very reason, the task of coordinating them became more complex and demanding. The first response was a refusal to recognize the problem: from the Stalinist point of view the socialist camp was a new world-system, complete with its own world market, obeying – in all essentials – the same laws as its Soviet core, and on collision course with the other international bloc. The relationship of the Soviet model to the West was, as has been seen, a mixture of antagonism and dependence. With the change in the global balance of power, both aspects were reproduced on a larger scale and at the same time distorted by a self-image which maximized the former and suppressed the latter. There was no coherent strategy behind the militant postures of late Stalinism; its power basis was too weak to warrant an offensive in support of its official claims, but the ideologically induced illusions were too entrenched to allow a retreat to more realistic policies. The post-Stalinist reappraisal resulted in a major strategic shift. Although some fundamental obstacles to rationalization remained in place, the oligarchic regime became – in comparison with its autocratic forerunner – not only more capable of defining and coordinating its imperial and developmental projects, but also more sensitive to backwardness and dependence as long-term problems. The first but short-lived result of these changes was a grand strategy of economic growth and rationalization (including a more rational division of labour within the Soviet imperial domain); by avoiding premature imperial confrontation and adopting more flexible methods of control over the periphery, more elbow-room was to be gained for a developmental offensive that would enable the Soviet bloc to outstrip the West and thus reach its imperial goal by a safer road. This project prevailed during the Khrushchev era, but failed because of its intrinsic flaws as well as the resistance of entrenched interests at all levels. The strategy that came to replace it during the Brezhnev era was a much more eclectic one. A more conservative regime now tried to maintain its imperial status through military parity with the other superpower, block all ambitious reform programmes within the bloc but rely on closer economic connections with the West and a more balanced pattern of growth as a partial substitute for them, and pursue a policy of cautious expansion within the underdeveloped periphery of the West. The short-term results of this balancing act were impressive enough to deceive both observers and performers, and when it began to falter, it took some time for the consequences to become visible. Their broader implications will be discussed below.

On the other hand, the Soviet centre insisted on the reproduction of basic structures of the model within each unit of the bloc. The emphasis, was in other words, on conformity and homogeneity rather than integration. But when the balance of power between the centre and the periphery was upset by crises or conflicts within the imperial apparatus, small-scale versions of the Soviet model could serve as a basis for separate strategies. An institutional complex that had originally taken shape in an imperial context and continued to embody an imperial logic was, in such cases, adapted to the more limited purposes of states in quest of autonomy from the imperial centre and trying to maximize both their power over their own societies and their position in the international arena. The imperial character of the model was, however, still reflected in the excessive ambitions and unbalanced policies which these second-ary centres tended to develop. The Soviet patterns of power could be turned against – or at least detached from – the imperial centre that had originally imposed them, but the attempt to adapt them to a more peripheral social basis gave rise to new problems and pathologies. From a historical point of view, the Soviet model is first and foremost an imperial formation, but for a typology of its variants, the contrast between its imperial versions and the more self-contained and isolationist ones is particularly interesting; the Soviet Union (and to a lesser extent China) is representative of the former, whereas Albania and Cambodia are the most striking examples of the latter.

Revisions of imperial strategy and their repercussions on the periphery were linked to changes at the centre. The absorption of the new empire and the reconsolidation of autocracy had gone hand in hand and reinforced each other. On both levels, the logic of the Soviet model thus took an extreme and potentially self-destructive turn. Whether it could have been halted if Stalin had lived to pursue his course further is a moot point; in any case, the contenders for power after his death shared the view that a readjustment of the regime was overdue, even if they disagreed on details and priorities. The arbitrary terror of the autocracy was threatening to escalate into a new massacre of the party-state élite, its foreign policies had brought the Soviet Union to the brink of global conflict, and its methods of economic mobilization were endangering the developmental project of the regime. For all these reasons (and, it seems, in this order of importance), Stalin's successors had to acknowledge the need for a rationalization of the Soviet model. But since there was no obvious or easy way of balancing the imperatives of change and control, different approaches to the problem could be invoked and instrumental-ized by competing factions within the apparatus; moreover, the impact of domestic concessions on the imperial environment raised new questions about the risks of chain reaction. The result was, as noted above, an irreversible reactivation of the idea of reform, but without a clear definition of acceptable limits, and a recurrent conflict between rival interpretations, but within a framework that favoured the conservative and minimalist versions. In the event, the most significant change was the transition from autocratic to oligarchic rule. Before discussing its long-term unintended consequences we need to take a closer look at the international background.

THE WESTERN PERIPHERY

The expansion of the Soviet model took various forms. Three main patterns can be distinguished, although some borderline cases blur the picture. In the first place, the Soviet regime imposed the model on other states that had come under its control. A second category differs from this openly imperial strategy in that it involved a more prolonged struggle for power by indigenous Communist parties: a counter-state with a territorial basis, however limited and insecure, pursued its political aims through a war (both civil and national, waged simultaneously or successively) that culminated in a complete takeover. China is, of course, the classic example. Finally, Soviet-type institutions could be adopted by regimes already in power (or factions within them) and in search of more effective ways to control and transform their societies. Cuba played a pioneering role in this regard, but its example was followed – often in more superficial ways – by other Third World states during the following two decades.

On closer inspection, however, these different processes have some fundamental characteristics in common. None of the transformations in question can be described as a *social* revolution in the more specific sense of the word, i.e. a structural change brought about by the autonomous action and progressive radicalization of social forces. For all their obvious diversity, the French, Russian and Spanish revolutions can be analysed in such terms (although the course of the last-named was cut short by a victorious counter-revolution). By contrast, all victories achieved by the Soviet model outside its original boundaries were takeovers rather than revolutions. The transformative processes took place under the control of a state or a state-like apparatus, whether it was the imperial Soviet state acting through domestic intermediaries, an embryonic but independent state on its way to total power, or an established state in the process of defining its identity and its aims. This pattern was to some extent prefigured by the Bolshevik seizure of power: as noted above, the 'dual power' that grew out of the February revolution enabled the Bolsheviks to build their own power base and prepare for a final offensive. But this was a takeover within a revolution, facilitated by social conflicts that did not come to an end with it and were only gradually brought under control after the monopolization of political power at the centre. Nothing similar occurred elsewhere; the 'October revolution' was therefore only a partial model for later takeovers. Its techniques of capturing and consolidating power could be successfully applied and developed in other places, but never in the same context of a revolution in progress. The Chinese counter-example is particularly striking: although the post-imperial crisis seemed to be taking a revolutionary turn in the mid-1920s, the conflict between the Communists and the Guomindang destroyed all chances of such a development, and the struggle for China became a contest between two rival centres of imperial reconstruction. The closest thing to a Communist takeover within a revolution outside Russia was the ascendancy of Spanish Communism during the civil war, but this is an inconclusive case: it is not clear how far the Soviet centre intended to pursue the takeover strategy, and it is a matter of debate whether the Communist bid for power failed because the war was lost or had been undermined from within before that.

Although the three above-mentioned forms of expansion should not be confused with chronological phases (as the case of Afghanistan shows, the first pattern was never definitively superseded, and in some other countries, it was to a greater or lesser extent superimposed on the third), they are, on the whole, typical of successive epochs and different regions. The postwar Sovietization of Eastern Europe was, first and foremost, an imperial takeover, the conquest from within was most characteristic of East Asian Communism, and the self-Sovietization of states in formation was a Third World phenomenon, linked to the last stages of a global confrontation. Our discussion must begin with Eastern Europe, which became the Western periphery of the Soviet bloc. It should be noted that the geographical category used here does not exclude other descriptions and divisions: recent events have again highlighted the differences between Central and Southeastern Europe, there are good reasons to set Poland apart from Central Europe, and the region that can be described both as the Far East of Europe and the Far West of the Soviet Union (Szporluk 1991), i.e. the area which extends from the Baltic states to Bessarabia, is both internally diverse and distinctive with regard to neighbours on both sides. But during the phase in question, these regions and sub-regions were unified under Soviet power, and it is therefore most convenient to refer to them as Eastern Europe. Even the sole country to secede from the Soviet bloc during its formative phase – Yugoslavia – retained some decisive features of the Soviet model and can therefore be regarded as a separate fragment of the Western periphery.

The imperial factor was decisive for the Eastern European region as a whole. It has often been claimed that the Yugoslav and Albanian Communists won power on their own, whereas the other 'people's democracies' were satellites from the very beginning. The contrast is, however, less fundamental than it may seem. In the first place, the Albanian takeover was only a sideshow within the Yugoslav one, and the Albanian regime was at first as dependent on Belgrade as the others were on Moscow. As for Yugoslavia, it is true that the strategy and tactics adopted by the Communist leadership in 1941 were in some ways similar to the Chinese experience, but their scope was more limited. The struggle for power was much shorter and more directly dependent on the international conjuncture than in China; the Soviet army played an important role in the last phase of the war (both the civil and the national one), and the consolidation of Tito's regime after the war was closely linked to the assertion of Soviet control over the whole region. For all these reasons, it seems more appropriate to describe Yugoslavia as an intermediate case, rather than – as suggested by some authors – the first revolution of a new type. On the other hand, there were significant differences between the countries that experienced a Soviet-directed takeover. The Bulgarian Communists played a more important role in the first moves towards Sovietization than the parties in Romania or Hungary; above all, the Czechoslovak Communists, who owed their initial position of strength largely to the Soviet connection that had been accepted by non-Communists leaders as a cornerstone of foreign policy, went on to complete the takeover in a more independent way than Stalin seems to have expected or wanted (the particularly bloody purge which later took place in Czechoslovakia may have been his way of acknowledging this fact).

In short, the techniques and details of the takeovers differed from country to country, and a simple dichotomy of dependent or independent roads to power is misleading. But the strategy of the imperial centre was concerned with the region as a whole. In the light of available evidence, it seems clear that Stalin was pursuing a strategy of total Sovietization from the outset – the export of the model seemed to be the only reliable way of keeping the new satellites within the orbit of the centre. If there was any hesitation on the part of the Soviet leadership, it concerned the boundaries of the new imperial domain (some analysts have argued that the direction of Soviet policies in Hungary was at first more uncertain than elsewhere, and it is a matter of debate whether a takeover was planned in Finland), as well as the timing of the Sovietizing process, rather than the institutional forms of control. Both these issues were in the event decided by the regional and international constellation of forces. But if there are some reasons to believe that global polarization and the beginning of the cold war prompted the Soviet leadership to speed up its absorption of Eastern Europe, there is no doubt that it wanted to keep open the possibility of further expansion, and the moves to tighten control had to be adjusted to this long-term goal. This seems to have been the main motive behind the ideological construction of 'people's democracy': as the growing strength of the Communist movement in some Western countries (and in some other parts of the world) held out the hope that the Soviet Union could benefit from further changes in the global balance of power, it was essential to minimize the adverse impact of the conquest in progress. The façade of a more benign and flexible regime (including a fictional multi-party system) was therefore preserved and propagated while the real structures of power were rapidly brought into line with the Soviet model. In comparison with the earlier slogan of socialism in one country, 'people's democracy' was – at least in the definitive shape which it took with the foundation of the Cominform in 1947 – a second-degree ideology: it played a more purely instrumental role, and it stood in starker contrast to the real course of events. But even if it was primarily a mystification aimed at an external audience, it imposed some constraints on the staging of the takeover; concrete circumstances, strategic considerations and ideological requirements thus combined to give a particular twist to the Soviet pursuit of power in Eastern Europe. There were, of course, some earlier experiences to draw on. Both the reconquest of the borderlands in the aftermath of the Russian civil war and the westward expansion after Stalin's arrangement with Hitler had allowed the Soviet centre to experiment with the techniques of imperial takeover, but on a smaller scale and in a more sheltered environment. These precedents did not add up to a ready-made model.[3]

Because of the historical vacuum in Eastern Europe, the first stage of the takeover was deceptively easy, and it was only later that the deep-seated obstacles became more visible. The Soviet model was imposed on paralysed states and disrupted societies; the Communist seizure of power did not follow a uniform pattern, but differences in pace and procedure had more to do with Soviet strategy than with the strength or weakness of domestic forces. And the stronger Communist parties in the region – the Czechoslovak, the Yugoslav and the Bulgarian – owed their success largely to conjunctural rather than structural factors: they had all lost much of their initial strength and regained ground during or after the war (a comparison with the other countries suggests, however, that past strength made it easier to take advantage of the new situation). For the same reason, the institutions of the new regimes were only loosely linked to the traditions of the region. It is true that statist projects of economic and social modernization had left their mark on Eastern European history, and it can be argued that this background facilitated the introduction of the Soviet model (the belief in the modernizing potential of the latter was much more widespread than the acceptance of its ideological claims), but the structures and strategies that were imported from the Soviet Union were imposed without any attempt to adapt them to the particular statist heritage of each country. It is also worth noting that the fortunes of domestic Communist movements did not depend primarily on the relative strength or weakness of statist traditions: Communism was strongest in Czechoslovakia, the most Westernized country of the region.

The regimes put in place throughout Eastern Europe after 1945 had a common institutional core, derived from the Soviet prototype; some of its chronic and structural problems – rooted in the interconnected dynamics of its economic, political and cultural components – were discussed above. The interaction between centre and periphery led to a further aggravation of these problems. In other words: the dissonance between the various aspects of the model became more acute as its imperial logic became more pronounced. On the political level, the rationale for expansion was built into the very foundations of the Soviet regime, and the conquest of Eastern Europe was the most tangible objective that it had achieved. The acquisition of a new imperial domain strengthened the international position of the Soviet state and reinforced its global ambitions. But the attempt to implant the Soviet model in all parts of the domain and at the same time control them from outside was self-undermining. The local centres lacked autonomy and therefore faced a permanent legitimation crisis; their subordination to the imperial centre limited their ability to adapt to their domestic environment and build a power basis of their own. The search for an escape from this predicament, perhaps best described as 'domesticism' (Brzezinski), took many forms and did not necessarily develop into fully-fledged national Communism, but it was an inevitable by-product of the very measures meant to discourage it.

If the political mechanisms of imperial control were double-edged, other factors added to their impact. Stalin's postwar economic strategy was based on massive exploitation of the satellites: resources were to be extracted from the periphery in order to aid the reconsolidation of the centre. As for the cultural aspects of Soviet imperialism, it was – first and foremost – evident in the dogmatic commitment to the Soviet model as a whole. The power structure of the centre was to be reproduced throughout the periphery without any regard to traditions or circumstances. Over and above that, however, there was a sustained but largely self-defeating effort to impose Soviet patterns on the cultural life of the countries in question . In brief, then, political imperatives were as fundamental to the expansion of the Soviet model as they were to its internal workings, but their logic was disturbed by short-term economic interests as well as by unquestioned ideological premises.

Soviet rule in Eastern Europe thus began with an uncompromising but unsustainable push for total control. Its subsequent history is marked by four successive defeats. The first blow was the emergence of a rival regional centre – Tito's Yugoslavia – that could neither be destroyed nor neutralized. A more global and conclusive failure had to be acknowledged after 1953: the Soviet leadership retreated from Stalin's strategy of complete assimilation and resigned itself to a system of more indirect control, coupled with more or less extensive concessions that opened the way for a 'return to diversity' (Rothschild 1989) within the bloc. This new policy defused some acute problems, but its ultimate limits became clear at the end of the 1960s. As the invasion of Czechoslovakia and the formulation of the Brezhnev doctrine showed, the Soviet centre had failed to stabilize a balance of power that would enable the peripheral regimes to reproduce themselves without military intervention. Finally, the Eastern European part of the empire collapsed at the end of the 1980s when the dependent party-states proved too fragile to survive a change of course at the centre.

The Yugoslav crisis and the Soviet reaction to it was a turning-point for the whole bloc; but it also set Yugoslavia apart from other Soviet-type regimes, and since its later development – as well as its particularly disastrous drift to self-destruction – was largely autonomous, a brief look at the Yugoslav experience is in order. It should first of all be noted that both the situation of the Yugoslav Communists and their response to it differed significantly from the rest of Eastern Europe. The Yugoslav state (which was, historically speaking, a combination of fragments from two empires) had been destroyed more thoroughly than any other in the region, and the Yugoslav party had from the outset contested its legitimacy. If it now came to see the rebuilding of this state as a road to power, that was obviously not because it accepted it as given or identified with its legacy. Rather, the reconstitution of Yugoslavia was seen as a first step towards more ambitious goals. The Yugoslav leadership would inevitably have played a dominant role in the union of Balkan states that was briefly envisaged after the war; within the emerging bloc, it aspired – on the strength of its revolutionary credentials and its autonomous power – to a special position which would have made it a junior partner rather than a mere instrument of the Soviet centre, and there even seems to have been some talk of Tito as a possible successor to Stalin. In short, the Yugoslav party-state had imperial designs of its own, and its domestic policies were correspondingly extreme: the 'construction of socialism' in Yugoslavia was to proceed along the lines of the Stalinist model, but with even greater speed. From this point of view, the description of Titoism as a 'premature form of Stalinism' (Brzezinski 1967: 63) is undoubtedly correct.

The crisis was thus the result of uncoordinated ambitions, rather than conflicting political orientations, and it began when the Soviet leadership decided to destroy a client that had become a potential rival. The Soviet approach to the problem was based on the assumption that the bloc could be treated as a Soviet state writ large; when this principle proved inapplicable to Yugoslavia, the Soviet response was to force the pace of assimilation in the other states, so that the centre could not be challenged again. On the Yugoslav side, the reaction was at first more confused: the leadership continued on its essentially imitative but exceptionally assertive and extreme course for some time after the break. In the long run, however, it was impossible to sustain the claim to autonomy without improving relations between state and society and adopting a more distinctive ideological stance. Because of the multinational character of the Yugoslav state, nationalism was not a viable alternative to orthodoxy (the attempt to foster a Yugoslav national identity, half-hearted at best, was abandoned in the early 1960s). A more original rationale was required; the solution devised by the leadership hinged on a selective relaxation of control and a new *modus vivendi* between state and society, as well as on the doctrine of self-management. Three main implications of the latter should be noted. It was, firstly, not unrelated to the earlier ambitions of the Yugoslav leadership: the claim to represent a more authentic version of socialism could serve to challenge the Soviet centre on its own ground. It was, in other words, inseparably linked to hegemonic aspirations that were to find expression in attempts to co-manage the crises of the bloc after Stalin's death. The belief that a transnational *raison d'état* was essential to the Yugoslav state (also reflected in Tito's efforts to build and lead a coalition of 'non-aligned' nations against the two superpowers) was a lasting obstacle to reabsorption into the bloc. As for the more specific content of the new official doctrine, it was an ingenious compromise between orthodoxy and innovation: the need to democratize the Soviet model was acknowledged, but given a restrictive economistic interpretation that sidestepped the crucial issue of party sovereignty (the nominal redefinition of the party's role as a matter of leadership rather than control did not endanger the monopoly of power). Finally, as the history of the following decades was to show, even this limited ideological opening could become the starting-point for conflicting visions and strategies of reform. The most ideologically minded part of the leadership seems to have been attracted to a corporatist model (Kardelj's 'pluralism of self-managing interests') which would lead to a significant redistribution of power but defuse both democratic and nationalist challenges. In the event, however, the doctrine of self-management was most effectively invoked and utilized by those who wanted to transfer more power to the individual republics and their political élites. This is not to say that the shift was uncontested or automatic. Demands for more managerial power also played a role and left their mark on Yugoslav society. The participation of workers in decision-making, officially central to the model and often over-emphasized by both critical and sympathetic observers, was much less significant in practice than in theory and more relevant to the distribution of income than to the power to determine economic strategies; the impact on society was, it seems, more conducive to localism and fragmentation than to grassroots democratization.

As a result of the reforms initiated at the beginning of the 1950s, the development of Yugoslav society diverged from the Soviet pattern. The mechanisms of the mobilized economy were largely demolished, and Marxism-Leninism no longer functioned as a monolithic ideology. On the other hand, the political core of the party-state remained intact, and its role was enhanced by charismatic leadership. The exceptional stability of the political centre throughout the successive phases of the 'Yugoslav road' – the premature Stalinism of the late 1940s, the tentative but ideologically amplified reforms of the 1950s, the more effective reformist offensives of the 1960s, and the abortive restoration of the 1970s – was a counterweight to changes in other areas. But the monopoly of political power was not wholly separable from the economic and cultural context. Attempts to shape the course of economic development and disagreements over the way to do so were an important part of the political process; a significant but unsuccessful attempt to reinforce ideological control was made in the 1970s. In comparative terms, Yugoslavia can certainly not be described as a fully-fledged Soviet-type regime. Rather, it represented an attempt to combine the political essentials of the Soviet model with an economy increasingly linked to the West and subject to market laws, and to embellish this balancing act with an ideology that protected the foundations of the regime from criticism but accepted cultural pluralism up to a point.

But although the centre survived major changes of policy, it was weakened by conflicts and gradually undermined by the ongoing redistribution of power. It was strong enough to decide the outcome of two major political crises, 1966 and 1971, but the long-term effects of its intervention strengthened the centrifugal forces. In 1966, a conflict at the top of the federal party ended with the apparent victory of a reformist coalition; yet the more lasting result was a strengthening of republican authorities, especially in the northern republics which had favoured reformist policies, and the beginning of a nationalist backlash on the Serbian side. The Croatian crisis of 1971 brought a republic-based reformist faction that had increasingly relied on nationalist support into open conflict with the federal leadership; the latter was, however, already too weak to embark on a full-scale restoration, and its victory led to a temporary reconsolidation of the party-state at the republican level. After Tito's death, the federal centre was no longer in a position to block the fragmenting process. But the transfer of power to the separate party-states made them more vulnerable to nationalism, rather than more capable of mobilizing it for their own purposes. The disintegration of the federal order had discredited its official ideology, and a return to more orthodox Soviet-style methods was impossible. This acute legitimation crisis was compounded by an economic one, due both to the worsening situation of Yugoslavia within the world economy and to the fragmentation of the internal Yugoslav market that had been brought about by separatist policies. The last-ditch defence against nationalism was an attempt to stabilize a division into territorial rather than ethnic units and to institutionalize the balance of power between them; but when the balancing mechanisms broke down, the discrepancy between ethnic and territorial boundaries made disaster inevitable.

This is not to suggest that the catastrophic course of events in the early 1990s was the only conceivable outcome. The ultranationalist forces that prevailed had benefited from the errors as well as the unfinished projects and ambiguous achievements of their rivals, and it is not impossible to imagine a less traumatic end to the 'Yugoslav experiment'. But in retrospect it seems clear that the Yugoslav regime never developed a coherent alternative to the Soviet model, never devised a viable formula for keeping a multi-national state together, and was structurally incapable of the mutation from imperial to national Communism which it helped to induce in other cases.

For Yugoslavia, the 1948 crisis marked the beginning of a more self-contained trajectory; for the rest of the bloc, it had the opposite effect. But the Stalinist strategy of imperial assimilation was, as we have seen, closely linked to autocratic rule at home and incompatible with the search for a new course after 1953. No similarly global and consistent project was ever developed during the post-Stalinist era. In that sense, the retreat was clearly the first step towards a final defeat. After 1968, it was at first widely believed that Soviet hegemony within the bloc had been stabilized as effectively and along the same lines as the oligarchic regime within the Soviet Union, but the diversity of the peripheral states – exemplified in different ways by Poland, Hungary and Romania – was already too great for this to be more than a short-term success. With regard to the Eastern European region and its post-1953 history as a whole, Soviet policies were a changing mixture of efforts to retain ultimate control and adaptation to irresistible trends. The changes which thus took place brought into play the different dynamics of economic, political and cultural factors. It would, however, be misleading to explain them in purely structural terms: the circumstances and direct consequences of the first moves had a lasting effect on later developments. The impact of de-Stalinization on the bloc was uneven, but in one case it did lead to the collapse of the local party-state. The Hungarian revolution of 1956 is the only example of a Soviet-type regime destroyed by popular revolt; its background and significance will be discussed in another context below, and for our present purposes it is enough to underline its impact on the emerging post-Stalinist pattern of imperial control. Given the Soviet procedures of policy-making, the reactions to it are not always easy to distinguish from the effects of other causes, but we must assume that it was a major factor. It showed how fragile the Sovietized states in Eastern Europe were, and how necessary it was to make concessions in time if their survival was to be ensured. Some concessions were easier to accept and control than others. In particular, the rationalization of repression was a relatively straightforward task, whereas economic measures to counter popular discontent posed a more serious problem.

The latter point is crucial to the understanding of Soviet policies in Eastern Europe. There is considerable disagreement on the details of economic relations between the Soviet centre and the various parts of the periphery, and the balance-sheet varies from country to country, but it seems clear that the empire as a whole gradually ceased to be an economic asset and became a liability. It would be implausible to explain this as the result of a conscious decision to separate the political purposes of empire from the more expendable economic ones. Rather, the economic concessions which the Soviet leadership had originally made for political reasons took an unexpectedly self-perpetuating turn and strengthened the bargaining position of the peripheral regimes; at the same time, the compensatory strategies which it tried to develop were obstructed by the very logic of Soviet institutions as well as by international factors. As noted above, the Hungarian experience highlighted the need for more flexible economic policies that could – at least in some cases – entail a shift from exploitation to subsidizing of the periphery. Because of the structural fragility of the Eastern European regimes and their intrinsic limits to development, this readjustment became a permanent drain on the centre; it was, moreover, incorporated (albeit not everywhere to the same degree) into the overall policy of party-states that were searching for a more balanced *modus vivendi* with their respective societies. A more systematic economic integration of the bloc around the Soviet centre would to some extent have counterbalanced this trend, but Comecon, the institutional framework for such a project, was never more than a halfway house. It was neither a supranational planning agency nor a common market: the first option was incompatible with the relative autonomy of the peripheral regimes, and the second was impracticable as long as the logic of the mobilized economy took precedence over that of the market. And it was neither a separate international system nor an effective link to the global economy. Regional autarky could never be achieved, and Comecon prices were 'derived from the very system that is economically, politically, and ideologically rejected' (Brown 1988: 148), but the relative closure of the bloc – together with belated and consistent attempts to overcome it – led to 'the worst of all possible outcomes: "double dependency" for Eastern Europe, the semiperipheralization of the entire bloc, and a sizable reduction for the Soviets in the gains from empire' (Bunce 1985: 42).

The economic dilemmas of the Soviet empire were aggravated by political and ideological instability. After the retreat from Stalin's strategy of total control, no stable formula was ever devised for the balance of power between centre and periphery. The Soviet Union had to intervene to prevent centrifugal processes from escalating out of control, and at the same time it had to come to terms with client regimes that challenged its primacy in a less frontal fashion. When the suppression of the Czechoslovak reform movement seemed to have led to the political stabilization of the whole bloc, the economic effects were destabilizing. The move towards closer economic contacts with the West in the 1970s was in all probability made on the assumption that Soviet rule in Eastern Europe was now firmly established and would not be threatened by a controlled economic opening to the capitalist world. But the pyrrhic political victory – the destruction of reform Communism – thus induced the Soviet leadership to embark on an economic gamble that proved self-defeating. International and domestic factors combined to limit the economic benefits of the new course; for some of the Eastern European countries a mounting foreign debt became an intractable problem; last but not least, the whole bloc became more dependent on the capitalist world economy, more vulnerable to its challenges, and more exposed to its fluctuations.

As for the ideological aspects of imperial rule, the main difference between Stalinist and post-Stalinist patterns was, roughly speaking, the same as within the Soviet Union: instead of assimilation through indoctrination, the centre fell back on more external and limited forms of control. The ideological parameters of public discourse remained in force, but the drive for a total cultural reorientation was abandoned. This retreat was, however, bound to have more far-reaching and threatening consequences on the periphery than on the internal front. As we have seen, nationalism and Westernism were the main currents with which the official ideology had to coexist, and in Eastern Europe both of them were inevitably opposed to the Soviet imperial order as well as to the Soviet model of development. For the satellite party-state, the obstacles to ideological penetration thus gave rise to more acute legitimation problems than in the original Soviet context. But if the problem was general, the solutions to it varied widely: from attempts to relegitimize the ideological monopoly through identification with nationalism (Albania and Romania) to the more dependent but also more adaptable regimes which combined further relaxation of ideological control with cautious measures to enlarge their margin of autonomy (Poland and Hungary).

In brief, then, the trajectory of the Soviet empire in Eastern Europe began with a short-sighted and short-lived strategy of political coloniz-ation, economic exploitation and cultural assimilation, followed by concessions and retrenchments which in the long run – through their unintended and uncontrollable consequences – undermined the whole imperial edifice. The autonomous dynamic of economic, political and cultural forces undermined all adaptive arrangements and worked (in the various ways outlined above) against the imperial extension of the Soviet model. The crisis which – as a result of successive setbacks – ultimately engulfed both centre and periphery will be discussed below; at this stage, our main concern is with the growing internal diversity of the empire, i.e. with the post-Stalinist versions of the Soviet model in Eastern Europe.

The most fundamental common characteristic which set them apart from the Soviet Union is best described in negative terms: rather than fully-fledged Soviet-type societies, they were Soviet-type regimes which differed from the original case in that they had a more tenuous grip and a more limited impact on their respective societies. Both their traditional roots and their transformative capacity were weaker than those of the centre on which they depended and to which they remained indebted even when they managed to escape from its orbit. Their imperial connection was, in other words, a handicap with regard to legitimation as well as to mobilization and development. The partial but genuine progress made during the Khrushchev era and the enforced stability of the Brezhnev era led many analysts to believe that this weakness had been overcome and that 'real socialism' had struck real roots in Eastern Europe; for some, this was primarily a result of its ongoing and supposedly irresistible identification with nationalism, while others stressed the creation of a new social structure and the emergence of a whole complex of interest groups which ensured its reproduction. The crisis at the end of the 1980s was to show how fragile both these footholds were. But it was at least true that the regimes in question had not simply resigned themselves to their inferior condition; their attempts to mitigate or overcome it were a crucial part of the postwar history of the region. To compensate for the built-in distortions of their developmental projects, they tried to establish a special relationship with the Soviet centre (Bulgaria) or, more significantly and fatefully, to intensify economic relations with the West (the growing dependence of the East German regime on the Federal Republic and the borrowing binge of the Gierek leadership in Poland are the most obvious cases in point). They also sought – and to some extent found – antidotes to their chronic legitimation crisis. The distinction between overt and covert modes of legitimation, suggested by Maria Markus (1982), is particularly relevant to Eastern Europe (it should not be confused with the above-mentioned difference between principal and auxiliary forms: the latter can be overt), but the most important covert claims could become more or less overt. A covert appeal to nationalism was ubiquitous; the most spectacular transition to overt embrace occurred in Romania. Consumerist concessions and promises became an important form of covert legitimation during the earlier phase of the Brezhnev era, and the more overt role which they played in Hungary and Poland left its mark on the cultural and political atmosphere of both countries.

These different responses to the common predicament of dependent Soviet-style regimes were, of course, linked to other effects of the 'return to diversity'. The differentiating process was the result of many factors, internal and external, and if it brought the historical individuality of the various countries in the region back to the surface, this also meant that domestic Communist traditions had some impact on the course of events.

It was not only their relative strength or weakness that mattered. In this regard, the contrast between the two weakest Communist parties brought to power by Soviet conquest is particularly interesting: the Polish one was – even during the Stalinist phase – the most reluctant to identify fully with the Soviet model (if it is true that national Communism never prevailed in Poland, it can also be argued that there was always an element of national distinctiveness), whereas the Romanian one went on to develop the most sustained and aberrant version of autonomous Stalinism. In more general terms, the legacy of local Communist movements reflected their internal history as well as the broader historical background to which they were related. The Czechoslovak party – the strongest in the region – was also the one with the most complex and ambiguous tradition. Alongside a strong domestic Stalinist current, it contained a more reformist one which retained some of its social democratic heritage and could be reactivated under post-Stalinist conditions. This helps to explain the subsequent polarization of Czechoslovak Communism, unparalleled elsewhere in the Soviet bloc: the party which at first resisted de-Stalinization and continued the purge which Stalin had started later became the exponent of the most ambitious and radical version of reform Communism. After the reformist wing had been defeated by foreign intervention and destroyed by the most massive of all post-Stalinist purges, the Stalinist wing was still strong enough to give a particularly retrograde twist to the strategy of restoration.

But even domestic Stalinism, as distinct from other aspects and potentialities of domestic Communist traditions, was not always conducive to a simple imitation of Soviet patterns. Its identification with the Soviet model was not incompatible with more or less significant reinterpretations of it. For one thing, the available evidence suggests that with regard to the distribution of wealth (not power), Stalinism in Eastern Europe was more egalitarian than in the Soviet Union (Wiles 1977: 443). There were, of course, significant differences between the various Eastern European countries (egalitarian trends were more pronounced where the regimes had stronger historical roots, especially in Czecho-slovakia), and it should also be noted that this egalitarian adjustment of the model could be a result of strategic calculations as well as a symptom of the underlying political culture. But it seems clear that traditions and ideology counted for something. Another source of variety was the changing relationship between Stalinism and nationalism: as the Albanian and Romanian experiences were to show, the autocratic power structures that had originally developed on an imperial basis in the Soviet Union could be adopted by refractory satellite regimes for their own purposes, and the defence of local Stalinism against Soviet-initiated reforms could become the starting point for a more far-reaching nationalist turn.

A detailed genealogy and inventory of the Eastern European variants is beyond the scope of this book. The following discussion will therefore be limited to a brief comparison of the two main directions of deviation from the Soviet model.[4] In the southern part of the region, dependent party-states rebelled against the centre and developed their own domestic and international strategies; this path was, as we have seen, first opened up by the Yugoslav leadership and later followed by Albania and Romania, but with less significant results in the former case and without a final break-out from the bloc in the latter. The loss of control over part of the periphery affected the whole context of Soviet power: the Yugoslav schism provoked an all-out but abortive effort to unify the bloc, the Albanian one added to the international impact of the Sino-Soviet rift, and the Romanian one seems to have been a major setback for Soviet plans to upgrade Comecon. On the other hand, the ruptures were neither caused nor accompanied by radical revisions of the Soviet model, and it was only in the Yugoslav case that the conflict took this turn at a later stage. By contrast, Albania and Romania took archaic versions of the model to extreme conclusions. In the more important northern tier of the bloc, the centre was confronted with much more serious problems. Three countries – Poland, Czechoslovakia and Hungary – went through a cycle of crisis, collapse and restoration; the course of events and the final results differed markedly from case to case, but each of them represented – at some stage or other – a frontal challenge to the Soviet model and opened up perspectives of fundamental change. Although the centrifugal forces were brought under control and contained within a more rigid imperial order than in the south, these three storm-centres had a more significant impact on developments within the Soviet Union.

Albania was widely regarded as the most extreme case of national Communism, and the Hoxha regime was credited with having secured the survival of Albania as a nation-state. The way in which Albanian Communism collapsed and the condition in which it left Albanian society showed that neither its national legitimacy nor its contribution to state-building had been as solid as they seemed in its heyday. To understand the particular fusion of nationalism and Communism that took place in Albania, both the characteristics of the pre-revolutionary nationalist tradition and the circumstances of its appropriation by the party-state must be taken into account. In the Balkan context, Albanian nationalism was a fragile latecomer with a weak social basis, marginalized by stronger rivals and handicapped by a long-lasting connection with the Ottoman imperial centre; it was thus all the more vulnerable to an ideological takeover that made it both more extreme and more manipulable. The Communist leadership which carried out this operation came to power as the client of a foreign state with hegemonic designs, and only a transfer of allegiance to a stronger and more distant patron protected it from total absorption. This is not to suggest that the relationship between Communism and nationalism was purely instrumental. The national identity of the regime was genuine, but it was also adapted to the interests of a leadership less committed to developmental goals than to the maintenance of total control; the isolationist policies that served the latter purpose were, in all probability, a mixture of nationalist reflexes and strategic calculations. In retrospect, the most noteworthy fact about Albanian Communism is that it was – uniquely – capable of breaking successively with three hegemonic centres within the Communist world (Yugoslavia, the Soviet Union and China) but incapable of surviving on its own when the bloc from which it had seceded broke up.

Romania is a more complex case. It is one of the striking paradoxes of Eastern European Communism that the most extreme attempt to overcome the twin defects mentioned above – lack of legitimacy and limits to mobilizing capacity – and at the same time to resist structural reform should have been made by the regime with the weakest domestic roots. It seems clear that this turn of events cannot be explained as the outcome of a national Communist strategy moving from covert to overt tactics. Rather, the initial weakness of 'domesticism' led the Soviet centre to tolerate anomalies which eventually developed into a deviation far beyond the projects of the first initiators. To begin with, the purge which followed the monopolization of power was atypical in that it strengthened a domestic faction at the expense of the 'Muscovites' (this may well have been a case of conflict between two main motives of Stalin's postwar purges, anti-domesticism and anti-Semitism). The next step was the defensive reaction of a particularly vulnerable leadership against Soviet moves towards de-Stalinization; this led to a more serious rift when the Romanian party opposed Soviet plans for economic integration and insisted on a more autarkic strategy of development. These cumulative changes were, however, only the prehistory of the full-scale national Communist phase which began with Ceausescu's rise to power and lasted for a quarter of a century. The exceptionally pathological features of this regime have attracted much attention; its highly syncretic character has perhaps been less generally understood. The quest for legitimacy led to a reactivation of the Romanian nationalist tradition and its political culture. As for economic policies, unusually incoherent and overambitious in comparison with other states in the region, they were essentially based on the Stalinist model of industrialization and in some ways even more unbalanced. Finally, both domestic and foreign analysts have suggested that there was an East Asian element in the Ceausescu syndrome: the Romanian version of Stalinist autocracy seems to have been inspired by Chinese and even more by North Korean precedents (the latter example was particularly attractive because it showed how an ultra-dependent satellite could take advantage of changing circumstances and assert its autonomy).

For all their differences in both degree and kind, the three Balkan deviants had a basic characteristic in common: the political factor played a particularly decisive role in their development. The modifications of the Soviet model were primarily due to the imperatives of party-states in quest of more power and independence. If the primacy of the political sphere (in a particular sense) is a constitutive feature of the Soviet model, it became more pronounced in these specific cases. But this did not mean that they all took the same direction or that the most basic choices predetermined all details. In Yugoslavia, an irremovable but adaptable political centre opted for a strategy of concessions and experiments; when the centre ceased to function, the struggle between the successor states overshadowed all other developments. In Albania, an all-round and extreme ideological dogmatism served to protect an autocratic regime against all challenges, at home or abroad, whereas the Romanian pattern combined autocracy with economic adventurism and ideological innovations which emphasized nationalistic themes and bent the rules of orthodoxy.

By contrast, the common characteristic of the northern countries was a fundamental fragility of the Soviet model as a whole and the political centre in particular. This condition was permanently acute in Poland, latent in Hungary after an early explosion, and successfully dissimulated in Czechoslovakia before and after a transitory crisis. But as I will try to show, the parallels are significant enough to justify the typology proposed above. The circumstances of the takeover differed widely, but in contrast to the southern area, the Soviet model was in all three cases imposed on more advanced societies with closer ties to the West, and the built-in tensions between the regime and the socio-cultural context were correspondingly harder to defuse. In this peripheral but refractory region, the model was therefore problematized to a higher degree than in the Soviet Union or elsewhere in Eastern Europe. The question of economic reform had to be put on the agenda and tackled in practice, even if radical answers were the exception rather than the rule; projects of political transformation clashed with the interests of the imperial centre and the structures which it had imposed, although the forms as well as the after-effects of the conflict depended on the historical conjuncture; finally, the dissonance between the Soviet model and national cultural traditions was a recurrent problem, notwithstanding the marked contrasts between the countries in question. At the same time, the crises and vicissitudes of the model gave rise to a counter-culture – more or less openly articulated, more broadly based in some cases than in others, but always a more serious threat than visible signs would suggest – which contested its basic principles. The description of Eastern European societies as 'blessed and damned, with a double and ironical vision, and with the inescapable compulsion to think in alternatives' (Hankiss 1990: 7) applies above all to Hungary, Czechoslovakia and Poland.

Their experience confirms the primacy of politics, albeit not in the same sense as that of the southern group: rather, it was the collapse, paralysis or incipient transformation of the political centre which most decisively set their overall record apart from more stable Soviet-type regimes. Although the political crisis of the party-state was everywhere followed by restoration, the de-legitimizing effect was irreversible. The illusion of total control over society had been shattered, and the imperial connection had been exposed. If the Eastern European regimes were from the outset troubled by more serious legitimation problems than their Soviet protector, the legitimation crisis of the restored regimes was inevitably more acute than that of the others. In that sense, it can be argued that Soviet-type regimes were by nature not fully restorable: the moral impact of breakdown was on a par with the aspirations and pretensions of the totalitarian project. But a more or less outwardly complete restoration was possible, and the strategies as well as the results differed from country to country. They depended on the historical background of each regime, the specific characteristics of the crisis, and on the condition of the whole bloc at the time. The following comparison will focus on the most salient contrasts.

Hungary was the first Eastern European country where the reaction against Stalinist excesses gave rise to a reformist project, but it was first blocked by an unreconstructed party leadership and then overtaken by a revolutionary explosion. The exceptionally rapid slide from crisis to collapse was then followed by imperial intervention and a restoration that lasted much longer and took a more original turn than any other. On the political level, the principle of party sovereignty remained in force; it was, however, applied in a more flexible way than elsewhere and translated into strategies of containment and neutralization, rather than mobilization. This redefinition of the relationship between party-state and society called for a corresponding ideological retreat: 'the official ideology no longer saw itself as the only possible world-view but only as the dominant one' (Hankiss 1990: 91). An unofficial pluralism was accepted as a fact of social life, but barred from public articulation. These changes paved the way for more significant innovations in the economic sphere. The Hungarian regime became, in a fundamental sense, more economy-centred than the others, and the economic reforms after 1968 were its most distinctive achievement, but they were made possible by the pre-established *modus vivendi* between a demoralized élite and a traumatized society, and it would seem that their most important effect was a further shift in this relationship, rather than the modest and inconclusive moves towards market regulation. The reform process led to the abolition of imperative planning as well as some other essential features of the mobilized economy; for the state-owned enterprise, the outcome was a condition of 'dual dependence' on bureaucracy and market, and the economy as a whole became 'a symbiosis of a state sector under indirect bureaucratic control and a nonstate sector, market oriented but operating under strong bureaucratic restrictions' (Kornai 1991: 62). The reformed system was thus a hybrid, rather than a clear-cut alternative to the Soviet model, and its overall performance did not differ significantly from more orthodox regimes. Bureaucratic control was perpetuated through more informal mechanisms. But although the symbiosis was asymmetric, it left its mark on the dominant partner. The ruling apparatus became 'more polycentric' (ibid.: 43), more receptive to managerial notions, and more attuned to bargaining rather than command. The economic reform was, in brief, conducive to an internal erosion of party-state power, all the more irresistible because of the particular political and ideological weakness of a regime restored from without. In this way, the groundwork was gradually – and in large measure unintentionally – laid for a more radical rupture with the Soviet model.

Although both the domestic power basis and the domestic Stalinist component of the Czechoslovak regime were much stronger than in Hungary or Poland, some early symptoms of fragility loom larger in retrospect than they did at the time. For one thing, the first mass protests by workers in Eastern Europe after Stalin's death took place in Czechoslovakia. The reform movement that came into the open during the first half of the 1960s grew out of a creeping legitimation crisis brought to a head by the joint impact of a new wave of de-Stalinization in the Soviet Union and economic setbacks at home. The Prague Spring was, as Strmiska (1988) has shown, a social movement *sui generis*, fuelled by widespread and increasingly vocal grassroots dissent. It was channelled into a reform Communist project that drew on an alternative tradition within the party and reactivated the political culture in which it was embedded. The strategy of the Prague reformers was exceptionally ambitious, but ultimately incoherent: as noted above, it involved a comprehensive revision of the economic, political and cultural patterns of the Soviet model as well as an attempt to conserve the leading role of the party in a new institutional context. If the project was self-contradictory, the contradiction proved productive: the result of the reformist breakthrough in 1968 was an 'interrupted revolution' (Skilling 1976), i.e. a transformative process that had clearly gone beyond the limits of the Soviet model before it was cut short by foreign intervention. This is, admittedly, a controversial issue, and we cannot go into details here, but it would seem that the break with the Leninist model of party organization was decisive (the invasion was timed to forestall a party congress which would have finalized this part of the reform). More generally speaking, the metamorphosis of the political centre was linked to an overall democratizing process which also affected the prospects and preconditions for economic reform. Earlier moves in that direction were overtaken by more radical projects, too far-reaching to be contained within the old framework but too short-lived for their institutional implications to become fully visible.

Because of the relative strength of domestic Stalinism and the conservative turn in the Soviet Union, the Czechoslovak pattern of Communist restoration was at first sight very different from the experience of the neighbouring countries. The post-1969 leadership tried to rebuild and perpetuate the orthodox model. But its response to the crisis which dislodged it twenty years later showed that the return in strength had been more apparent than real. And some major flaws had been obvious well before that. Rising living standards during the 1970s helped to establish what dissident observers described as a 'new contract' between regime and society; the discrepancy between overt and covert legitimation was probably greater than in any other Communist country. Restoration was, in other words, inevitably accompanied by a strategic retreat from the political to the economic sphere, although it did not take the same form as in Hungary. This made the regime all the more vulnerable when economic decline set in during its second decade in power, and the reopened question of economic reform became a permanent threat to stability. The ideological rationale of 'normalization'

– a particularly conservative version of 'really existing socialism' as a social formation in its own right, rather than a transitional form – crumbled when the Soviet centre changed course and used the same premise to justify the opposite conclusion: the redefinition of socialism as a long-term project now served to de-legitimize the regimes that had supposedly failed to advance beyond its beginnings.

Poland was, as is well known, more resistant to the Soviet model than any other country on which it was imposed, and the record of Polish Communism in power comes closest to a permanent crisis. But it can also be argued that early adjustments enabled the regime to postpone an acute crisis for longer than in the two other countries. A modest but not insignificant departure from the Soviet pattern was already evident in the treatment of domesticism during the Stalin era. As a result, a domesticist leadership could return to power in 1956 and defuse the more radical reformist challenge. The public resonance of the latter was more important than its practical effects: it gave rise to debates and projects which affected developments elsewhere in the bloc (in particular, Polish proposals for economic reform anticipated the policies later adopted in Czechoslovakia and Hungary), and it put the regime irreversibly on the ideological defensive, but it did not lead to a reformist takeover of the party leadership. Contestatory currents within and outside the party were kept under control for a quarter of a century, and in retrospect, it must – for all the obvious moral and material weaknesses of Polish Communism – be admitted that the apparatus evinced a surprising staying power. Its strategy was a varying mixture of concessions and counter-attacks; the most fateful turn was taken at the beginning of the 1970s, when a new leadership tried to use foreign loans to finance rapid industrial growth and rising living standards at the same time, but succeeded only in setting off an explosion of mismanagement and corruption which damaged the regime beyond repair.

The long-drawn-out effort to contain reformism widened the gap between party-state and society. When the conflict could no longer be averted, the underlying problems were already too serious for a reformist strategy to be viable; the result, unique in the history of the bloc, was the emergence of a mass movement which became the acknowledged representative of society against the regime. This new version of dual power was tantamount to a breakdown of the Soviet model. No self-limiting strategy on the part of Solidarnosc could alter the basic facts of the matter: for the party-state, mere coexistence with a self-limiting rival meant a loss of sovereignty and a crisis of identity. Restoration was the only real alternative to capitulation. In this case, imperial control was reasserted through a domestic intermediary, but that was only a minor advantage in comparison with the Hungarian and Czechoslovak crises, and other factors – a shattered economy, an atrophied ideology, a totally alienated society, and a global decline of the empire – made restoration more difficult in Poland than in other countries at an earlier stage. The social movement which had destroyed the old order could be suppressed, but a return to the *status quo ante* was impossible; neither Czechoslovak nor Hungarian methods were applicable. Because of the political impasse, party institutions could not even resume their normal role, and the military remained in control. For all these reasons, but contrary to the views of most contemporary observers, the Jaruzelski regime was – as A. Walicki (1991) has shown – in some ways a first step towards post-Communism, rather than a last stand of totalitarianism. The pseudo-restoration paved the way for a programmed transition. During the 1980s, convergent ideological shifts brought the regime and its adversaries closer to agreement on a radical reorganization of the economy.

When the military leaders forced the remnant of the party to negotiate with the opposition, the ground had thus been cleared for a transfer of power, more rapid and complete than expected, but prearranged in principle and unsurprising in retrospect. The beneficiary was a counter-élite (or, more precisely, a coalition of counter-élites) which derived its prestige and legitimacy from an extinct social movement; the movement itself had disappeared together with its adversary.

THE EASTERN ARENA

Chinese Communism was indisputably the most significant non-Russian version of the Soviet model. It represented the most effective challenge to Soviet hegemony within the Communist world and was for some time widely regarded as the most serious attempt to develop a counter-model. In retrospect, however, its record is more confused and its achievements more problematic than they often seemed to earlier observers. Its deviations from the orthodox pattern never added up to a coherent and viable alternative; its decomposition reached a critical point well before the Soviet Union and its satellites. On the other hand, the terminal crisis has yet to run its course, and the final outcome seems more uncertain than elsewhere.

The following reflections will focus on some key aspects of the Chinese trajectory, but all that can be attempted here is a cursory and selective analysis, more limited in scope than our discussion of the original Soviet experience. In line with the general perspective, our main concern will be with the imperial context of revolution and post-revolutionary modernization. China was not the only country outside Russia where the Soviet model became a vehicle for imperial traditions and aspirations, but it was the only one where this happened on a scale comparable to the original and led to the reconstitution of a separate imperial centre. Despite this overall similarity, there were some major contrasts between the two cases; they have to do with different characteristics of the imperial legacies, different backgrounds to the fusion of revolutionary projects and imperial traditions, and different results of this combination.

The interrelations between Chinese Communism and the imperial past have never gone unnoticed. During the more orthodox phase, the apparent success of Leninism in China – in contrast to other non-Western civilizations – was often explained in terms of affinities with pre-modern political culture. Both the Confucian version of the unity of power and knowledge, embodied in bureaucratic domination, and the traditional link between popular rebellion and dynastic change had, in this view, made Chinese society particularly receptive to the idea of the revolutionary party-state. When the original and heterodox aspects of Maoism became more conspicuous, they too seemed reminiscent of more remote ancestors. Mao's conception of revolutionary leadership could be compared with ideals of imperial sovereignty as well as with the charismatic rebels of the past, and the fusion of the two models was not without precedent. As for the revolutionary project that was first translated into an effective strategy and then revived in a disastrously regressive form within the post-revolutionary power structure, it was obviously indebted to a millenarian tradition which had grown out of early crises of the imperial order and accompanied the latter throughout its history. Whether Mao's 'Sinified' version of Marxism in general and dialectics in particular owes more to the Confucian mainstream or to alternative traditions has been a matter of debate. But the analysis of underlying connections is further complicated by the fluctuating attitudes of the post-revolutionary regime to the cultural heritage. If the nihilist crusade against the 'four olds' (thinking, culture, customs and habits) during the cultural revolution represents one extreme, the opportunistic rehabilitation of Confucius and his legacy in the 1980s can perhaps be seen as the other, and both are – at least on the level of official policies – equally unparalleled in the history of Soviet revisions of the Russian past.

In short, the picture is confusing, and different views of it can lead to starkly contrasting conclusions. The disagreement is, moreover, less structured than in the other crucial case: as far as I can judge, interpretations of the relationship between imperial and Communist China have not crystallized into the clear-cut alternatives that the above discussion of Russian and Soviet history could start with. This suggests that the connection might be structurally more problematic, and perhaps even – in some respects – an open and as yet undecidable question. Whether or to what extent that is the case should become clearer if we consider some key aspects of the Chinese transformation. To begin with, the argument must be linked to earlier debates about the Chinese imperial tradition – in the broad sense, i.e. as a complex of cultural orientations and power structures – and its impact on the modernizing process. But the transition to modernity and the conflict between different projects of modernization were not only influenced by an exceptionally powerful tradition; they also took place in the context of a particularly prolonged and severe imperial crisis. This background explains the initial response to the Soviet model. The most salient episode in the history of Chinese Communism, however, is the subsequent deviation from Soviet patterns; the dynamics and implications of this development are still obscure in many respects. Finally, the post-Maoist phase is, as I will try to show, best understood as a new turn in an ongoing and conflictual transition, rather than an internal reform of the Sinified Soviet model.

The imperial tradition

The Chinese imperial tradition was, as is well known, more continuous and self-contained than any other; it was not immune to centrifugal forces, but its ability to survive crises and temporary breakdowns is unique. This long history was reflected in the cultural unity and homogeneity that had been superimposed on China's underlying diversity. Furthermore, the Chinese imperial order was at the centre of a whole civilizational complex within which its cultural authority proved more compelling and durable than its political power. In all these respects, it stands in marked contrast to the more discontinuous, composite and heteronomous tradition of the Russian empire, and the different background was not irrelevant to post-revolutionary developments. In China, the revolutionary detour to imperial restoration was completed after a much more prolonged crisis than in Russia, but once in place, the imperial party-state could build on more solid traditional foundations of unity. Although it was established on a less developed economic and technological basis, it had an advantage over its Russian precursor in that it was to a greater extent able to draw on techniques of power (such as methods of bureaucratic control and mutual surveillance) which had been developed for the purpose of perfecting traditional domination but could now be put to more effective use on a modern basis. Finally, the strength of the imperial legacy militated against the unconditional acceptance of an imported model, and even more so against the political tutelage which had from the Soviet point of view become an integral part of the model. The disparity of imperial traditions was thus one of the roots of the later Sino–Soviet conflict.

But if we want to situate the Chinese variant of the Soviet model within a more complex interplay of tradition and modernity, something must first be said about the theoretical frame of reference. Max Weber's comparative analysis of China is an obligatory (even if not always explicitly acknowledged) starting-point for any discussion of this subject. More precisely, the comparison of China and the West can now be undertaken in a perspective that incorporates Weber's basic insights but relates them to new developments and avoids his conceptual slippages. The Weberian focus on the Western breakthrough to modernity (as a background to the interpretation of other civilizations) is justified in principle; Weber's own understanding of it is, however, open to some objections. In the light of the reconceptualization of modernity, proposed in the introduction, the main problem with Weber's approach is his one-sided emphasis on modern capitalism and his failure to integrate the analyses of its cultural and political preconditions and counterweights into a coherent picture. Further elaboration of the multidimensional image of modernity that was adumbrated in Weber's writings (more so than in the work of the other classics) would have helped to problematize its predominant Western patterns, and thus also to distinguish between Westernization and modernization. The comparison with non-Western civilizations could, by the same token, have taken a more explicitly self-relativizing turn. As for China, its crucial importance for comparative analysis is now – in the light of later research – more obvious than it was for Weber: the fact that China was – especially with regard to technological and organizational capacities – so far ahead of the West for such a long time makes its later inability to achieve a comparable breakthrough all the more striking. Because of its longevity, autonomous history, initial lead and limited contact with the West, Chinese civilization is arguably the most revealing alternative with which the West can be confronted. But if we can still follow Weber in the very general sense of trying to account for the contrast between Western self-transcendence and Chinese self-containment, his way of posing the problem must nevertheless be qualified in several significant respects. In view of the major transformations which now are known to have taken place in traditional China, the focus must be on the particular directions and inherent limits of change, rather than any absolute obstacles to it. And on the other hand, the developmental or modernizing potential of the Chinese tradition must now also be judged on the basis of more recent changes; they include the emergence of new models of capitalist development on the periphery of the Chinese world, but also – and for our purposes primarily – the adoption and adaptation of the Soviet model by a resurgent Chinese centre.

Although more or less systematic revisions of Weber's interpretation of China have been undertaken by many scholars, some of the key issues are still controversial. The following discussion (drawing on the work of Etienne Balazs, Wolfram Eberhard, S.N. Eisenstadt, Mark Elvin, John Fairbank, Thomas Metzger, Benjamin Schwartz et al.) will be limited to a few points where the debate has taken a clear direction and highlighted connections between the pre-modern past and the post-revolutionary present. There is, first, no doubt that the notion of the patrimonial state was in this case even more conducive to the neglect of specifics than it was with regard to Russia. Weber's concern with the general problematic of patrimonialism led him to pay less attention to imperial patterns in general as well as to the Chinese imperial order in particular; and since the impact of cultural orientations on social order and change was mediated by the political centre, a diluted conception of the latter was bound to affect the overall picture. A stronger emphasis on the imperial order and its dominant role has opened up two complementary lines of inquiry. On the one hand, many historians have stressed the diversity and dynamism which the empire managed to contain. Greater awareness of the contrasts between geographical regions and historical epochs has revolutionized the received image of traditional China. On the other hand, this context makes the staying power of the imperial centre and its institutional framework all the more striking, and the implications of different explanations of this phenomenon for the present version of the empire all the more relevant. If the maintenance of imperial continuity in the face of formidable obstacles and challenges must be regarded as a historical achievement, rather than a case of historical inertia, the question of its preconditions also bears upon the prospect of further survival.

There is no general agreement on this issue; but to argue that a comparison with Europe (where the Roman imperial myth survived the fall of the empire but did not lead to a durable restoration) shows the relative insignificance of imperial traditions, in contrast to structural factors (Elvin 1973: 22), is to beg the question: to what extent was the different record of imperial myths in East and West due to their different content? Moreover, it would seem that this aspect of the phenomenon – the specific cultural model or models of power that was or were embodied in the Chinese imperial order – is particularly illustrative of the logic which links its origins to the most recent past. The cultural framework of the imperial structure which took shape under the Qin and Han dynasties (221–206 BC and 206 BC–220 AD) consisted of two layers. The unification of China was the crowning achievement of a strategy pursued most effectively by the state of Qin and articulated most clearly by the Legalist school; this project was arguably the most accomplished prefiguration of totalitarianism in the pre-modern world (for a particularly interesting interpretation, cf. Lévi 1989). But it was too unbalanced to survive intact and on its own. To stabilize the empire, an older and more diverse tradition had to be reconstructed. Its centre-piece was the 'general idea of the primacy of order in both the cosmic and human spheres' (Schwartz 1985a: 413), translated into the more specific model of an all-encompassing sacred political order. The rationalization of archaic notions of order had given rise to rival models and visions which could now serve as sources for an eclectic synthesis; the result was the syncretic cultural formation known as imperial Confucianism. This second layer helped to consolidate the viable core of the original imperial project and at the same time to scale down its more extreme aspirations. But the duality of the imperial institution – and the imperial imaginary – was also a source of tensions and conflicts that could be exacerbated by other factors.

This formative phase of the imperial tradition was re-mythicized during the most extreme phase of the Chinese revolution. Mao and his associates referred to the first Qin emperor as a model of revolutionary leadership and linked their offensive against the party-state apparatus to a critique of Confucianism. It goes without saying that the historical interpretations built on this basis were worthless, and that the ideological use of the past was geared to less publicized political goals. But it seems nevertheless highly significant that conflicts within the post-revolutionary regime could be represented in terms of archaic precedents. The imaginary connection with the foundation of the empire was used to legitimize the search for a more effective strategy of political control and mobilization (by contrast, Stalin's imperial role models were more recent and genuine), and dissatisfaction with some aspects of the Soviet model found an outlet in the attack on traditional patterns of bureaucratic domination. In both respects, the invocation of the past can be seen as an attempt to disguise or exorcize the contradictions of an incoherent project: the combination of a partial repudiation of the Soviet model with a radicalization of its essentials.

The problematic of the imperial legacy is closely linked to another Weberian theme. As Weber saw it, the most distinctive feature of the Confucian tradition was its systematic effort to minimize the tensions between man and world; the cultural model constructed on this foundation was translated into a comprehensive social order which functioned – on all levels – in such a way that tensions and their trans-formative potential were minimized. This view is no longer tenable. The traditional order was, as more recent research has shown, characterized by a whole complex of interrelated tensions. There was, for one thing, no pre-established harmony between the two components of the imperial centre: a pre- or infra-Confucian foundation and a syncretic Confucian framework (or, in more institutional terms, between the autocratic and the bureaucratic patterns of power). But there were also tensions – analysed and interpreted in somewhat different terms by Eisenstadt (1983) and Metzger – within the Confucian tradition. Visions of cosmic order were never adequately embodied in mundane orders, and political reforms fell short of the cultural ideals of moral perfection. The Confucian tradition seems, in short, to have institutionalized the possibility of immanent and permanent critique. With regard to the relationship between imperial state and society, it is true that there was no 'plurality of centres', but the claims of sacred and centralized authority had to coexist with and adjust to 'a variety of commitments ranging from the familistic to the metaphysical' (Metzger 1984: 360). The imperial centre finally triumphed over the refeudalizing trends and aristocratic forces which had been a recurrent threat to the early and middle empire (i.e. roughly during the first millennium after unification), but it remained dependent on mediating élites and structures. As for the geopolitical context, tensions between the empire and its environment were evident on two fronts. On the one hand, the Chinese state was permanently threatened and periodically conquered by the nomadic imperial formations which grew up alongside it (Barfield 1989); its military vulnerability was offset by its civilizational superior-ity, but not always to the same extent or with the same results. On the other hand, the empire was – especially from the eleventh century onwards – increasingly drawn into an international trade system centred on South China; the later imperial dynasties tried, with varying success, to limit this involvement, but they could not block a development which led to growing divergences between interior and maritime regions.

Finally, a few words should be said about a further structural tension that seems particularly relevant to the crisis and reconstruction of the

Chinese empire. It might be described as an inbuilt imbalance between the foundations of imperial order and the more elementary imperatives of state formation. Elias's analysis on the twin monopolies of taxation and violence as the keys to state formation is a convenient guide to this problematic. The state which unified China owed its success to particularly effective ways of extracting resources and organizing warfare. But its imperial successors faced permanent problems and suffered from structural weaknesses in both respects. The crisis of the middle empire in the eighth and ninth centuries was due to the collapse of its solutions to these problems (the complementary institutions of the peasant militia and the equal-field system). No comparable breakdown occurred under later rulers, but neither was there a comparably ambitious attempt to tackle the problems of a fragile infrastructure. On the military level, the empire had to cope with threats from the imperial nomads of Inner Asia as well as domestic rebellions (the last dynasty neutralized the former problem through a definitive merger of the two imperial traditions, but had to confront the second one at its most explosive – the Taiping and Nian rebellions – and solve it in a way that strengthened local militarism and paved the way for separatist forces). As to the imperial taxation systems, they were notoriously resistant to reform and always combined with additional exploitation of taxpayers by officials; this was one of the intrinsic destabilizing mechanisms of dynastic rule. Lucian Pye's (1990) description of China as a 'civilization pretending to be a state' can perhaps be understood as an allusion to these problems: in historical perspective, China was an exceptionally durable imperial formation backed up by a correspondingly powerful cultural model, but the basic mechanisms of state formation were underdeveloped and their scope limited by the very forces and traditions on which the imperial edifice rested. Strategies of imperial reconstruction and modernization thus faced the primary task of building more effective state structures.

These multiple tensions make it easier to understand the pattern of crises, breakdowns and restorations which found its official expression in the dynastic cycle (imperial continuity was not, as in some other cases, matched by dynastic continuity). But with regard to the challenges and upheavals of the last two centuries, some further implications should be noted. The structural problems of the imperial order had, on the one hand, given rise to traditions of both reform and rebellion; their legacy and their interaction on the eve of the final breakdown had a major impact on the subsequent course of events. On the other hand, internal tensions and latent crises could be brought to a head by external factors and thus result in changes that could neither be controlled nor comprehended in the traditional way. The conceptual scheme of 'Western impact' and 'Chinese response' is an oversimplification of this process: the events set in motion were often disproportionate to the impact and only in part reducible to a response. This applies to social transformations as well as to ideological developments. If there was – as Metzger (1977) has emphasized – always a tension between accommodative and trans-formative tendencies within the Confucian tradition, it became much more acute when confronted with the Western challenge, and the transformative potential thus released was reflected in various attempts to adapt modernizing strategies to Chinese premises. And a programmatic break with the past did not exclude an implicit continuity: the apparent triumph of the ostensibly most radical Western alternative became the starting-point for a new cycle of assimilation.

If the traditional Chinese world was much more tension-ridden than Weber thought, it was also – and in large measure for that reason – much more dynamic. On this point, however, the Weberian legacy is ambiguous. Weber's interpretation of China allows for rationalizing processes which differ in content and direction from those of the West. In this general sense, his approach is relevant to current debates: if there is a 'paradigmatic crisis in Chinese studies' (Huang 1991) brought about by the discovery of developments which seem paradoxical from the view-point of both Marxist and liberal orthodoxy, the notion of contextual and culture-specific rationalization might point the way for a third alternative. But the specific phenomena in question are beyond the scope of Weber's argument, and it remains to be seen whether they could be integrated into a suitably revised civilizational analysis. They can, in brief, be described as patterns of self-limiting or self-containing change, incompatible with older views of a stagnant China, yet not conducive to a developmental breakthrough on a par with the Western one. Historians have noted such trends in the economic, political and cultural spheres. They are doubly relevant to the understanding of the Chinese revolution and its sequel: as aspects of a historical background that is far too complex to fit with overgeneralized notions of underdevelopment or backwardness, and as parts of a historical heritage that may be perpetuated by post-revolutionary policies. The latter point will be briefly considered below.

On the economic level, the most conspicuous paradox is that of 'growth without development' in the late imperial era (1600–1911). This epoch saw a demographic explosion, extensive commercialization without significant capitalist development, and a new wave of urbanization which led to the growth of market towns rather than metropolitan centres. Mark Elvin's (1973: 298–316) theory of the 'high equilibrium trap' (diminishing returns for traditional inputs, accompanied by steady population growth and cheapening labour) is the most technical attempt to explain why there was no qualitative change; the Marxist emphasis on 'a fairly complete separation between large-scale owners and production processes' (Lippit 1978: 305) and the resultant lack of economic dynamism is another answer to the same question. But no built-in barriers to economic innovation can explain the failure of the political centre to develop a transformative strategy comparable to the policies of the Meiji era in Japan. The paralysis of the imperial institution was partly due to developments which had occurred at an earlier stage. The Northern Song era (960–1125) had seen a simultaneous strengthening of emperor and bureaucracy, accompanied by economic growth and all-round civilizational progress as well as the emergence of a world trade system centred on China. The significance of these changes was first recognized by Japanese historians who saw them as an incipient transition to modernity, well in advance of the Western breakthrough, and drew parallels with European absolutism. But the sequel suggests that the affinities should not be overestimated. John Fairbank describes it as the 'paradox of Song China and Inner Asia': the era which began with China's greatest civilizational achievements ended with the most complete takeover by conquerors from the Inner Asian periphery. And this was only the first phase of a long-term process which culminated – after a temporary reassertion of Chinese supremacy, but this time in a more imitative, defensive and inward-looking way – in the Manchu conquest and the final fusion of Chinese and Inner Asian imperial traditions under the Qing dynasty (1644–1911). Fairbank's thesis is that the outcome is best understood as a merger of the Inner Asian component with the imperial-autocratic counterpart to China's civil bureaucracy. It was the result of complex developments within both regions as well as their ongoing interaction, but what concerns us here is the adverse impact which it had on the adaptive and transformative capacity of the empire. The Chinese imperial formation as a whole became more continental, inward-looking and unresponsive to the possibilities of maritime expansion that had seemed to be opening up during its most dynamic phase; the structural conservatism of the imperial order was strengthened by the measures taken to maintain a regime born of conquest; and notwithstanding the sustained effort to combine the military resources of the conquerors with Confucian models of civilization and statecraft, the failure to achieve full assimilation made the dynasty vulnerable to a Chinese national backlash. All these factors proved to be major obstacles to imperial modernization.

The self-reproducing and synthesizing capacity of the imperial order was in large measure due to its cultural context. The political centre was, in other words, reinforced by a complex of 'persistent and dominant orientations' (Schwartz 1985b: 4); they could be interpreted in different ways, and countertendencies could develop up to a point, but a strong case has been made for the exceptional continuity of the core components. A recent analysis refers to them as 'the secret of social immortality' (Graham 1989: 372). They include, in particular, strong assumptions about the primacy of order and the key role of a sacred political order as a link between human and cosmic levels; an intuitive and holistic approach more conducive to the elaboration than the questioning of primordial conceptions of order; and last but not least, the projection of an ideal order into the past. The paradox involved here can perhaps be described as rationalization through archaization. It was central to a cultural pattern which did not preclude cognitive progress, but constituted an obstacle to the objectification of nature as well as to visions of individual or social autonomy.

These various paradoxes seem to have converged in the most striking developmental pattern of late imperial China: economic and social life became less dependent on the imperial state, but this did not lead to a redistribution or restructuring of political power. The primacy of the political centre remained uncontested despite a decline of strength *vis-à-vis* society. Huang (1991: 320) calls this 'the paradox of the expansion of the public realm without the assertion of civic power against the state'. The forces that disrupted this constellation threatened both the state and the social order, and they were galvanized into action by external factors.

The modern crisis

Etienne Balazs once suggested that it would be easier to compare the relations between China and the West with those of Russia and the West, if only one century had elapsed between the Peter the Great and Stalin. It would – with more wisdom of hindsight – seem easier to argue that China had neither a Peter nor a Stalin. The transformation induced by its interaction with the West was not simply more rapid and traumatic; its context and direction differed from Russia, and its major turning-points are not of the same kind as the Russian ones. There was no early breakthrough to imperial modernization comparable to the Petrine revolution. And the Maoist interlude does not bear comparison with Stalin's second revolution: neither the transformative impact nor the institutional legacy was of the same calibre. The centennial landmarks that stand out in the Chinese context are, rather, the Taiping rebellion (1850–64) and the cultural revolution of the late 1960s. As we have seen, the historical background to this trajectory was complex and distinctive. But although there are good reasons to revise the over-Westernized vision of modern Chinese history, based on the misconception of an inert civilization overwhelmed by a dynamic one, the result should not be a 'China-centered history of China' (Cohen 1984). The intrusion of the ascendant West was an essential part of the process; the focus should, in other words, be on interaction rather than on an internal unfolding or an external impetus, and it is the unique pattern of this interaction that has been obscured by oversimplifying notions of imperialism, colonialism or underdevelopment. It is better described as a civilizational collision than as a civilizational encounter: the outcome was, to quote one of the foremost Western observers, 'a disaster so comprehensive and appalling that we are still incapable of fully describing it' (Fairbank 1992: 189).

Economic dislocation was not the most important aspect of the Western impact on China. It is now well established that the effects of foreign capitalist penetration on the Chinese economy were limited and double-edged, disruptive in some respects but stimulating in others. But the significance of Western economic outposts on Chinese territory lay partly in the backing they gave to non-economic forces. The treaty ports were both symptoms of the inferior condition to which stronger (and, for the Chinese, upstart) states had reduced the empire and intermediary spaces where the appropriation of Western ideas and techniques could progress more rapidly than elsewhere. The cultural and political effects of the collision were more dramatic than the economic ones. Chinese cultural orientations, grounded in the most autochthonous and self-contained civilizational complex in the non-Western world, were exposed to a frontal and global challenge; selective borrowing from Western traditions (Christian or Marxist) could have rapid and spectacular effects, but the ideological formations to which it gave rise were extremely unstable. Both the self-image and the legitimacy of the imperial order were undermined by defeat at the hand of Western states; to regain the lost ground, state structures had to be rebuilt on firmer foundations and adapted to Western models, but these imperatives of rationalization have yet to be reconciled with the maintenance of imperial unity.

The view that the modern crisis of imperial China began in 1840 with the Opium War seems to have gone out of fashion, but there is no doubt that its acute phase began ten years later with the Taiping rebellion. The latter event – a social and cultural explosion unparalleled anywhere else in the nineteenth century – was the result of cumulative developments during the Qing era as well as of the new turn which relations with the West had taken. In the present context, the ideological syncretism of the Taiping is of particular interest. Their version of Christianity was obviously essential to the formation of the movement as well as to its ability to contest some key aspects of the Chinese social order. This brief but massive impact of Sinified Christian beliefs stands in marked contrast to earlier and later failures of orthodox Christianity (it might be added that with regard to both short-term dynamism and inability to survive, Maoist Marxism now seems more comparable to Taiping Christianity than it may have appeared at the peak of its power). On the other hand, the mixture of hierarchic and egalitarian elements in the political programme of the Taiping was reminiscent of Chinese traditions, and the closer they came to building a state apparatus, the stronger was the tendency to fall back on indigenous and archaic models. In the later phase of the movement, its nationalist appeal was increasingly overshadowed by theocratic claims; moves towards Westernizing reforms came too late to improve its chances. Strategic errors and lost opportunities have been stressed by later historians, and a Taiping victory does not seem to have been structurally impossible, but the record of the movement is too varied and ambiguous to permit any plausible speculation about further conse-quences. And in view of the original ideological ambitions, it is all the more striking that the movement did not give birth to a tradition. It had lasting effects, but left no durable legacy; this is, as we shall see, important for the comparison with Russia.

Both the handicaps and the achievements of the 'self-strengthening' modernizers of the late nineteenth century stand out more clearly when set against the background of the Taiping upheaval. In terms of Russian parallels, it could be argued that the late Qing statesmen had to tackle simultaneously the tasks that Tsarist Russia had faced at the beginning and at the end of the seventeenth century (i.e. after the 'time of troubles' and in the course of the Petrine revolution): the rebuilding of a traditional order which had been brought to the brink of destruction and the adaptation of internal power structures to standards set by more advanced rivals. The two goals were incompatible, and it was the first one that prevailed. In contrast to the Petrine revolution, the conservative strategy of the Tongzhi Restoration of the 1860s allowed for the borrowing of Western technology but excluded the adoption of Western models of state-building as well as the systematic development of the infrastructure which they would have required. When an attempt was made to meet these twin requirements (first by a weak reformist élite during the 'hundred days' of 1898 and then by an exhausted dynasty after 1901), it was too late: as a result of its attempts at reform, the imperial centre lost control over provincial élites and capitulated without resistance. This was the real meaning of the 'revolution' of 1911, often misleadingly compared to the French and Russian ones.

Initial responses to the Soviet model

Chinese responses to the Soviet model were thus conditioned by a very specific and traumatic historical background. The Bolshevik regime represented an imperial formation that had overcome its crisis through political reconstitution as well as social renewal and seemed to have found a formula for further progress. By contrast, the crisis of the Chinese empire had deepened until it destroyed the centre, and no adequate remedies had been invented. As noted above, the Confucian strategy of restoration through reform – impressive enough in its own right – did not measure up to the demands of imperial modernization. Revolutionary alternatives were equally retarded: limited contact with the West had been enough to give new content to the Chinese millenarian tradition and trigger its most massive outbreak, but not to transform it into a revolutionary counter-culture with modernizing ambitions. There was, in other words, no Chinese equivalent of the Russian revolutionary tradition in its capacity as an inter-civilizational articulation of radical perspectives. If China had neither a Peter nor a Stalin, it is equally true that it had neither a Herzen nor a Lenin (the widely held view of Mao as the Lenin of the Chinese revolution is highly misleading: apart from other crucial contrasts, Mao's historical role differed from Lenin's in that it began with the conversion to an already existing model of imperial power bent on revolution from above, rather than the construction of an imaginary union of knowledge and power, and an effort to adapt it to a project of national transformation, rather than a vision of world revolution; the wish to restore China to former greatness and global pre-eminence seems to have been one of the constant motives in his otherwise chequered intellectual career).

In the Chinese context, the Soviet model thus became a substitute for defeated or discredited strategies of regeneration from within. But this development must also be related to the more specific situation which took shape after the imperial collapse. The interlude between the abdication of the dynasty in 1912 and the nationalist revolution of 1927 has been described in many different ways, and the various labels reflect the conflicting forces at work. It became known as the 'warlord era' because of the fragmentation of China into smaller units ruled by military strongmen. In a long-term perspective, warlordism can be seen as a regressive episode in the process of state formation that had to begin anew after the disintegration of the empire; in this respect, the warlords were not all of the same stamp, but they lacked the ideological and organizational resources to compete with the forces which eventually emerged as the main contenders for the imperial succession. On the other hand, these years were also the 'golden age of the Chinese bourgeoisie' (Bergère 1989) and a particularly dynamic phase of capitalist development; although the results were short-lived, the question of their historical significance must now be reconsidered in the light of the post-Maoist transformation of China. At the same time, a new wave of iconoclastic anti-traditionalism made the intelligentsia more receptive to Western thought. This gave an added impetus to Chinese Marxism, which could thus – during its early days – claim the dual legitimacy of revolutionary power and radical critique (there was no Marxist tradition prior to or independent of the Bolshevik connection, and no conflict between Western and Russian versions of Marxism before the emergence of a marginal Trotskyist current after 1927). Last but not least, the absence of centralized authority opened up new possibilities for collective action. The workers' and peasant movements of the 1920s played an important if indirect role in the history of Chinese Communism: the involvement in their struggles enabled the party to develop a self-image and an ideological language which could later be adjusted to the policies of an apparatus that had to control rural society from above and conquer urban society from without. But it should be emphasized that the connection between Communist strategy and social movements was much more limited and artificial in China than in Russia. The formation of the party was less dependent on an urban working-class background than pre-revolutionary Bolshevism had been, and its rise to power, which took place in an altogether different environment, was not a 'peasant revolution'; the decisive step was, rather, the takeover of rural society in peripheral regions by an embryonic party-state which could draw on its earlier urban experience. Class categories became an integral part of official doctrine, but because of the tenuous link to their original context, they were more malleable and adaptable to other perspectives than in the orthodox Soviet pattern.

It was not only through Communist channels that the Soviet model affected the course of Chinese history. It had also been a source of inspiration for the Guomindang, and although this common orientation was no obstacle to all-out war between the two parties, it gave them both a decisive advantage over other forces. The victory of the Communists was, as is now generally acknowledged, largely due to external factors, but that is not the whole story; their ability to take advantage of the new historical conjuncture reflects the intrinsic superiority of their institutional and ideological basis. The Guomindang regime was, by comparison, a much more fragile construction. Lessons learnt from the Soviet experience had been essential to its promising start in the 1920s, but the victory of its militarist wing blocked further progress towards party-state rule. As for later attempts to imitate European fascism, they did not lead to any significant changes, and the wartime alliance with the West did nothing to Westernize the regime. After 1927, the foreign elements – including the Soviet ones – were never more than surface trappings of a more autochthonous dictatorship that is best described as warlordism writ large.

The invention of a more effective strategy of state-building was the most significant aspect of the Yan'an phase in the history of Chinese Communism. Limited information and lingering myths about this episode make its details difficult to assess, but some starting-points for later developments should be noted. It seems clear that there was no dissent in principle from the Soviet model which had taken shape a few years earlier. The Chinese Communists identified with Stalin's second revolution (or, more precisely, with their own image of it) as a strategy of social transformation, and they did not question the hegemonic role of the Soviet Union. But in building their own power basis they took some steps towards partial autonomy and thus paved the way for the more radical deviations of the post-Stalinist phase. In particular, they avoided a complete political takeover and a full ideological assimilation. The Moscow-trained leadership which the Soviet centre tried to impose (the 'twenty-eight Bolsheviks') was neutralized, and Mao gradually emerged as a supreme leader, uncontested from within and uncontrolled from without. His road to power was, however, indirect and to some extent extra-institutional: from 1938 to 1945 the party had no official leader (Ladany 1988: 52). The stage was thus set for later conflicts between an autocratic ruler with extreme ambitions and a party-state apparatus which tried to absorb him and convert him into a symbol of collective authority. This unorthodox political pattern was reflected in ideological orientations. Mao's ascendancy put an end to the systematic appropriation of Soviet Marxism and led to the imposition of 'Mao Zedong thought' as the only legitimate Chinese version of Marxism-Leninism, but the immediate result was impoverishment rather than innovation. Although it has proved difficult to separate the original content of Mao's Yan'an writings from later revisions, it can hardly be claimed that his theoretical frame of reference was anything more than an ultra-simplistic version of official Soviet thought. By enforcing this elementary transcript as the only authoritative interpretation and blocking the development of a more elaborate doctrine, Mao could combine ideological authority with strategic flexibility (that was one of the purposes of the 'rectification campaign' of 1942–4; as this operation showed, Mao and his associates had managed to develop their own version of the Stalinist technique of the purge, adapt it to more constraining conditions, and use it to protect themselves against excessive Soviet interference). As Benjamin Schwartz (1989: 21) has argued, Mao's thought is marked by 'the plasticity and malleability of his entire arsenal of categories'; but it needs to be added that the plastic categories were the shrunken contents of an imported orthodoxy which was thus made more adaptable to domestic interests.

If some developments within the Yan'an regime can now be seen as prefigurations of later events, it was the relationship to its broader social context that was most essential to survival and victory. To solve the twin problems of recruiting an army and mobilizing popular support in a rural environment, the Chinese Communists had to depart from Soviet precedents and devise their own rules, but it can hardly be said that the secret of their success has been clarified: there has, as an authoritative source puts it, 'been no significant work on what happened when the revolutionary movement actually met rural society' (Huang 1991: 327). But although the relative importance of reforms and anti-Japanese resistance is a matter of debate, it seems clear that flexible socio-economic policies were a crucial part of Communist strategy. The 'Yan'an way' can perhaps be described as a war economy *sui generis*, but without massive redistribution and large-scale developmental projects. The Soviet model was, in other words, implemented in a structurally unbalanced way: its ideological and political essentials (the party-state, legitimated by Marxism-Leninism) were accepted, whereas the construction of their economic counterpart had to be postponed. Although this disconnection of base and superstructure (to use the official language) was primarily due to practical constraints, it was – in the long run – conducive to a more detached and critical view of Soviet economic institutions. Liu Shaoqi is reported to have said in 1957 that the Soviet Union had only the planning side of a socialist economy (MacFarquhar 1974: 313), and this probably reflected a more widespread attitude of the leadership.

The Maoist project

The image of the Chinese revolution as a successful guerrilla war has played a prominent role in twentieth-century revolutionary mythology, but it is not founded on fact. It was a conventional war on a very large scale – and with exceptionally rapid turns of the tide – that brought the Communists to power. In the aftermath of the Japanese surrender, their counter-state had – with some Soviet aid – acquired a new territorial basis in Manchuria, and this was a much more important asset than later accounts of the 'Yan'an way' would suggest. The civil war thus came to an end with a definitive victory of one successor state and one strategy of imperial reunification over another. When the Guomindang regime collapsed, the Communists faced two interconnected tasks: to bring the whole imperial domain under the control of an apparatus which had hitherto operated on a regional basis, and to apply the Soviet model in a more systematic fashion. Later crises of Chinese Communism reflect – among other things – the tension between these equally pressing but not automatically compatible demands. Unification was, of course, easier to achieve than Sovietization. The transitional regime of the first few years after 1949 differed from Soviet practices in some crucial respects. As a result of the unexpectedly rapid takeover, the military had to be charged with administrative tasks, and the subsequent failure to complete the institutionalization of the Soviet model left the military with a greater share of power and a higher level of autonomy than in more orthodox Soviet-type regimes. The new regime inherited some mechanisms of state control over the economy from its statist predecessor, but it had to resign itself to temporary coexistence with the private sector; although it soon moved to absorb the latter (through the 'Five Anti' campaign of 1952), this process was more gradual and controlled than in Russia, and the model of unequal partnership rather than total control could be reactivated when the retreat from the Maoist impasse began in the late 1970s. On the other hand, the reference to 'Mao Zedong thought', enshrined in the party constitution since 1945, indicated a claim to originality, autonomy and self-defining orthodoxy that found no expression in the pragmatic arrangements of the early 1950s.

The first five-year plan, beginning in 1953, seemed to mark the beginning of full-scale Sovietization. Given the advantages which the regime enjoyed, there was every prospect of success: popular support was incomparably stronger than it had been in Russia, the rural background of the party enabled it to carry out the collectivization of agriculture in a less destructive and chaotic way, and it had been much easier to bring the urban economy under state control. In short, several factors combined to smooth the way for a complete and definitive alignment with the Soviet model. It is significant that 'Mao Zedong thought' was dropped from the party constitution in 1956: a standard Soviet-type regime would have no need of an ideological simulacrum. But in the course of this transformation, the regime took a more radical turn which soon escalated out of control and derailed the whole project. The process which culminated in the cultural revolution began with the decision to quicken the pace of 'socialist construction', taken before the first plan was completed. In retrospect, it would thus seem that the Chinese version of the Soviet model began to self-destruct at the very moment of its apparent consolidation. As a recent analysis puts it, 'one of the great mysteries of twentieth-century history is why the rulers of China decided to plunge into an entirely socialist economy when they were doing so well with a mixed one' (Jenner 1992: 161). It may be argued that the economic policies of the early years were not an unqualified success, and that the first steps towards a more systematic application of Soviet precepts had highlighted both the intrinsic problems of the model and the additional difficulties arising from its imposition on a more backward economy. But then the logical response would have been a shift to more cautious approaches and an attempt to adapt the details of the model to Chinese conditions. This was in fact the reaction of the bureaucrats most directly involved in planning; they were, however, overruled by a political leadership which first tried to speed up the transformation along Soviet lines and then went on to experiment with much less orthodox techniques of control and mobilization. No threats or setbacks forced Mao and his associates to make this choice (such arguments are even more obviously untenable than in the case of Stalin's second revolution); the only plausible explanation is that they wanted an economic breakthrough that would match their political and ideological aspirations. The imperial legacy, translated into visions of overtaking more advanced patrons and rivals, was more conducive to imaginary shortcuts than to rational strategies.

With the passage of time, it has become easier to see the two Maoist decades – from the socialist upsurge of the mid-1950s to the liquidation of the 'gang of four' in 1976 – as a whole, and to dispose of some earlier interpretations. The dominant motive behind the upheaval was not, as many observers believed, the search for a Chinese alternative to the Soviet model of development. For the Chinese leadership, the essentials of development – rapid industrialization with particular emphasis on heavy industry and a fetishistic commitment to steel production – were the same as in the Soviet case, and the radicalizing process began with an effort to accelerate the standard procedures; as the results proved unsatisfactory, political and ideological instruments came to be substituted for the economic ones. The upshot was a schizophrenic combination: the underlying developmental goals were grounded in an unreconstructed Stalinist outlook, but the specific Chinese way of pursuing them was both increasingly divorced from objective conditions and incompatible with the routinized version of the Soviet model. During the Great Leap Forward of 1958–60, political and ideological visions were projected onto the economic plane and presented as an economic strategy, but the result was a major disaster. By contrast (and probably because of this experience), the cultural revolution was devoid of any specific economic policies, although it was clearly launched with the expectation that its mobilizing effect would eventually lead to more rapid development.

It is equally misleading to describe the Maoist phenomenon as the reaction of a rural revolutionary movement against the constraints of modernization. Agricultural policies were always subordinated to the industrializing drive; in that sense, Maoism never departed from the Soviet mainstream of modernization. And if it is true that the leadership was (at least intermittently) concerned about the dangers of a developmental rupture between rural and urban society, this awareness was no guarantee of effective remedies. Misguided efforts to bridge the gap – through the construction of rural industries and the transfer of rural models of mobilization to the cities – contributed to the catastrophe of 1958–60. On the other hand, it can be argued that a major collision with urban society led Mao to take a turn which is perhaps best described as an imaginary re-ruralization: a suitably mythologized version of the party's rural detour to power was to be reactivated against a refractory urban environment. This is the most convincing interpretation of the 'hundred flowers campaign' of 1956–7 and its aftermath. It was, to begin with, an integral part of Mao's mobilization strategy. Intellectuals and specialists were to be induced to participate more effectively in the social transformation supervised by the party. The wave of criticism with which they responded to the relaxation of control was symptomatic of a more far-reaching rejection of the party-state by urban society, and it had a lasting effect on the policies of the leadership.

The crucial importance of the 'Mao factor' is beyond dispute. Mao's initiatives were decisive at all stages of the radicalizing process. But further contextualization is necessary to explain their impact. Something must, in other words, be said about the sources on which Mao drew in constructing his self-image and the forces which he mobilized to implement his strategies. With regard to the former question, the affinities between the Maoist conception of leadership and the traditional ideal of the unity of ruling and teaching are obvious. In the imperial tradition, however, the image of the sovereign who was both supreme ruler and supreme teacher (Schwartz 1985b) had been associated with a mythical past, and to reorient it towards the present was to pave the way for a particularly extreme version of the totalitarian project. Mao's vision of himself as 'alone with the masses' is revealing. A leader who ruled through teaching did not need and could not accept the constraints of a bureaucratic apparatus of control, and a teaching embodied in a ruler was not bound by the rules of a codified and institutionalized ideology. This was a way of neutralizing both the prescriptions of Marxist-Leninist doctrine and the Chinese tradition of cultural limitations of autocratic power. From this point of view, Maoism can perhaps be described as the lowest common denominator of the Soviet model and the Chinese imperial tradition, but also as a result of the mutual reinforcement of their most extreme potentialities.

On the other hand, Mao was never in complete control of the party. In terms of his self-image and the political conclusions he drew from it, his claims to autocratic authority went beyond those of Stalin, but he never succeeded in concentrating power in his hands to the same extent as Stalin had done in the 1930s. He had to seek allies, protect himself against potential rivals, and adjust his policies to changing constellations. More importantly, his most significant initiatives depended on support from forces outside the central power élite. The first attempt to find such a basis (the 'hundred flowers') was a total failure. The next one was more successful in the short run, but eventually took a more catastrophic turn. The 'great leap' was a social movement *sui generis*, animated by local cadres who followed the 'logic of decentralized mobilization' (Fairbank 1992: 371) but lacked a coherent developmental project. Finally, the third and last offensive – the cultural revolution – was launched with the aid of a very disparate coalition which fell apart as generational and social conflicts became more acute. Maoism did not reflect any specific social interests or represent any clearly defined social forces; the most remarkable thing about it is, rather, its ability to construct unnatural alliances and switch from one set of supporters to another. The protest movements which it used so effectively during the first phase of the cultural revolution were to a large extent directed against the post-revolutionary patterns of inequality and privilege. As we have seen, the combination of hierarchical and egalitarian strategies is a general characteristic of the totalitarian project, but the fluctuations and conflicts between them are particularly pronounced in the Chinese case.

Despite this lack of social identity, it is possible to speak of a Maoist project, but it is easier to define in negative than in positive terms. It might be characterized as a systematic attempt to short-circuit the institutional interconnections of the Soviet model on all the three levels analysed above. The fully developed version of the mobilized economy combined the central mechanisms of command with remnants and fragments of the market; Mao's economic vision has, by contrast, been aptly described as 'neither plan nor market' (Riskin 1991). An uncompromising rejection of market forces was accompanied by administrative decentralization and a weakening of the bureaucratic apparatus that was essential to planning. Problems of coordination were to be solved through ideological and political homogenization. Analogously, Mao's political conceptions might be summed up as 'neither party nor state'. The fusion of party and state institutions in the apparatus was, as already noted, at the centre of Soviet-type power structures. Mao came to see both layers of the apparatus as obstacles to the more authentic direct and effective authority of the leader (i.e. himself) over the masses. Attempts to translate this phantasm into practice led to an explosion of grassroots violence and a proliferation of local despotisms; to bring these centrifugal forces under control, the Maoist leadership had to fall back on an alliance with the military establishment and give the latter a much greater share of power than it had originally envisaged. Finally (and most paradoxically), the ultimate logic of 'Mao Zedong thought' was, in a sense, neither ideology nor culture. In the archetypal form of the Soviet model, a systematized ideology is embedded in a more complex and heterogeneous cultural formation. Mao's peculiar version of the unity of theory and practice bypassed both levels. This resulted in the wholesale liquidation of culture and neglect of education during the last and more militant phase; and although ideology was absolutized as an instrument, it was devalued as an institution and a specialized sphere of activity. Direct communication between the leader and the masses was to replace the ideological mechanisms of control.

This systematic de-differentiation of the Soviet model was, of course, a self-defeating utopia. In the first place, Mao's enduring commitment to essential parts of the model – in particular, as we have seen, to its developmental goals – was a counterweight to his deviations in other areas and an obstacle to definitive breaks. In addition, the disruption caused by his incoherent policies repeatedly forced him to retreat to more orthodox positions. And other factions in the leadership, less inclined to depart from Soviet precedents, could then bring their influence to bear and reimpose the party-state routines. But after the last outburst and final defeat of Maoism, it was too late for a full restoration.

The post-Maoist phase

The problematic of the 'reform decade' and the political crisis in which it culminated is beyond the scope of this book. It is an established fact that China has confounded all diagnoses: it has disappointed both those who expected it to invent or reinvent market socialism and those who believed that concessions to capitalism would not be possible without further progress towards democracy. The continuation of economic growth and transformation after the crackdown of 1989 shows that the relationship between political and economic structures differs from both Western and Soviet patterns. And if Mao's formula for a socialist economy was 'neither plan nor market', then the contemporary Chinese economy has both plan and market, but without effective coordination. The central authorities no longer exercise the overall control that is essential to a Soviet-type mobilized economy.

But although economic de-Sovietization – the decollectivization of agriculture, the partial de-statization of the urban economy, and the opening to foreign capital – has not led to political democratization, it has had other repercussions. The abandonment of earlier visions of 'socialist construction' could not but undermine ideological orthodoxy; the post-Maoist policies were too pragmatic and their direction too uncertain for the rationalization of 'socialism with Chinese characteristics' to be effective. Marxist-Leninist doctrine now plays a much less important role in the self-representation and legitimation of the regime than it ever did in the Soviet Union and claims to national and imperial legitimacy are correspondingly more important. In brief, what seems to be going on is an attempt to reconcile the survival of a party-state which (although nominally intact) is now returning more explicitly to its imperial sources with the development of an economy which is becoming an integral and dynamic part of East Asian capitalism. The political centre is, in other words, faced with an uncontrollable economic transformation and an irresistible ideological erosion, but its imperial foundations are more solid than in the Soviet Union and its chances of survival through adaptation correspondingly better. Whether it can, in the long run, mutate into a neo-authoritarian regime presiding over an East Asian-style capitalist economy must be regarded as an open question. There are at least three major destabilizing factors that will inevitably complicate the search for such a model. In contrast to the Soviet Union, China has never completed the transition from autocracy to oligarchy: if it can be argued that Mao's rule was never as effectively autocratic as Stalin's, it also seems clear that the post-Maoist leadership is still a semi-autocracy and its power basis partly external to party institutions. This unstable balance of power at the top could, especially in conjunction with other factors, lead to a major political crisis. Second, the threat of fragmentation may be less acute than in the Soviet Union, but the possibility of uneven development and devolution of power to regional centres leading to a break-up of the Chinese state cannot be ignored. Finally, some observers take the view that the joint effects of overpopulation and unbalanced development might result in an environmental disaster with much more massive social consequences than the Soviet one.

In a sense, the post-Maoist phase of Chinese Communism has brought its historical background into sharper focus. The vicissitudes of the Soviet model in China are only one aspect of the encounter of the world's oldest civilization and most enduring imperial formation with Western modernity.[5] Their interaction has now taken a new turn, and there are too many contingent factors, internal and external, for any grounded predictions to be possible. And as for the trajectory of Chinese Communism, it can perhaps be added to the above list of paradoxes: the most autonomous variant of the Soviet model was also the most massively self-destabilizing one.[6]

Chapter 4

Crisis and collapse

The events of 1989–91 are generally regarded as a global and terminal crisis of Communism. A closer look at their background and outcome raises some doubts about this conventional diagnosis: it can be argued that the coincidence of major turning-points in Eastern and Western regions of the Communist world led to the artificial assimilation of crises that were in fact developing along different lines and at a different pace. This is not to deny that the optical illusion had some real and important consequences. The vision of a uniform crisis, affecting all versions of the Soviet model for the same reasons, became a de-legitimizing factor in its own right; it reinforced the disintegrative trends and undermined the power structures. Moreover, the initiatives and reactions of the main protagonists were partly determined by their perceptions of the international context. It seems likely that the protest movement in China was encouraged by the reform process in the Soviet Union; Eastern European leaders were probably more demoralized than comforted by the Chinese way of restoring order; and there can be no doubt about the impact of Eastern European precedents on developments inside the Soviet Union. But the underlying trends were more varied than overdramatized accounts of the collapse would suggest. The transformation of Chinese Communism had, as argued above, passed a critical point some time before the Soviet crisis turned into a decomposing process. On this view, the Chinese prelude to the Eastern European revolutions of 1989 was a turning-point in the prolonged conflict between the Soviet model and the Chinese environment, but neither the beginning nor the end of structural change. The pattern of the Chinese crisis, markedly different from the course of events in the Soviet bloc, reflected both its direct antecedents and its broader background. The 'pro-democracy movement' (as it is usually described, although its diverse components were neither equally committed to this goal nor in agreement about its meaning) demanded reforms, but it also represented a backlash against unbalanced reform policies and their uncontrollable consequences. This constellation was unique to China. It led to a mass mobilization of urban society, but the passivity of the much larger rural population helped the regime to resist and mount a counter-offensive. In the much more urbanized societies of the Soviet Union and Eastern Europe, a lower (and sometimes very low) level of popular mobilization was enough to reinforce the self-destructive trends within the apparatus. Last but not least, the imperial factor as such played no role in the Chinese crisis: the main conflict took place in the metropolitan centres and had nothing to do with trouble on the periphery.

As for the Eastern European states, their divergent roads had in some cases led to crisis and collapse at an earlier stage, and the restored order was a shadow of its former self; even the regimes that had avoided breakdown were congenitally fragile and doubly crisis-prone because of their derivative character. In this regional context, the final crisis therefore took a distinctive turn. But although the differences between centre and periphery were reflected in their respective patterns of disintegration, the two processes – the loss of the external empire and the self-liquidation of the centre – were closely interconnected, and their mutually reinforcing dynamic is the main subject of the following discussion. Our task is not to explain the events of 1989–91 in terms of a general and systemic collapse of the Soviet model; the focus will, rather, be on the interaction between its original imperial version and its most important peripheral variants, as well as on the broader historical constellation which brought the built-in problems of this relationship to a head.

The roles which different accounts of the Soviet crisis assign to structural and historical factors depend on their theoretical presuppositions. There is, in particular, a link between interpretations of modernity and explanations of what happened to its Soviet version. If the Parsonian vision of a functionally balanced and normatively integrated modernity is taken for granted, it is tempting to reduce the whole Soviet trajectory to a misdirected detour or a failed leap forward: from this point of view, the Soviet model was structurally unsustainable because it lacked some essential ingredients of the 'main pattern' and could not compete with the 'lead societies' of the West. Against the background of a normative telos of modernity, the historical details of deviant forms seem less significant. The Soviet experience may have discredited the evolutionist axioms of earlier modernization theory, but the same course can still be prescribed for political action. A standardized image of modernity serves to justify post-Communist strategies of 'normalization' which differ from the Soviet model in that they aspire to rejoin rather than redirect the mainstream of development, but resemble it in that political intervention guided by expert knowledge is expected to lay the foundations of a new social order. For the advocates of classical modernization theory, the verdict of history is ambiguous: while they can draw comfort from the post-Communist reinvention of the Western paradigm, neither the experience which preceded it nor the effects that it is now having are easy to fit into the received picture.

The conceptual scheme outlined in the introduction centres on the idea of modernity as a multidimensional and open-ended process of differentiation, conditioned rather than contained by partial and fragile patterns of integration, and co-determined by diverse civilizational legacies. This frame of reference makes it easier to see structural crises and disintegrative dynamics as part and parcel of the modern constellation. The Soviet model can then be regarded as an extreme case of more general trends. It was, as we have seen, based on a particularly explosive combination of traditional and modern factors; its logic maximized some aspects of the global modernizing process and suppressed others; the integrative mechanisms which kept the built-in tensions in check were at the same time conducive to imbalances at another level. But to argue that the self-destructive potential grew together with the accumulation of power is not to explain why the collapse occurred at the time and in the way it did. In retrospect, it is easy to imagine Stalin's second revolution culminating in a complete breakdown of the regime. And the unintended disruptive consequences of the Khrushchev interlude might have gone beyond breaking-point. On the other hand, Gorbachev's victory was not the only conceivable outcome of the succession struggles between 1982 and 1985, and the more radical turn taken in 1987 was not the only option open to him. The scenario which Timothy Garton Ash (1989: 252–5) described as an 'Ottomanization of the Soviet empire' (a long-drawn-out decay of the centre and a gradual loss of control over the periphery) did not materialize, but this does not prove that it was structurally impossible. In brief, the historical life-span of the Soviet model was not predetermined by its structural logic; there were always counterweights to its self-destructive tendencies, and the balance between the two sides was never independent of the global environment.

The above analysis of the model, its core structures and its variants may have thrown some light on the background to its demise. But it should also help to understand why the search for an exhaustive theoretical explanation would be misguided. On the other hand, a detailed historical reconstruction of the events in question is beyond the scope of this book, and it is in any case doubtful whether enough evidence will ever be available for historians to put together a convincing account of the 'death of Communism'. All that can be attempted here is a partial clarification of a specific issue: the combination of structural problems, long-term processes and contingent circumstances that first prompted and then thwarted the move towards a new strategy of imperial modernization. To begin with, however, I will briefly review some current approaches and consider the questions they have raised.

VISIONS OF BREAKDOWN

In analysing the events of 1989–91, four main factors must be taken into account, and our view of their respective role is bound to affect the interpretation of the process as a whole. There is, first of all, the question of self-destructive trends and mechanisms. On the day of reckoning, the self-destructive dispositions of Soviet-type regimes were too obvious to ignore, but it is a matter of debate how deeply rooted and decisive they were. The mobilization of social forces against the regimes, less important in retrospect than some contemporary observers came to believe, cannot be omitted from the picture. It is generally agreed that the Soviet empire lost the 'great contest' with the West, and that this failure sealed its fate, but when, how and why it happened is somewhat more controversial. Finally, a geopolitical perspective on the crisis must also take note of the internal divisions of the Communist world and the interaction between its different parts; this applies especially to the relationship between the Soviet centre and the Eastern European periphery, but also – as we shall see – to the Sino-Soviet rift and its consequences. Each of these four factors has been singled out by some analysts, and the theories developed on that basis draw – in a similarly selective fashion – on the experience of particular countries. Apart from the Soviet Union, the three states discussed at the end of the section on Eastern Europe seem to offer the most suggestive record. A closer examination should help to disentangle historical lessons and theoretical issues from the ideological constructions that have been grafted onto them.

The rapid collapse of the power structures and capitulation of the power élites in the Soviet Union and Eastern Europe surprised most observers. It seems obvious that the self-destructive dynamic that so suddenly became visible had been undermining the party-state for some time before its demise. The internal erosion and external ritualization of

Marxist-Leninist ideology had impaired the ability of the apparatus to resist challenges and devise counterstrategies. Behind the façade of the monolithic regime, there was a welter of rival factions and interest groups, unable to pursue a coherent course of collective action. Some of them were more willing than others to accept or even initiate radical change, and their various strategies of survival and adaptation in the post-Communist phase have shown how illusory their erstwhile unity was. The economic crisis that spread and deepened during the last decade before the collapse was doubly damaging to the party-state establishment: economic performance had from the outset been one of the systemic priorities of the Soviet model, and economic concessions had been essential to its techniques of crisis management. Failure on this level was therefore bound to have a demoralizing as well as a destabilizing effect. Ideological and political decay, together with imperial overstretch (the latter factor will be discussed below), had made it more and more difficult to cope with or compensate for the economic downturn.

All these trends were enhanced and brought into the open at the end of the 1980s, but their impact can only be understood in a long-term perspective. This valid point has, however, been used to back up less plausible theories of a pre-programmed collapse, caused by systemic flaws in Soviet-type regimes. Such lines of argument refer to 'the logic of a closed system', fundamentally incapable of adaptation or self-transformation, and 'the vicious cycle of decline', leading to the exhaustion of resources and the reinforcement of blockages (Kaminski 1991). Before discussing the more specific questions at issue, the changing function of 'closed system logic' should be noted. It is now invoked to explain why command economies and party-states could not survive, but the original emphasis was on their ability to resist reform and perpetuate the status quo. After the 'restoration of order' (Šimečka 1984) in Czechoslovakia, the Eastern European opposition had lost confidence in reformist projects; Soviet rule over the bloc as a whole seemed unchallengeable and the Soviet model came to be seen as a total institution within which no radical change could be envisaged. Theories of totalitarianism became more popular in oppositional circles. This ideological reorientation was based on a somewhat one-sided reading of the Czechoslovak experience. The defeat and destruction of reform Communism obscured the fact that a mutation of the model had already been in progress. Selective learning from history led to simplifying conclusions: the Czechoslovak reform movement had shown how fragile the core structures of Communist power could become, but the collective memory of the opposition took less note of this than of the subsequent reversal, and when the underlying fragility of the Eastern European regimes became evident again in a very different situation, the earlier experience had been discounted. Needless to say, there is no suggestion that the victorious dissidents of 1989 could or should have returned to the policies of the Prague Spring. But it can hardly be denied that a levelling vision of the past helped to justify oversimplified and exclusivistic notions of the one and only road back to normality. For a comparative study of crises and transformative processes in Soviet-type regimes, the Czechoslovak case is of the highest importance, and for the political debates of the post-Communist phase, it could at least serve as a reminder of unsolved problems and underlying realities which the dominant liberal utopia prefers to ignore. We can only speculate about the course which the reform movement would have taken if it had been left alone, but it is hard to imagine anything other than a multi-party system with strong statist tendencies and a mixed economy operating within a global capitalist framework (in both respects, the contrast between this abortive precedent and the present transition may be less radical than the accompanying rhetoric would suggest). These changes would, however, have taken place in a more promising context. A less obsolescent economy, a less demoralized society and a less constrained political imagination might have made for a more inventive democratizing process than the one which is now going on.

In more recent diagnoses the model of the closed system is used to explain self-destruction rather than self-perpetuation. On this view, the subordination of the economy to the state paralysed the former and saddled the latter with responsibilities far beyond its real capacity to intervene; the structural inability to coordinate individual and collective interests led to an organizational as well as a moral breakdown; and ideological closure resulted in an all-round adaptive downgrading. The tendency to focus on economic failure reflects the experiences of the 1980s, particularly the Polish crisis (its exceptionally dramatic character has made it a favourite case in point for analysts of collapse), but it is reinforced by an economic reductionism which sometimes seems to be the lowest common denominator of old and new ideologies. The retrospective explanations offered by post-Communist liberals often amount to little more than the claim that really existing socialism failed because it did not measure up to an ideal image of capitalism.

There is no denying that the more sophisticated theories of collapse have thrown some light on the last days of the Soviet model. They are less convincing when they try to encompass its whole history.[1] If the internal constitution of the Soviet model is – as I have tried to show – irreducible to a systemic logic, it is by the same token impossible to explain its global trajectory in terms of a prolonged systemic self-destruction. And a brief glance at the main landmarks will show how implausible such attempts are. The adaptability and transformative capacity of the model must be given its due. It served to reconstruct the Russian empire and raise it to the level of a superpower; within the Soviet Union, it survived the transition from autocracy to oligarchy and the concomitant scaling down of the totalitarian project. During the first phase of the oligarchic regime, imperial expansion and domestic consolidation went hand in hand (it was this temporary success which led some analysts to portray the 'Soviet way of life' as a distinctive cultural model with significant legitimatory resources; the fact that it was overrated at the time is not a reason to forget it now). As for the record of other Soviet-type regimes, within and outside the imperial domain, we have seen that the variants of the model differed as much from each other as from the original version, and that their distinctive features affected both the developmental strategies and the structural problems of the regimes in question. These considerations do not cast any doubt on the disastrous balance sheet of the Soviet experience as a whole, but they should caution against simple scenarios and short-term perspectives. A convincing account of the self-destructive dynamic that intertwined with a formative impact on world history has yet to be given.

It might be suggested that a theory of systemic exhaustion rather than collapse would be more adequate. On this view, the Soviet collapse was caused not so much by fundamental and permanent flaws as by the widening gap between basic goals on the one hand and increasingly overstrained capacities and resources on the other. In an elementary sense, the point is beyond dispute: the Soviet model was less attuned to the challenges which it faced in the 1980s than to the problems which it had been devised to solve during the 1930s. The question is whether we can explain this shift in terms of specific purposes and predetermined limits. As argued above, the transformative potential of the Soviet model was grounded in an extreme and unbalanced interpretation of the horizon of modernity; it maximized the momentum of some modernizing processes while suppressing or deforming others; and the different aspects – economic, political and cultural – of the overall pattern were combined in a way that gave rise to tensions and conflicts. The model generated obstacles to its own aspirations, but it also showed an impressive ability to capitalize on historical conjunctures. A reconstruction of its history must take note of its trans-systemic as well as its infra-systemic features; it was, in other words, characterized by a structural hubris, incoherence and indeterminacy that could not be contained within systemic parameters. This suggests that its trajectory (including the terminal crisis) is best understood as an ongoing interaction between enduring but unsettled patterns and contingent historical situations.

Some attempts to explain the collapse of Soviet-type regimes have – more or less explicitly – drawn on classical Marxist assumptions about the self-destructive dynamic of capitalism.[2] The second interpretive model mentioned above also has some affinity with Marxist ideas: the vision of social forces revolting against the party-state is reminiscent of the claim that political and ideological superstructures are transformed by the dynamic of the base. The element of truth is as obvious as in the first case. For all the impact and influence of the Soviet model, it could never achieve the aim of recreating society in its own image. With regard to the relationship between regime and society, there are – as we have seen – fundamental differences not only between the Soviet prototype and its later offshoots, but also between Western and Eastern variants. But in the last instance, and in the most general sense, it is true that party-state power always fell short of complete control over and absorption of social life; it had to adapt to social contexts which proved less malleable than expected; and the modernizing processes which it set in motion gave rise to new social forces which posed new problems for the power structure. From this point of view, it can be argued that the collapse of the Soviet model was the final solution of a chronic conflict between state and society. However, some major qualifications must be added, and an overall description should not be mistaken for an explanatory argument. In the first place, it would be misleading to claim that the party-state was engaged in a losing battle against society from beginning to end. The relationship was always conflictual, but phases of relative calm and partial compromise alternated with more acute tensions. In the Soviet Union, the ups and downs would seem to have been particularly marked, and major shifts towards a truce occurred during World War II as well as in connection with the reforms of the Khrushchev era and the initially successful consolidating moves of the post-1964 oligarchy. Some significant changes also took place in the Eastern European context (the Polish pattern of prolonged and open discord between regime and society was the exception rather than the rule). The contrast between initial levels of legitimacy and subsequent alienation from society may have been most pronounced in China, but the Chinese regime could then – as we have seen – fall back on more solid foundations and flexible strategies than the Soviet one.

More importantly, the diagnosis of an enduring but largely latent conflict between regime and society does not explain why it took the particular turn which led to breakdown and mutation at the end of the 1980s. Was the crisis a logical outcome of long-term processes which polarized a changing society and a stagnant regime, or was it rather the result of a more contingent historical constellation that brought about the convergence of experiment from above and protest from below? Some early interpretations of Gorbachev's perestroika took the former view and tried to show that the maturation of Soviet society – more precisely: the changes caused by industrialization, organization, and educational revolution – had reached a point where a radical transformation of the political system could no longer be postponed (Lewin 1988). Later developments have made this line of argument untenable. The reform which resulted in the collapse of the regime and the ruin of the empire was not a response to the demands or pressures of rising social forces; rather, it revealed the predicament of a political centre in search of a social basis for its new modernizing strategy, and the absence of any social actors that could have sustained a progressive radicalization of the reform project. In the event, the political vacuum created by a partial self-liquidation of the centre could only be filled at the regional level, and the twin forces (sometimes in tandem, sometimes in conflict) of integral nationalism and a fragmented apparatus overshadowed all other candidates for the succession.

In comparison with the Soviet Union, the exit from Communism in Eastern Europe (or at least in its northern region) was easier to construe as a victory of society over the party-state, and a more specific emphasis on civil society served to signalize dissent from both Marxist and mainstream perspectives. In the present context, neither the history nor the recent revival of this concept can be discussed in detail; all that can be attempted is a brief review of its changing role in the self-interpretation as well as the Western understanding of the Eastern (more precisely: Eastern Central) European opposition. Visions of self-organization, emancipation from state control, and a publicly articulated pluralism of ideas and interests were always central to it, but their connotations varied. Four successive phases should be distinguished. At the beginning, the idea of civil society was complementary to that of the totalitarian or post-totalitarian state: it referred to the social space which the opposition could hope to protect or reclaim from a totalitarian adversary in retreat, but incapable of reform and immune to revolution. This cautious and defensive approach was central to the strategy of the opposition after 1970. A second phase began with the Polish crisis of 1980–1. Some analysts – active participants as well as Western observers – saw the rise of Solidarnosc as a great leap forward in the struggle of civil society against state and empire. The Polish situation was, however, unique in that a mass movement of industrial workers found an ally in the Catholic establishment and became a vehicle for national aspirations. A conjunction of class, church and nation can hardly be regarded as an embodiment of the ideals that have traditionally been linked to the concept of civil society; in retrospect, it would seem that this reading of the Polish experience obscured its exceptional and problematic character.

The events of 1989 and their immediate aftermath constituted a third phase. In this case, the invocation of civil society as an explanatory factor – supposedly the driving force behind the upheavals which destroyed one party-state after another – was easier at a distance than on the spot. It became a common theme of theorists who otherwise disagreed on major points. But on closer examination, the argument is unconvincing. Briefly, the mobilization of social forces for collective action played a limited role in the last stage of the crisis; within these limits both its level and its character varied significantly from case to case, and the circumstances under which it became most important were not the most conducive to an autonomous development of civil society. The precondition for the demise of the Soviet model in Eastern Europe was a stalemate within the Soviet leadership. The more radical reformers had outmanoeuvred the conservative wing and initiated a transfer of power from the party apparatus to other institutions, but found themselves in a social void and without a coherent strategy. This paralysis of the centre affected the peripheral regimes and made them all more vulnerable to popular protest, although the same constellation was not reproduced throughout the bloc. Bulgaria came closest to repeating the Soviet scenario; in East Germany, mass emigration preceded and sparked mass protest, while the rift at the top was slow to develop. The anomalous course of events in Romania is perhaps best described as a local inversion of the general pattern: a popular revolt precipitated a move against the autocracy from within the apparatus. It is noteworthy that the countries where popular action was least important to the actual transfer of power were those where the discourse of civil society had been most developed and seemed most apposite. In Hungary, the pattern of self-liquidation was more clear-cut than anywhere else, even if the strategy of those who engineered the transition from party-state to pluralism was clearly based on erroneous assumptions about their prospects of survival. In Poland, the organized mass movement of 1980–1 and the protest wave of 1988 had set the scene for the final act, but in the end, the militarized rump of the party-state relinquished power to a counter-élite with a broad but increasingly passive social basis. On the other hand, the higher level of mobilization in some other countries (this was, albeit in different ways, characteristic of East Germany and Czechoslovakia) did not have any lasting impact on the post-Communist constellation.

As the rough outlines of a new order have taken shape, the discourse of civil society seems to have entered a fourth and final phase: there is now a stark contrast between the domestic and dominant tendency to equate civil society (when the label is used at all) with a supposedly standard version of liberal democracy, and the attempt – more often made by disappointed Western observers – to retain the idea of civil society as a codeword for 'daring more democracy'. It is the former current that concerns us here. The 'liberal utopia' (Sgard 1992) which has, at least for the time being, become the dominant political culture in Eastern Europe is a more artificial and incoherent construct than its advocates like to admit. It takes a fundamentally harmonious relationship between capitalism and democracy for granted and subsumes both sides under an idealized model of the market. But this economistic vision of society is put forward as a political project and incorporated into the strategy of political élites: the new developmental model is 'capitalism by design' (Offe 1991). Finally, this amalgamation of economics and politics is presented as part of the normal order of things and – more or less explicitly – as a return to the evolutionary mainstream from which the socialist experiment had deviated. The whole project is thus given a meta-social grounding. As for its practical consequences, it is obviously too early to tell; the only safe guess is that this new version of world-historical planning will meet with some new surprises.

The liberal utopia is, among other things, an answer to the third question raised above: to what extent was the collapse a result of rivalry with the West? For a doctrinaire liberal diagnosis, it is not so much the fact of collapse as the illusion of a rivalry based on alternative models that needs explanation. The theoretical premises of the present inquiry do not lead to such conclusions, but there can be no doubt about the importance of the issues. It is obvious that the demise of the Soviet model was also a defeat in its contest with the West. But it is more difficult to explain how the two sides of the problem – internal breakdown and external failure – are related to each other. Did the West win by default, or did the Soviet model fail because it was outdistanced by a more dynamic rival? The question is still open and it seems likely that it will have to be reconsidered in the light of both further developments in post-Soviet societies and Western responses to the problems that are now emerging. Our present task is not so much to answer it as to combat the widespread tendency to oversimplify it. The need for a multidimensional approach –

one which does justice to the various aspects of intersystemic competition as well as the interaction between domestic and international, structural and conjunctural factors – has been obscured by the conventional wisdom which tends to reduce the whole problematic to economic issues. In this view, it was first and foremost an economic system that failed; the Soviet model proved least effective in the area where its adversary was most innovative and where it was most directly exposed to shared criteria of performance. The connection between internal shortcomings and comparative backwardness thus becomes a simple and direct one, and if the system which found itself unable to compete with the West was by the same token failing to meet its own demands, it is easier to understand why its central authorities should have started experimenting with a new strategy. There is no denying the crucial role of economic factors in bringing about the collapse, but there are – as I will try to show – some reasons to question the economic-reductionist orthodoxy. Rather than adopting an inverted Marxist viewpoint and taking the primacy of the economy for granted, we should try to analyse the broader context which added weight to it and channelled its impact in a particular direction. To begin with, a brief glance at the historical background may help to explain the appeal of the economistic view.

As we have seen, transitional crises or chronically unstable conditions made some Soviet-type regimes more open to critical reflection and 'thinking in alternatives'. The projects that developed under such circumstances tended to focus on the rationalization of specific aspects of the model; this applies, in particular, to the Eastern European blueprints for economic reform. The economists who elaborated them saw the subsequent practical measures as experimental tests and fitted them into a narrative of 'socialism in search of an economic system' (Brus and Laski 1989); the pre-reform regime was thus credited with an economic logic which it had never possessed and the reform process with a more definite direction than it ever had. For obvious reasons, the Hungarian experience lent itself most easily to this reading. The vicissitudes of the 'new economic mechanism' were taken to exemplify the divergent logics, conflicting demands and ultimate incompatibility of two forms of economic coordination, market and bureaucratic. Such descriptions are largely convincing, and they have – in particular – shown how some basic mechanisms of bureaucratic coordination could outlast the more formal institutions of the mobilized economy. The question is, however, how much they explain. If we follow the above analysis of the Soviet model, with its emphasis on trans-economic determinants, it is easier to agree with the economists who argue that 'inability to perform and/or reform is a fact for which no explanation is found in economic theory' (Drewnowski 1982: 72). The Soviet model never followed the rules of an economic system, and its transformations were never geared to the search for new rules. Both the goals and the limits of Soviet economic performance were determined by an institutional context whose core components were extra-economic; both the social space available for economic innovations and the use made of it depended on the changing constellations of these background factors; and the long-term results of reform policies must be judged on the basis of their overall social impact. In the case of the Hungarian reform, its effects on the socio-cultural fabric may – as suggested above – have been more important than the strictly economic achievements.

If the Soviet pattern of modernity must be analysed from a multidimensional perspective, the same applies to its confrontation with the pre-existent and more resilient pattern; and if the economic dimension of rivalry, which was always present, became particularly critical at a decisive moment, the political and cultural background to this turn of events should not be overlooked. The contrast between the 1970s and the 1980s is a convenient starting-point. Ten years before the collapse, the Soviet challenge to the West was widely perceived as an acute threat, and this was due to the political and ideological forces that still seemed to be sustaining a drive for global hegemony, rather than to any surviving illusions about the economic offensive that had already faltered. But the twin pillars of Soviet power had now taken new forms. On the political side, it was the commitment to global expansion, rather than to radical transformation, that seemed most characteristic of the Soviet state; it had grown more conservative at home as it became more enterprising abroad. As for the ideological (or, as some commentators preferred to call it, the ideocratic) foundations, their strength now appeared to lie in the articulation of an unrestrained will to power, rather than in the perverted universalism which had once been described as an 'opium of the intellectuals'. Both these changes converged in a more visibly and conventionally imperial strategy. The underlying nature of the Soviet phenomenon remained as controversial as before, but the affinities with historical empires were now in some ways more obvious and the analogies more tempting.

It is the rapid descent from this imperial apogee to terminal crisis that calls for closer examination. But the global aspect of the process must also be related to the intra-imperial connection that was the fourth and last explanatory factor mentioned above. There can be no doubt about the close link between the crisis patterns of centre and periphery. Yet it is by no means obvious that the two phases of the collapse were simply two steps of a dismantling operation, as argued by those who ascribe to Gorbachev the insight 'that the Europeanization of the Soviet Union could not proceed without the de-Sovietization of Eastern Europe' (Dawisha 1990: 198). Gorbachev's policies were too inconsistent and underwent too many changes for them to be summed up so easily. The available evidence suggests that his original project is best described as a new strategy of imperial modernization (in his own words, used in an early speech, the aim was to 'enable the Soviet Union to enter the twenty-first century in a manner worthy of a great power'). It may be appropriate to talk about 'Europeanization' in the sense of seeking closer contact with the West, but not in the sense of the adaptation of Soviet institutions to Western models, and neither the external nor the internal empire were meant to be liquidated. Rather, it would seem that Gorbachev misjudged the condition of both parts in curiously contrasting ways. With regard to Eastern Europe, he was more aware of the diversity of the region and of the need for a nuanced approach than of the underlying fragility of the regimes; with regard to the Soviet Union, it has often been pointed out that he clearly underestimated the gravity of the national problem and was more concerned with the general backwardness of Soviet society than with the centrifugal forces which a reform from above might release. The overall strategy unravelled because of its inner contradictions and was never replaced with a more coherent one. For our present purposes, it is enough to note three crucial turning-points on the road from restructuring to disintegration. A belated and mismanaged push for reforms in Eastern Europe triggered a crisis which the local regimes could not survive (the de-Sovietization of the region was an unintended consequence, rather than a price which the Soviet leadership had accepted to pay for higher priorities); a military intervention could not be envisaged because it would have put an end to perestroika both at home and abroad; but the domestic backlash caused by the loss of the Eastern European domain proved no easier to contain than the reform process on the periphery and led – in conjunction with other factors – to a paralysis of the centre and a fragmentation of the internal empire. The demoralization of the Soviet apparatus after 1989, most evident in the stillborn restoration of August 1991, can only be explained as a consequence of the defeat which the empire had suffered on its Western flank, and it confirmed – ex post – that the rationale for Soviet rule in Eastern Europe had not been merely a matter of strategic calculations. The territorial spoils of victory in a global war and the seemingly permanent division of Europe had been crucial to the self-definition of the

Soviet Union as a superpower. When this achievement was undone, the effects went beyond a loss of legitimacy; they are perhaps best described as a crisis of identity.

Both the beginning and the end of the process in question are easy to date. It is the constitutional abolition of the 'leading role of the party' in Hungary in February 1989, rather than the more spectacular sequel in other countries, that must be regarded as the starting-point. When the Soviet leadership accepted this unprecedented step, it had become clear that maintenance of the essentials of the Soviet model in Eastern Europe was no longer a matter of principle, and it was inevitable that the limits of the imperial retreat would be put to further tests. Given the internal atrophy and the impossibility of intervention, the result was a chain reaction throughout the bloc. The last act was the Moscow coup of August 1991. It was, of course, a coup from within and above, engineered from the very summit of the apparatus which saw power slipping from its hands; its failure was foreshadowed by exceptionally inept conduct and finalized when the military did not follow suit. A symbolic show of popular resistance was enough to seal its fate. Its defeat cleared the way for a counter-coup: the final dismantling of the imperial centre by a coalition of political élites that had gained or retained control at the republican level. Some of them had stronger democratic credentials than others, some were more closely allied to nationalist movements than others, but the common ground was a strategy of redistributing power to the emergent post-imperial states. There is, however, a major qualification to be added to this account: Russia is still a state of imperial dimensions, and it is an open question whether its present crisis will lead to consolidation, resurgence, or further fragmentation.

The consequences of the retreat from the periphery should be seen against the background of competition with the West. As many former dissidents and foreign observers have pointed out, the political defeat of the Eastern European regimes was preceded by a cultural one. But this did not – as has sometimes been suggested – primarily mean that the ruling élites were becoming more receptive to a 'culture of critical discourse'. Rather, the cultural model that was gaining ground was an image of the West as a more advanced and more authentically modern society. Its progress prior to the final crisis helps to explain the inability of the party-state to put up active resistance and the adaptability of significant sections of the apparatus. This political sequel to a cultural abdication was bound to reinforce similar but less prominent trends within the Soviet Union. The shortcomings of the model were highlighted and brought closer to home.

A brief comparison with the role of the Eastern European connection in earlier Russian history may help to clarify this point. As Marc Raeff (1989) has argued, one of the main motives behind Russian conquests in Eastern Europe – from the sixteenth-century Livonian War to the annexation of the Ukraine and the division of Poland – was the need to acquire a 'cultural glacis' that would facilitate contact with Western civilization and at the same time make cultural borrowing more controllable. The original function of Eastern Europe in Stalin's international strategy was also – among other things – that of a cultural glacis, but for the opposite purpose: the construction of satellite regimes was to be the first step towards a globalization of the Soviet model that would in particular involve further advance towards the West. This project proved illusory and the Western periphery became an internally disruptive rather than outward-oriented cultural glacis. The ongoing delegitimation of the Soviet model in Eastern Europe and the growing identification with the West as a counter-model put the imperial centre on the defensive. Later Soviet policies were to some extent aimed at neutralizing this threat. The offensive strategy of the early 1980s was – in the European context – an attempt to use military strength to compensate for weakness in all other areas, more particularly to gain the political influence needed to develop economic contacts with Western Europe on more favourable terms; in a long-term perspective, the problems of Eastern Europe – a political periphery of the Soviet empire that was irresistibly becoming a cultural periphery of the West and increasingly exposed to 'double peripheralization' on the economic level – would have been defused through the expansion of Soviet control over Europe as a whole. But it soon became clear that the domestic basis was too weak to sustain such ambitions. A new European strategy and a new conception of the role of Eastern Europe in that regard was obviously in the making during the reformist interlude of the late 1980s. It was overtaken by events, and if the contribution of Eastern Europe to the present Westernizing push in Russia is to some extent reminiscent of earlier precedents, the situation differs from the traditional pattern in that a cultural turn to the West is accompanied by political fragmentation. In brief, Soviet expansion towards the West never achieved the balance between political control and cultural opening that was characteristic of the Petrine empire.

On balance, the internal tensions of the empire would seem to be the most visibly decisive reason for its rapid demise. But the process which led to their aggravation beyond breaking-point was to a very significant extent the outcome of imperial strategies in the external arena.

FROM EXPANSION TO EXTINCTION

The collapse of the Soviet model may appear less dramatic if we pay more attention to some structural shifts and historical setbacks that preceded it. There were, in particular, three major and interconnected changes which occurred during the last quarter of a century before the final crisis and can now be seen as a background to it. They did not predetermine the conjuncture of the late 1980s, but their long-term undermining effects are more obvious in retrospect than at the time.

First, the Sino–Soviet rift – it came into the open at the beginning of the 1960s and had escalated beyond repair by the middle of the decade – had a destabilizing impact, hard to measure but impossible to deny. As the unity of the Soviet bloc broke down, it became more difficult to defend the project which it was supposed to embody as a global alternative to Western institutions and Western hegemony. Both the ideological polemics and the manifest power politics with which the dispute became entwined threw further discredit on the official doctrine invoked on both sides. The rivalry between the two centres made their imperial heritage and character harder to conceal. But if we want to go beyond these general comments, we must distinguish more clearly between Soviet and Chinese responses to the break-up.

On the Soviet side, the conflict with China seemed at first to be an incentive to more open criticism of the Stalinist legacy, but this was only a passing episode: the main effect was to reinforce the trend towards oligarchic restabilization that prevailed in 1964. The demand for an end to experiments and controversies which the Chinese could exploit for their own purposes was clearly one of the motives behind the revolt of the apparatus against Khrushchev's policies, and the perpetuation of the conflict helped to consolidate a conservative leadership. At the same time the expansionism that came to characterize Soviet policies during the Brezhnev era was in part a reaction to the Chinese challenge in the Third World. It is true that the Chinese attempt to acquire an international clientele during the first half of the 1960s was a complete failure, but the danger had to be taken seriously and pre-emptive activism – motivated by other factors as well – was an obvious way of dealing with it. In sum, the lasting and overall effect of the rivalry with China was to strengthen a structural drift towards conservatism at home and expansionism abroad. By contrast, the development of Chinese policies after the rift was characterized by more rapid changes and took a more acutely destabilizing turn. Four successive landmarks should be noted. At first, the Chinese leadership sought allies against the Soviet Union and tried to lay the foundations for its own rival bloc, but this strategy proved ineffective and came to an end with the destruction of the Indonesian Communist party in 1965. The setbacks abroad strengthened the isolationist and exclusivistic tendencies at home; the next phase – the cultural revolution – was marked by the most uncompromising claims to represent an ideological and political alternative to Soviet 'revisionism'. As we have seen, the manifest extremism masked an enduring dependence on the Soviet model. It was, paradoxically, a further aggravation of the conflict that brought about a return to more orthodox Soviet methods on the Chinese side: the military threat from the Soviet Union led the Maoist faction to call a halt to the cultural revolution and share power with the party apparatus which they had set out to purge. But the restoration of traditional party-state structures was only one aspect of an unstable compromise. The fourth and last phase, beginning in the late 1970s, gave a new twist to the Sino–Soviet rift. An informal alliance with America was now seen as the best protection against the Soviet threat and an opening to the capitalist world economy as the best way of overcoming the developmental blockages of the Soviet model. All in all, the break-up of the bloc made the crisis of its less developed part more acute and the search for solutions more urgent; there was thus an underlying logic to the oscillations which began with an attempt to maximize the mobilizing capacity of the Soviet model and ended – for the time being – with efforts to keep the remodelling of its economic institutions under political control.

The Sino–Soviet conflict and its immediate consequences were highly visible and widely perceived as a historical turning-point. The second development to be discussed was limited to the Soviet sphere of influence, and it is only after the collapse that it can be seen in proper perspective. As noted above, the reorientation of Soviet strategy after 1964 was not unrelated to the Chinese challenge, but the new constellation had a broader background and a pattern of its own. The consolidation of the Soviet model within its original domain went hand in hand with a more ambitious global strategy; as internal stabilization turned to stagnation, the expansionist drive continued and led to the conquest of a new periphery. It is this aspect of the trajectory of the Soviet model – a growing discrepancy between domestic and international dynamics – that must now be reconsidered in the light of its demise.

In the mid-1960s the economic infrastructure of the Soviet empire was still strong enough to meet the demands of a more active global strategy while leaving some scope for concessions and readjustments at home (even if the latter sometimes proved to be futile exercises, as was the case with the massive increase of investment in Soviet agriculture). This fact should not be forgotten because of the economic failure which became evident during the final decade. As Sapir (1990) has argued, both the temporary success and the definitive failure may be easier to understand if we locate the economic alternatives of plan and market within the more comprehensive forms of social regulation of the economy. He distinguishes two possible ways of regulating the mobilized economy: a voluntaristic one, exemplified by the policies of the Stalin era, and a consensual one, never implemented on the same scale and best defined as a project inherent in partial revisions of the voluntaristic model. On this view, the attempts to strike a new balance between coercion and bargaining (and therefore also between vertical and horizontal mechanisms of coordination, political strategies and social needs) can be interpreted as a search for more consensual forms of regulation. The progress made in this regard during the 1960s is as undeniable as the failure to follow it up with further reforms; and although the contrast between the two modes of regulation is not reducible to the dichotomy of plan and market, a decisive break with the voluntaristic mode would have required a more thoroughgoing reactivation of the market. But this does not mean that the persistent imbalance between bureaucratic controls and market mechanisms is self-explanatory. Rather, the decisive obstacle was political: the primacy of the power structure which had imposed its laws on the mobilized economy (Sapir's thesis is that the partial shift from voluntaristic to consensual regulation came to an end with the destruction of the Czechoslovak reform movement; from now on, the limits to change were clearly defined, and further experiments – as in Hungary – would only be tolerated if political containment was assured).

The balance-sheet of the 1960s is a matter of debate. But it is now generally accepted that the economic crisis which spread throughout the bloc in the late 1970s was not fully reflected in official statistics and that the underlying condition was too serious to be diagnosed as a mere failure to move from extensive to intensive growth. The Soviet economic model had not simply exhausted its potential or reached limits which it could not transcend; it was decomposing. It seems, however, that the economists who have tried to explain this development have been faced with a dilemma: some built-in dysfunctionalities of the model are now well-known, but they explain bad performance, rather than declining performance (Wiles 1982), and are easier to relate to the conjunctural fluctuations of Soviet-type economies than to their terminal crisis; on the other hand, some crucial aspects of the latter – such as the decline of labour discipline, the loss of power and authority by the coordinating centre, growing corruption, and the adverse impact of demographic trends – are hard to measure in economic terms and obviously linked to the political and cultural background. Our analysis of the Soviet model as a whole points to an explanation in terms of extra-economic contexts rather than intra-economic mechanisms, but it must leave more specific questions open. In conclusion, however, it may be useful to note the diversity of the crisis patterns – a point often overlooked by those who now see the Soviet economic model as a recipe for disaster and nothing else. In general, the gradual decline was accompanied by cyclical fluctuations, but the breakdowns were more pronounced in some countries than others; some of the regimes in question embarked on adventurous and mismanaged projects which aggravated the crisis (as the Polish and Romanian experience shows, this could be done in different ways), whereas others decayed in a less dramatic fashion; the foreign debt problem, a major factor in some cases, was of very minor importance elsewhere; the widely accepted view that agriculture is the most insoluble problem of command economies proved more valid for the Soviet Union than for some of the satellites (Hungary and Czechoslovakia are conspicuous cases in point). All in all, it seems clear that both economic conditions and crisis symptoms in the various countries of the bloc were more diverse than their subsequent paths of political transition.

In the political sphere, oligarchic stabilization marked the end of revolutions from above. The changes designed to protect the apparatus against autocratic excesses went hand in hand with a strategic retrenchment: the reproduction of the existing power structure now took precedence over any transformative projects. Over and above that, however, the leadership which presided over the transition managed to stay in place for two decades and tie the stability of the regime to its own survival. This immobility at the top led, in the end, to a paralysis of the political centre and an uncontrollable growth of the pathologies that threatened the party-state from within: patrimonialism, gerontocracy, clientelism and corruption. At the same time, the ideological framework was undergoing a similar change. With the new emphasis on the defence and glorification of 'really existing socialism', Marxism-Leninism took a more conservative turn. It became a formula for the transfiguration rather than the transformation of the status quo, and although it had now been codified in greater detail and thus rendered less susceptible to arbitrary revisions than it had been during the Stalin era, its ritual functions overshadowed its doctrinal content. If it could still be used to define the limits of legitimate public discourse, it could no longer impose an ideological programme on scientific research and cultural creation.

In the international arena, there were two sides to the seemingly irresistible advance of Soviet power. On the one hand, the Soviet Union maintained and consolidated its position as a military superpower. Whether it had achieved or was about to achieve military superiority over its main rival was a matter of debate in the late 1970s and early 1980s, but the question is now academic, and the details of the controversy are irrelevant to our present purposes. Some basic facts can, however, be regarded as beyond dispute. During the Brezhnev era, the Soviet Union entered into a more global rivalry with the United States than before; although the bipolar pattern of world politics had taken shape in the aftermath of the war (as a result of the balance of forces between the two main victorious powers and their quasi-monopoly of nuclear weapons), the most sustained Soviet efforts to exploit its potential and contest its original terms took place during the last two decades before the breakdown. In pursuing this course, the Soviet regime proved incomparably more competitive in the military field than in any other area; its military buildup was more continuous than that of the other superpower and imposed much heavier burdens on economy and society. Last but not least, the Soviet leadership repeatedly tried to score gains that would result in major strategic advantages. The 'battle of the Euromissiles' in the early 1980s was the last significant initiative of this kind.

But it was the connection between growing military strength and political gains on the periphery that most impressed contemporary observers. The emergence of the 'New Communist Third World', i.e. the proliferation of ostensibly Marxist-Leninist regimes under more or less effective Soviet control, was the most visible symptom of the new expansionism. With this development, Soviet strategy in the Third World took a new turn: it became more concerned with the institutional assimilation of client states, but also more adaptable to unorthodox detours and shortcuts towards this goal. Once again, it was a contingent and external development that opened up new possibilities. The Cuban example of self-imposed Sovietization inspired various post-colonial or post-revolutionary regimes to follow suit; although the Cuban regime had conspicuously failed to achieve the developmental aims which it had set itself, the adoption of the Soviet model and the entry into the Soviet sphere of influence had enabled the Cuban state to play an international role out of all proportion to its previous record, and this was an attractive precedent for political élites whose ambitions exceeded their resources. The resultant 'roads to socialism' had little in common with traditional Marxist-Leninist recipes, and the 'leading role of the party' seemed to be degenerating into a ritual formula on a par with the 'dictatorship of the proletariat'. But from the Soviet point of view, that was not an acceptable price to pay for political support. The institutional core of the party-state was less negotiable than the ideological fiction of proletarian power, and the Soviet leadership did not take all conversions at face value. Rather, it tried to distinguish between various levels of 'socialist orientation' and supervise the Sovietizing process, directly or through intermediaries.[3]

Although the two aspects of the expansionist drive – the maximization of military strength and the export of the Soviet model – were closely related, it now seems clear that they were not as rationally coordinated as they appeared to Western observers. The invasion of Afghanistan, widely seen as a spectacular turn towards a more unified and aggressive strategy, was a local operation that got out of control: it was, to begin with, primarily directed against a national Communist regime with real or suspected pro-Chinese inclinations (this was largely overlooked at the time), but it brought the Soviet Union into direct conflict with a religious and ethnic revolt that called for intervention on a much larger scale.

The discrepancy between domestic failure and global advance did not go unnoticed. Severyn Bialer (1986) described it as the 'Soviet paradox' of external expansion and internal decline. Some observers saw it as a particularly dangerous turn: in this view (forcefully argued, among others, by Edward Luttwak (1983)), the 'regime pessimism' which would inevitably result from a growing awareness of decline was likely to prompt the Soviet leaders to make full use of their military advantages before it was too late. With the wisdom of hindsight, it can be argued that the phenomenon was less paradoxical and the danger less acute than it may have seemed at the time. On the one hand, the success of the expansionist strategy was short-lived and superficial. The Soviet Union could not remain a military match for the other superpower if it continued to lose ground on other levels, especially the economic one; if the imbalance between military buildup and relative or absolute regression in other areas was nevertheless allowed to develop as far as it did and undermine the very achievements to which all else had been subordinated, this must in part have been due to ideological factors. There is, in other words, no doubt that the Soviet leadership failed to grasp the complex dynamics of interstate – especially interhegemonic – competition and overestimated its own ability to offset structural weaknesses through strategic gains. Ideological visions had become much less important for the self-representation of the regime, but ideological delusions about its performance and potential were slow to disappear. As for the other form of expansion, the acquisition of new client states, more recent events have shown how fragile the foundations and identities of Third World Marxist-Leninist regimes were (the Cuban exception is more apparent than real: the Castro regime owes its strength to a unique combination of Soviet and Latin American elements, rather than a successful adaptation of the Soviet model en bloc). And Soviet policies in this area also had an ideological background. In particular cases, political calculations could take precedence over ideological principles, but in view of the resources devoted to the Third World offensive, it must be assumed that the overall strategy was based on a double illusion: about the applicability of the Soviet model to different regions of the developing world and about the impact which loss of control over parts of the periphery would have on the central Western powers.

On the other hand, it is true that domestic problems eventually became too urgent to be ignored and proved too serious to be solved within the framework of the regime, but 'regime pessimism' is hardly the right word for the reaction which they provoked, and the road from decline to fall took an unexpected detour. The regime did not disintegrate as a result of irresistible decay; it self-destructed in the course of an ambitious but abortive reform. It was not uncommon for observers to consider the collapse of the Soviet empire as a theoretical possibility, but it was very rarely seen as imminent, and nobody seems to have expected it to happen in the way it did. The reformist interlude may, in retrospect, seem less significant than the more long-drawn-out crisis which preceded it and the more spectacular breakdown that followed. But the 'revolution from within' (Gooding 1992), launched by a leadership which had become dissatisfied with the performance of the regime but not lost confidence in its potential, was in reality the decisive episode in a decomposing process that is still going on. The 'new thinking' of Gorbachev and his associates was a partial self-critique of the Soviet model, innovative in some respects but fatally retarded in others, and the learning processes which followed the first unsuccessful moves never added up to a coherent project. Despite the loss of meaning and momentum, the official self-image of the regime was still a serious obstacle to a diagnosis of its trouble. And since ideological barriers were easier to overcome in some areas than others, the reform strategy was permanently off balance. Its successive phases are perhaps best described as different approaches to the twin problems of rebuilding the mechanisms of control and reviving the project of mobilization. In the present context, it is above all the starting-point of this process that should be noted. During the first phase, characterized by the slogan of 'acceleration' (*uskorenie*), rather than glasnost or perestroika, the two strategic goals were hardly distinguishable. This was evident in the attempts to restore labour discipline, bring the second economy under more effective control, and – last but not least – to link the struggle against corruption to a reaffirmation of central authority over the national power élites (Carrère d'Encausse 1990). In fact, the imperial and Russocentric character of Gorbachev's strategy was at this stage so pronounced that one can almost speak of a reconquest of the internal periphery.

It soon became clear that a re-mobilization of society would not be possible without relaxation of control. But the first steps towards reform were clearly more than a reaction to perceived decline. The problem was rather – as the leadership saw it – a disconnection of regime and society, and in that sense, the condition of the Soviet model in its heartland was not altogether unlike the situation which it faced in newly conquered domains: a diminishing capacity to impose its logic on a changing social environment. In the last instance, then, the parallels between external and internal development were more decisive than the apparent paradox. If we use Michael Mann's distinction between extensive and intensive power, i.e. 'the ability to organize large numbers of people over far-flung territories', and 'the ability to command a high level of mobilization or commitment from the participants' (Mann 1986: 7), the overall change which the Soviet model was undergoing can perhaps be described as a hypertrophy of extensive power accompanied by an erosion of intensive power. And in this way, it was becoming more similar to traditional imperial structures.

This line of argument calls for a closer look at a third aspect of the above-mentioned changes: a structural shift that was, as has now become clear, closely linked to the geopolitical ruptures and displacements, but had to do with the interaction and relative weight of the components of the Soviet model as such, rather than its performance and position in the global arena. From our point of view, the changing relationship between totalitarian power and its imperial context, as well as between economic, political and cultural patterns, is of particular significance. And in both respects, it can be shown that real trends gave rise to rival and one-sided interpretations which must now be reconsidered in the light of later developments.

The imperial legacy was, as we have seen, essential to the totalitarian project; it could re-emerge as a more independent factor when the latter had to be downgraded. As the Soviet regime entered the phase of oligarchic stabilization, global expansionism became easier to sustain than internal mobilization. The focus of rivalry with the West shifted from the self-strengthening of the Soviet Union (pursued in different ways during the Stalin and Khrushchev eras) towards a strategy of extending Soviet influence and exporting Soviet institutions. With the increasing reliance on military strength and direct or indirect conquest, rather than developmental performance, the Soviet empire took a more traditional turn; ideological control over oppositional movements in the enemy camp became less important than the political techniques which served both to attract and to assimilate peripheral states. But if the imperial activism of the Brezhnev era was a substitute for more ambitious original goals and a sign of reorientation towards the pursuit of extensive rather than intensive power, this did not mean that no significant developments took place within Soviet society. V. Zaslavsky (1982: 66–8) distinguishes two phases in the history of the Soviet Union: a revolutionary one which lasted until the end of the 1950s, and a stationary one which followed. This dichotomy seems questionable. Both before and after the quarter-century from the beginning of the second revolution to Stalin's death, Soviet society went through transitional phases that can certainly not be described as revolutionary in the same sense as the Stalin era, but that were not stationary either. During the 1920s, politics and society were changing along several divergent lines, and the second revolution took some of these trends to extreme lengths while it cut others short; as for the Khrushchev era, it was characterized by attempts to continue mobilization without terror and rapid change without revolution from above. The political stability of the oligarchic regime which put an end to this balancing act should not be equated with a stationary state of the whole society. Rather, the retreat from mobilization and the diminishing dynamism of core institutions changed the balance between dominant and subordinate mechanisms of the system and thus opened the way for an overall involution. The imperatives of self-reproduction prevailed over those of social transformation, but at the same time a less perceptible trend towards self-decomposition became harder to resist. As argued above, the economic, political and cultural changes that took place during the misnamed 'era of stagnation' (1964–85) were confined within the limits of the Soviet model; we now have to consider the undermining effect which they nevertheless had on its basic structures, and this may be easier to understand if we relate the discussion to some earlier interpretations.

The worsening condition of the Soviet economy during the later years of the Brezhnev era can also be diagnosed as an institutional problem: a failure of the regulative mechanisms of the mobilized economy to maintain the developmental pattern to which they had originally been tailored. Their loss of strength automatically entailed an upgrading of other forces. It led, in short, to an increase in the relative weight of horizontal forms of coordination, as against vertical ones, and of the second economy in contrast to the official one. Gorbachev's economic policies were at first aimed at reversing this trend. His references to 'new thinking' may be understood as a less articulate response to a similar predicament on the ideological level. If we follow Zaslavsky's analysis of ideological developments during the 1960s and 1970s, two dominant tendencies can be distinguished. On the one hand, the ritualization and 'fictionalization' of the official doctrine, now reduced to the defence of an established order rather than the advocacy of a programme, enabled the unofficial (or, as Zaslavsky (1982: 81) calls it, 'operative') ideology of Russian nationalism and imperialism to play a more independent role. On the other hand, the regime tried to use the notion of the Soviet way of life, a loosely defined mixture of traditional and modern elements, as a bridge between official and unofficial ideologies, but its appeal was limited. Later events have, however, highlighted some other changes that were less obvious at the time. Apart from the connection with Russian nationalism, the propaganda for the 'Soviet way of life' also served – less visibly and less effectively – to counter the revival of non-Russian identities and aspirations. And if the national-imperial ingredients of the decaying Stalinist synthesis had now become a separate but subliminal ideology, something similar seems to have happened to its Westernist component. In view of the almost instant extinction of 'scientific socialism' we must assume that visions of Western alternatives had been gaining ground behind the official façade. The manifest inability of the Soviet model to complete its self-declared historical mission – to overtake the West – made it vulnerable to conversion from within. It might be suggested that Soviet versions of technocratic ideology, centred on the vague notion of the scientific-technological revolution, were meant to provide the same defence against this trend as the 'Soviet way of life' against nationalist currents, but proved even less effective.

Both economic and ideological structures were thus undergoing a change which affected the internal balance as well as the overall dynamics of the regime. And since the mechanisms that were running down had been essential to political control over economic and cultural life, the political centre was by the same token losing power. It was – as noted above – also exposed to the disintegrative forces which the transition to oligarchy had released. But although the power basis of the party-state was thus crumbling from within and without, its institutional framework remained the most firmly entrenched part of the Soviet model.

The decline of Soviet economy and ideology had gone too far for a purely internal solution to their problems to be plausible, but it was still possible to envisage – if not to achieve – a politically programmed restructuration of society as a whole. This residual primacy of politics is crucial to the understanding of the 'Gorbachev phenomenon' and its consequences.

At this point, a brief glance at the sovietological debates of the early and mid-1980s may be useful; none of the conflicting schools of thought can claim much credit for prognostic insight, but their incompatible images of Soviet society can still serve as a reminder of unanswered questions. We can, broadly speaking, divide the interpretations in question into two groups: some of them focused on the global growth of Soviet power but disagreed on its implications, whereas others tried – in varying ways – to explain the more elusive forces at work within the Soviet Union. The following comments will be limited to two contrasting examples of each approach.

Castoriadis's theory of stratocracy has already been discussed in connection with the legitimation crisis of late Communism; its main aim, however, was to clarify the socio-cultural meaning of Soviet imperialism and militarism. Expansion abroad and stagnation at home were, in this view, the two main symptoms of a social mutation: terror and ideology, the twin instruments of the party-state, had ceased to function and left the field to a military apparatus which could impose its logic on the party without any overt transfer of power. The strategic reorientation – from an internal to an external pursuit of power – and the institutional shift were thus two sides of the same phenomenon. Its significance was evident in the fact that the Soviet regime could still aim at military superiority over the West despite a hopelessly inferior performance in all other areas. But the concentration of efforts and resources in the military sector was predicated on complete control over everything else: the Soviet Union was an 'ossified society' with overdeveloped destructive forces. In short, this analysis led to the conclusion that control and mobilization were now less closely linked than before. The regime remained in control of social life, but its mobilizing capacity was now restricted to imperial rivalry.

A very different interpretation of the Soviet military buildup was proposed by Jacques Sapir, who saw it as a continuation of the much older Russian tradition of 'paradoxical militarism'. The paradox consisted in the fact that an 'overdeveloped military apparatus' did not 'reflect the social supremacy of a military group or caste' (Sapir 1991: 225). In this view, the original rationale for Russian militarism was political: it was meant to compensate for the economic and social backwardness that threatened to undermine the imperial strategy. But although the military apparatus was kept under political control, it had a dynamic of its own and a distinctive impact on its social environment. Vested interests, institutional inertia and routinized approaches gave it a staying power which no strategic revisions could break; more importantly, the methods used to enhance military strength could become models for more comprehensive developmental projects. According to Sapir, paradoxical militarism was not simply inherited by the Soviet regime; rather, it was revived by the Stalinist leadership in the course of the second revolution, after a brief but unequivocal break and on the basis of a strategy which took both aspects of the tradition – the subaltern and the unbalanced character of militarism – to extreme lengths. The military apparatus was more thoroughly subordinated to the political centre than ever before; at the same time, the political need for rapid militarization and an offensive strategy was more urgent than in pre-revolutionary Russia (it was now a matter of compensating for acute crisis and disruption, rather than persistent backwardness), and the military paradigm of mobilization was imposed on economy and society with unprecedented thoroughness. But the primacy of politics was never in doubt: the maximization of military resources and the militarization of society were the result of political decisions, and if it could be argued that 'the most militarized aspects of the Soviet system have nothing to do with the military in any real sense' (Sapir 1991: 267), this was another way of saying that they obeyed a political logic. In stark contrast to the theory of stratocracy, Sapir claims that the fundamental relationship between political and military factors remained unchanged during the later phases of the Soviet regime and that the persistence of paradoxical militarism was at least partly due to political and ideological priorities of the leadership, rather than to structural causes.

As we have seen, modern attempts to organize economy and society for military purposes belong to the prehistory of the Soviet model, but its institutional patterns are far too complex and their background too broad to be reduced to an extension of the war economy or the 'warfare state'. There is no need to reconsider this issue. What concerns us here is the question whether 'stratocracy' or 'paradoxical militarism' is a more adequate description of the Soviet regime in its most openly imperialist and least developmentalist phase. There are, at first sight, strong arguments against the stratocracy thesis. The whole history of the failed reform and its aftermath shows that the military apparatus had not become a dominant force in Soviet society. Support from higher echelons of the military may have been essential to the first moves of the reformist leadership, but the military as such was neither the prime mover of reform nor the main obstacle to it. The social and political paralysis of the armed forces, both before and after the collapse of the centre in 1991, seems easier to explain if we accept the notion of paradoxical militarism. In its most general sense, this concept refers to a combination of hypertrophy and heteronomy: military power is overdeveloped and overemphasized at the expense of other forms of social power, but military actors and institutions remain subordinate to an external authority. It can hardly be doubted that this applies to relations between army and party-state in the Soviet Union until the very end. On the other hand, a closer look at the last phase suggests that paradoxical militarism had in some ways taken a new turn, different from the traditional pattern which Sapir describes, and that the stratocracy thesis – even if untenable in a literal sense – can be read as an attempt to grasp this new constellation. Three interconnected aspects of the change should be noted.

First, paradoxical militarism had always been closely linked to economic weaknesses but not always in the same way (it had originally developed as an imperial response to economic backwardness, and it had been revived in connection with a risky and disruptive strategy of economic development), and this connection took a particularly ominous turn during the 1970s and 1980s. The overdeveloped military apparatus continued to expand at a time when the regime was confronted with economic challenges that could no longer be tackled in the traditional way. Most importantly, the shift towards a more interventionist global strategy coincided with developments which made the economic foundations of Soviet power more vulnerable to external pressures. Both interdependence and rivalry posed new problems. But if it is a matter of debate how much the exposure to a volatile world market had to do with the Soviet crisis, it is much easier to grasp the role of economic factors in interstate and inter-imperial competition: the economic shortcomings of the Soviet model were reflected in a growing technological gap and a worsening geopolitical position. Contrary to official – and to some extent genuine – Soviet expectations, the 1970s were not marked by a deepening crisis of capitalism, but by a new wave of technological innovation that made it much more difficult to catch up with the West. As has often been pointed out, the political constraints of the Soviet model were the most decisive obstacle to the absorption and diffusion of information technology. The core structure of the regime was thus having a more visibly adverse effect on its competitiveness than ever before. And since there could, in the long run, be no complete separation of civil and military sectors, the ability of the latter to compensate for the underdevelopment of the former was thus called into question. No redistribution of resources could make up for a structurally retarded technology. At the same time, the global balance of power was becoming less favourable to the Soviet empire. Although the basic bipolarity of the postwar world remained intact, there were some shifts towards a more multipolar configuration, and they were more threatening to the Soviet Union than to the other superpower. One such development was the Sino–Soviet rift, which we have already discussed. But in the present context, the emergence of new economic power centres within the capitalist world is more directly relevant. America was the main adversary of the Soviet Union as a hegemonic power, but the comparison with Western Europe and Japan was perhaps even more damaging to the Soviet model as a social alternative. It seems probable that the Soviet leadership was particularly disturbed by the rise of Japan as an economic superpower: as it overtook the Soviet Union and became the world's second largest economy, Japan was in fact doing to the Soviet Union what the Soviet Union had previously – during the Khrushchev era – proposed to do to America. And at a time when the demands of imperial strategy were overstraining a stagnant economic base, such setbacks could hardly be ignored.

These considerations support the view that it is 'in the perceived inability of the Soviet system to catch up, let alone overtake, the West that a central aspect of the Soviet collapse must be seen' (Halliday 1992: 133). But if the emphasis is on 'perceived', the obstacles to perception must also be taken into account. The first response to the problems which the Soviet rulers faced during the 1970s had been an intensification of paradoxical militarism; they continued, in other words, to rely on the compensatory function of military power in a situation that was less and less amenable to such solutions. Most observers were surprised when Soviet leaders became critical of their own system, but in view of what is now known about the condition of Soviet society, it is rather the ability of their predecessors to ignore, minimize or misunderstand the malfunctions of the regime that needs explanation. If we approach the question from this angle, it may help to put a further aspect of Soviet militarism in its true light. There is no doubt that ideological residues, however atrophied, were still conducive to illusions about the viability and potential superiority of the Soviet model. Ideological constraints could not be imposed on society without having some repercussions on the regime. But the self-deluding effects of official doctrines are easier to understand if we relate them to the social and historical background. As we have seen, the confidence of Soviet leaders was largely due to the victory over Germany and the conquest of Eastern Europe; this apparent proof of the essential superiority of the regime was central to its self-image, and since military performance had thus become the main test of ideological claims, further accumulation of military power could by the same token serve to confirm that the system was fulfilling its historical mission. This ideological militarization did not only apply to the international context. The armed forces were a crucial instrument of control and integration within the Soviet Union, and if they functioned as a 'socialization agency' (Sapir), i.e. as a transmission belt between regime and society, it seems clear that there was another side to this: they also became a smokescreen between society and regime. In other words: the army represented an imaginary model of Soviet society (most importantly with regard to its supposedly trans-ethnic identity) which desensitized the regime to its problems. From this point of view, it could be argued that the stratocracy thesis was based on a misreading of the relationship which it had rightly singled out as crucial. What had happened was not so much a transfer of power from the party-state to the military apparatus as an ideological overidentification of the former with the latter. In that sense, the problem was cultural rather than political: the potential which the Soviet model had shown in military competition became the basis of a self-interpretation which obscured its inferiority and irrationality in other areas.

When this ideological shield could no longer conceal the inability to compete and the urgent need for a strategic reorientation, the structural weight of the military apparatus was still an intractable problem. The third and last point to be made in relation to the stratocracy thesis is that it conflated two levels of the power structure. The disproportionate development of the military sector did not lead to the displacement of political institutions by military ones, but it proved to be a decisive obstacle to reform. One of the most striking weaknesses of the Gorbachev leadership was its inability to achieve the conversion of the military-industrial complex that was clearly essential to its domestic as well as its international policies. Sapir's analysis of the mobilized economy may help to put this fact into perspective. There is no reason to disagree with the claim that the imperatives of mobilization applied, in the first instance, to Soviet economy and society as a whole, and that the distinctive features of Soviet militarism are related to this broader context. But it needs to be added that the Soviet model proved incapable of balancing socio-economic mobilization and military buildup, and that this developmental dislocation made the transition to a less militarized version of the mobilized economy impossible (if we follow Sapir, the reorientation of the Japanese economy is the prime example of such a change).

Neither of the theories we have discussed can explain the revolution from within. The reformist turn showed that the party-state was more intact and independent than the stratocracy thesis had assumed, but the sequel soon made clear that it had lost the ability to control and mobilize which is taken for granted in the model of paradoxical militarism. At this point, some questions must be asked about the society that the regime was trying to re-mobilize. If the failure of this attempt revealed the fragility of the centre, it also brought the shortcomings of social actors and structures into the open. Earlier interpretations of Soviet society, especially those inspired by the prima facie promising changes of the early Gorbachev years, must now be confronted with the last act of its history.

For optimistic observers, the reformist turn was the triumph of a civil society that had been taking shape below the surface of Soviet institutions. We should distinguish this use of the term from the oppositional concepts of civil society, discussed above: it reflects the experience – and even more the expectations – of the second half of the 1980s, but it was meant to explain the gradual and irresistible developments which had supposedly paved the way for more radical change. S. Frederick Starr's (1988) account of the birth of civil society during the Brezhnev era is perhaps the most extreme version of this view, but others have argued in a similar vein. Urbanization, an expanding 'second economy', the diffusion of a global youth culture and the growing influence of public opinion have been seen as aspects of a social transformation that was undermining the party-state; those who emphasized actors rather than structures often focused on the middle class as 'at once the most important and the most overlooked social class in Soviet society' (Rywkin 1989: 65; Jerry Hough's description of Gorbachev's reforms as a revolt of the middle classes is another well-known example).

Far from acting on behalf of or in response to civil society, the reformist centre was – as events were to show – pursuing a strategy of its own for which it could not find a social basis. But in view of conditions in post-Soviet Russia, it would not be easy to argue that the party-state has been defeated or displaced by civil society. The collapsed regime was a configuration of state and society, and both sides have been drawn into the decomposing process. If the methods of those who are now trying to bring capitalism to Russia bear some resemblance to early Bolshevik visions of a shortcut to socialism (Gellner 1991), this reflects not only the social vacuum which the Soviet model left behind, but also the continuity of some underlying attitudes and relationships. As we have noted, the concept of a state-conditioned society can serve to describe the specific institutional pattern which emerged in Russia during the Muscovite phase; the Petrine revolution from above can then be seen as an attempt to move towards a more fully state- controlled society, and the Stalinist synthesis of imperial and revolutionary projects was to lay the foundations for a state-programmed society. During the Brezhnev era, the mechanisms of control and mobilization lost much of their earlier strength, but the result was not so much a birth of civil society as a reversal to the state-conditioned mode. The Gorbachev leadership reacted to this trend and tried to reactivate society without falling back on the traditional patterns of mobilization. In so doing, it brought down the whole imperial edifice. The post-imperial but still state-conditioned society, disjointed by the crisis which destroyed the regime, has yet to rebuild a durable institutional framework, and it remains to be seen how much of the traditional basis (with its pre-Soviet as well as Soviet layers) will survive. But the present transformation should, in any case, be seen as a new phase of the ongoing interaction between the Russian and the Western trajectory, rather than as the coming of age of an indigenous society or a wholesale conversion to an imported model.

Those who greeted the rise of civil society in the Soviet Union tended to take the unity of Soviet society as such – or at least the stability of some shared and essential characteristics – for granted. For obvious reasons, this assumption is no longer tenable, and the fragmentation of the Soviet state suggests that another view may have been much better founded. It would, in other words, seem that the erosion of state power over social life did not lead to a general and uniform strengthening of civil society, but to a reconstitution of national societies and identities; by implication, it depended on the different socio-cultural contexts which thus were brought into play how much scope there was for developments along the lines of civil society in the more specific sense. This line of argument was, in particular, developed by Hélène Carrère d'Encausse (1978, 1990) well before the reformist turn and updated to explain the events that followed. But as she saw it, the Soviet project had not only been undermined by the revival of nations and nationalism. It had also suffered another defeat in that the most vigorous trans-national cultural community – the Islamic region of the empire – was particularly resistant to Soviet strategies of assimilation and Soviet visions of progress.

There is no doubt much more to be said for this analysis than for the oversimplified and over-optimistic projections of a post-Communist Soviet society. More generally speaking, it seems clear that the formation or restoration of states and the constitution or reconstitution of national identities is the crucial aspect of the 'exit from Communism'; the moves towards liberal democracy and a market economy may figure more prominently in mainstream commentaries, but they are a dependent rather than a dominant variable, and their outcome will be determined by unpredictable combinations of global and internal factors. However, the fact that the nation-state has become the main beneficiary of the demise of the Soviet model should not lead us to mistake it for the historical subject of the transformation. In view of present conditions, it may be tempting to explain the crisis and collapse of the Soviet empire as a revolt of national realities against ideological constructs, and as a victory of more or less particularistic national aspirations over imperial pseudo-universalism. But the interpretation which I have been trying to develop runs counter to such claims. If the Soviet model collapsed under the strain of its inbuilt tensions and imbalances, we should try to explain how its disintegration opened up a new space for nationalism and co-determined the direction now taken by the latter, rather than mythicizing nationalism into an indomitable and ultimately victorious adversary of empire. The Eastern European crisis has already been discussed; what concerns us now is primarily the fate of the internal empire. In this regard, there are two obvious objections to the narratives which reduce the collapse of the Soviet Union to a contest between nationalism and the imperial centre.

First, the reformist push from the centre had to reach a certain level before nationalist movements could take shape. In retrospect, the turning-point stands out very clearly: it was the organization of popular fronts in support of perestroika, orchestrated from the centre, which made the public articulation of nationalist views possible. But this step was taken because earlier setbacks had brought the reformist policies to a critical juncture. The attempt to mobilize support outside the conventional channels of the party-state was the first step towards a de-monopolization of power, and as such, it reflected the radicalization of the reformers in the face of continuing obstruction by the apparatus, but also the absence of clearly defined ideological and political parameters for a more radical strategy. How the 'revolution from within' reached this point and took this turn is a question which only a more concrete historical analysis could answer; for our present purposes, it is enough to note that it precedes the problem of nationalism and its contribution to the crisis. Second, the break-up of the Soviet Union did not represent an outright victory for nationalism. Some of the post-imperial states are dominated by reconverted sections of the apparatus; in other cases, nationalist movements allied with cadres of the old regime to pursue a strategy of state-building (Ukraine is the prime example); finally, even where secessionist nationalism triumphed in the first round (as in Georgia and the Baltic states), it has already become clear that the vicissitudes of state formation will confront it with new problems and rival forces. In brief, post-Soviet nationalism is part of a complex and changing constellation which, in turn, is still subject to after-effects of the collapse.

To conclude this discussion, we should therefore take another look at the 'revolution from within' and its detonating impact. The implications of the above analysis may be summed up in shortened form. From the mid-1960s to the mid-1980s, two dominant but divergent trends shaped the course of Soviet history; the political centre, most directly exposed but at first oblivious to the growing tensions between them, finally responded in a way that brought the conflict to a head and broke the mainsprings of the regime.

I have already used the term 're-traditionalization' in connection with the Stalinist reactivation of the imperial legacy. But in a more conventional and comprehensive sense, and with the connotations of a process rather than a strategy, this concept might also serve to describe the changing forms and functions of the Soviet model during the Brezhnev era. The involution of the regime was, in other words, leading to a closure of its historical horizon. The joint effect of economic, political and ideological trends was – as noted above – a reduction of trans- formative potential and a reorientation towards self-reproduction on a 'really existing' basis. This conservative turn followed a developmental strategy which had in some respects endangered the foundations of long- term reproduction. As the persistent but unavailing efforts to improve the condition of Soviet agriculture show, the ruling oligarchy was not wholly unaware of this problem; it was much less responsive to the ecological crisis, but the aggravation of the latter became one of the main concerns of a nascent public opinion and one of the most explosive issues brought to the fore after 1985. More generally speaking, the retreat from mobilization to stabilization highlighted some previously neglected problems and exposed the regime to new dangers. The ideological pendant to the structural change – most clearly evident in attempts to portray the 'Soviet way of life' as a fully-fledged civilizational alternative and a tradition in its own right – can be seen as a pre-emptive response to these prospects. As we now know, it failed on two fronts: it was as incapable of open competition with Western models as it was of containing or absorbing the resurgent national forces. But the work of dissidents and exiles (Heller, Nekrich, Sinyavsky, Zinoviev et al.) can still serve as a reminder of how different the outlook seemed on the eve of the crisis, and how seriously the self-perpetuating capacity of 'homo sovieticus' and 'Soviet civilization' was taken by their bitterest critics.

If re-traditionalization was the dominant internal trend, the external change which accompanied it is perhaps best described as globalization. Soviet expansion, political and military, was only the active side of this process, and its obverse was in the long run more significant. The Soviet empire was drawn further and further into a global struggle with a more advanced adversary, disadvantaged in some respects but still capable of imposing – in all essentials – its terms of competition; at the same time, the uneven development of Soviet power undermined its hegemonic pretensions and made it more vulnerable to new challenges from more adaptable rivals (such as the East Asian centres of capitalist development). In short, the growing involvement in global affairs called for a more complex and innovative strategy at the very time when the Soviet regime was regressing towards a more stagnant state. The closure at home coincided with increasing exposure abroad.

The political centre, faced with the demands of global competition and the impediments of a decaying power structure, found itself in a situation which called for a radical change of course. Some reasons for the delayed reaction have already been discussed; to explain what happened after the obstacles to a reformist turn at the top had been overcome, both the strengths and the weaknesses of the leadership must be taken into account. Because of its privileged position at the apex of the mono-organizational structure, it was the only institution capable of initiating change. But the model of a revolution from above, geared to specific and imperative goals, was no longer applicable. Rather, the first precondition for further changes was a redefinition of the relationship between regime and society. If the aims of a reform strategy were to be articulated and its addressees identified, the political constraints on the public sphere had to be softened. The policy of glasnost, adopted after a brief experiment with more authoritarian notions of reform, was meant to meet this need. It led to a relaxation of ideological control and thus to put the ideological resources of the centre to a more severe test. The reformist leadership did not, as some analysts have suggested – and some of those involved probably believed – have an alternative tradition at its disposal. The reform episodes in Soviet history were too discontinuous, inconclusive and under-theorized to add up to anything of the kind. There was, at best, an ideological substratum – the Leninist legacy – that had been adapted to the strategies of the autocratic and oligarchic regimes, but could to a certain extent be reprocessed for other purposes. Although the 'return to Leninism' was an obligatory starting-point for any political changes and a potential opening to reform, its real meaning depended on the preferences of those who proclaimed it. A rhetoric of Leninist revival could easily have served to legitimize policies very different from those of Gorbachev and his associates. And neither the course adopted in 1985 nor the subsequent revisions are fully explicable in terms of the force of circumstances. A combination of sensitivity to some problems with blindness to others is as characteristic of Gorbachev's early years in power as a rapid but increasingly disoriented learning process was of his more radical phase. The most momentous turn was, it seems, the attempt to outmanoeuvre opposition within the party leadership by transferring more power to state institutions; there is no reason to doubt that Gorbachev intended to put the party-state together again in a more effective form, but the unintended effect was to paralyse the centre and pave the way for a devolution of power from imperial to national authorities.

These considerations may help to understand how the Soviet collapse could happen, but they do not explain why it happened at the time and in the way it did. The escalating crisis was a result of cumulative developments, but not the only conceivable outcome; a different mode of crisis management might have led to a more long-drawn-out decline. Historical contingency must be given its due, and the trajectory of the Soviet model exemplifies the two faces of contingency: the emergence and the extinction of formative patterns that can be related but not reduced to pre-existent sources. From this point of view, complaints about the failure of historians and social scientists to foresee the collapse seem misguided. There is no reason to believe that the end of Communism should have been more predictable than the beginning.

Notes

1 INTRODUCTION: THEORETICAL PERSPECTIVES

1 It might be objected that the Eliasian theory of state formation (discussed and applied in the following chapter) relativizes the distinction between states, state systems and empires: if states emerge and maintain themselves through the absorption and integration of less developed power centres, empires would seem to be nothing more than a continuation of the same process, and state systems appear to follow the same patterns of interaction and rivalry as the smaller units involved in state formation. There is no denying that a processual approach necessitates some rethinking of all three categories. But it should not lead to the blurring of boundaries between them, and the levelling turn is easier to avoid if the cultural dimension of the process – i.e., in particular, the cultural frameworks of state systems and empires – is given its due. Briefly, the subordination of pre-existing state systems to imperial centres involves specific forms and figures (organizational patterns and cultural definitions) of power, and they differ from the more elementary mechanisms which operate at the level of state formation. As for state systems (or, in other words, relatively stable patterns of interstate competition), they presuppose a more regular interaction and a stronger admixture of mutual recognition than a plurality of pre- or proto-state centres. These suggestions raise a number of problems that cannot be discussed here, and the conceptual boundaries in question should be drawn on the basis of historical comparisons rather than prior to them. It may be useful to indicate some of the most salient historical landmarks for a comparative analysis.

   The distinction between state systems and empires goes back to the very beginnings of civilization: the first conclusive transition from the former pattern to the latter (or to use Michael Mann's terms, from multi-power-actor civilizations to 'empires of domination') took place in Mesopotamia, and one way of elaborating the distinction would be to trace the development of more complex imperial formations on the basis of this initial breakthrough. The well-known contrast between the Chinese record of imperial continuity and the Western pattern of fragmentation is more directly relevant to the genesis of modernity, and the consolidation of the European state system after the failure of the sixteenth-century attempt at imperial restoration can serve to highlight the difference between two very different power structures with different implications for social development. But there is also a distinction to be made between interstate and inter-imperial relationships: a comparison of processes within the core of the European state system and the interaction between the imperial formations on its Eastern fringe would throw light on this point. Finally, it should be added that the distinction is relative in that an empire can also become one of the actors of a state system. In this respect, there is a striking contract between Russian and the Chinese empire: the expansion of the former led to a growing involvement in the European state system which it could not control, whereas the latter absorbed a more self-contained state system and was not confronted with a global one until much later.

2   The legacy of the two other empires is also relevant to the later history of the Soviet model: the restored and restructured Russian empire expanded into regions which had been under Habsburg and Ottoman control, and as we shall see, the construction of Soviet-type regimes faced specific problems in each domain. One link to the Habsburg past was the idea of Central Europe which became a common theme of dissident subcultures in several countries during the 1980s; it played a certain role in the cultural de-legitimation of the Soviet model, but it has had no impact on developments after the collapse.

2   SOURCES AND COMPONENTS

1   The view that cultural conceptions of power are central to political culture has been defended by Lucian Pye; as he sees it, 'political power is extraordinarily sensitive to cultural nuances, and... therefore cultural variations are decisive in determining the course of political development' (Pye 1985: vii). But his work also shows that if this insight is not linked to recent attempts to rethink both power and culture, the focus of concrete analyses can easily shift from institutional patterns to personality structures. An argument which begins with a strong emphasis on cultural differences then ends with the notion of 'paternalistic authority and the triumph of dependency' (312).

2   The reign of Ivan the Terrible is one of the most puzzling episodes in Russian history, and it is of interest here both because of the connection with Stalinism (cf. Tucker 1990: 482–86 on 'Iosif Grozny') and as a particularly striking example of the pathologies of state formation. For convincing arguments against over-rationalizing interpretations, cf. Richard Hellie's introduction and contribution to a special issue of *Russian History*, vol. 14 (1987) no. 1–7. For a recent rehabilitation which differs from both conservative and traditional Marxist views, cf. Wallerstein's account of sixteenth-century Russian history (1974: 313–24). On this view Ivan can be credited with 'trying to establish the autonomy of the Russian state from the European world economy' and succeeding at least in postponing integration until it could be achieved on more favourable terms. But this claim is unconvincing: if the Livonian war was an attempt to bring Russia closer to Europe, it would make more sense to describe Ivan's policies as an unsuccessful bid to join the world economy. Moreover, his strategy of state-building culminated in a crisis which exposed Russia to more serious threats from the European state-system than ever before.

3   The oversimplified notion of a struggle between society and the patrimonial state is reflected in Pipes's inconsistent views on the bureaucracy and its role.

In his well-known analysis of the old regime (1974: 134–38), the bureaucracy figures on the list of social forces which began to press the state for concessions. But in a later work on the revolution (1990: 65), it is described as 'a carryover from medieval times, before the emergence of a distinction between the person of the ruler and the institution of the state'.

4   The same author has also undertaken a comparative analysis of Russia and Iran as examples (and, in his view, the only clear-cut cases) of autocratic modernization (McDaniel 1991). This parallel is much less convincing than his analysis of Russia. The Pahlevi regime in Iran was not a traditional autocracy (the old regime had collapsed during the first two decades of the century), and its modernizing efforts were too short-lived and dependent on contingent circumstances (oil revenue and the American connection) to be comparable to the Russian process of imperial modernization. Both the autocratic power and the modernizing project were, in other words, fundamentally inauthentic.

3   THE MODEL AND ITS VARIANTS

1   Edgar Morin has repeatedly emphasized this point. His analysis of the Soviet Union (Morin 1983) is also one of the few attempts to do justice to both the totalitarian and the imperial aspects of the Soviet phenomenon. But as far as the latter issue is concerned, he deals primarily with the postwar expansion of the Soviet empire and neglects the original imperial source of the totalitarian project.

2   For the most sustained attempt to analyse the great purge as a conflict within the apparatus, rather than an offensive of the autocracy against both apparatus and society, cf. Rittersporn (1991). He argues that behind the external mechanics of the purge there was 'virtually a civil war being waged within the apparatus' (65). On the other hand, he is forced to admit that 'one should not imagine two clearly delimited camps, facing each other on definite political lines' (76). It is hard to conceive of a civil war without clearly delimited camps; it seems more likely that a whole complex of interconnected conflicts was utilized and manipulated by the autocracy.

3   It has been suggested (Hammond 1975) that the takeover of Mongolia in the 1920s became a model for the later Sovietization of Eastern Europe, but the differences between the two operations are too fundamental for this claim to be convincing. Most importantly, the restoration of Russian hegemony in Mongolia preceded the definitive crystallization of the Soviet model, whereas the imposition of an existing model was central to Soviet strategy in Eastern Europe from the outset. The creation of the Mongolian party-state was essentially a part of the Bolshevik reconquest, although its nominal status as the second Marxist-Leninist state has led to some misleading comparisons with later developments.

4   Each of the two regional types described here has its exception. The stability and conformity of the Bulgarian and East German regimes set them apart from their neighbours (the 1953 revolt in East Germany was merely the last upset before the consolidation of a regime which had developed later than the others). It would nevertheless be misleading to lump the two cases together as

examples of internally stable and externally controlled Soviet-type regimes. Each of them developed its distinctive strategies of stabilization and conformity, and thus gave a distinctive twist to its version of the Soviet model. In the Bulgarian case, the unique background of a party which emerged as an offshoot of Bolshevism before the Russian revolution was reflected in a strong domestic Stalinist tradition as well as in a particularly close connection with the Soviet centre. These two factors reinforced each other, but they could also come into conflict. If there was a pro-Chinese undercurrent within the Bulgarian regime (its strategies of economic reorganization showed some signs of Chinese influence, and one might even speculate that the abortive military coup of 1965 had something to do with the Chinese example of a more autonomous military), this is most plausibly explained as the response of a local Stalinist subculture to the international constellation after 1956. But the Stalinist legacy also helped a semi-autocratic leadership to survive and adapt to changing policies of the Soviet centre; the typical pattern of the Balkan party-states was thus repeated under more restrictive conditions.

As for the GDR, Sigrid Meuschel (1992) has shown that the image of a permanently dependent and conservative regime calls for some qualifications. The party leadership tried to compensate for its particularly subaltern and fragile condition by developing its own depoliticized model of reform and using it to establish a distinctive position within the bloc. Two sharply different phases of this strategy can be distinguished. During the Ulbricht era (i.e. until 1971), the idea of the scientific and technological revolution was used to legitimize projects of party-controlled technocratic reforms and – less explicitly – visions of the GDR as the most advanced socialist society. The distinctive ideological perspective of this phase can be described as 'a symbiosis of technology and community' (Meuschel 1992: 215). By contrast, the official ideology of the 1970s and 1980s was more defensive: the emphasis on economic equality and security as socialist values, stronger than elsewhere in the bloc and translated into the official slogan of 'unity of economic and social policy', was meant to compensate for the double dependence on the Soviet Union and West Germany.

5 For a very interesting attempt by a Western scholar to construct a Chinese perspective on this process, cf. Schrecker (1991).

6 One of the crucial differences between Soviet and Chinese Communism was that the latter did not acquire an external periphery (the reconquest of the internal one was a minor operation), and was therefore not faced with the problems which this achievement created for the Soviet centre. The smaller party-states in the East Asian region did not come under Chinese control. But although the extent of Chinese influence varied from case to case, it was strong enough to limit the expansion of Soviet power. This did not mean that the region was simply a contested domain between the two imperial centres. Rather, the mutually neutralizing effect of the latter opened the way for more independent developments, and in this regard, the record of the three regimes in question (North Korea, Vietnam and Cambodia – Laos can hardly be regarded as a separate political entity) is strikingly different. The rule of the Khmer Rouge in Cambodia was the most destructive episode in the whole history of the Soviet model, and their strategy the most overtly anti-developmental, but the available evidence does not suggest a radical

break with the developmental imaginary: rather, the destruction of urban civilization and the elimination of Western influence was to clear the way for a new start. The regime was too short-lived and too consumed with its own violence for a distinctive variant of the Soviet model to emerge. As for Vietnam, the most salient fact is a fundamental inability to complete the transition from war to a functioning party-state; economic collapse undermined the pretensions to orthodoxy, and the regime now seems to be repeating the Chinese turn to capitalism on a smaller scale and a more fragile basis. Finally, North Korea became the most absolute and durable autocracy in the whole Communist world. The isolationist and independent course of this regime is all the more striking because of its beginning as a satellite par excellence, installed by the Soviets and reinstated by the Chinese. But it is arguably the least known variant of the Soviet model, and its real performance – as distinct from its mythical image – may become easier to assess when it has run its course.

4 CRISIS AND COLLAPSE

1 Cf. Kaminski (1991: 19) on state socialism: 'Although the economic system has become a caricature of command planning, and its polity has become a caricature of totalitarianism, the mechanisms have remained essentially intact, particularly in the economic system.' What kind of essence is it that can become a caricature of itself and still remain intact?

2 The application of Marxist theories of crises and contradictions to Soviet-type societies was pioneered by the radical left, but it can be adapted to a liberal perspective; cf. Clark and Wildawsky (1990).

3 A comparative analysis of Third World versions of the Soviet model could start with the problems of state formation: if the apparent efficiency of Soviet techniques of power made the model attractive to state-building élites with developmental ambitions, the extreme fragility of the regimes in question is largely due to the tensions which developed between local conditions and the misunderstood and misplaced party-state paradigm. The extent of Soviet influence, as well as the details of the combination with traditional patterns, vary from case to case. Ethiopia is one of the most noteworthy examples; here the Soviet model was adopted by a military dictatorship in order to contain a radical social transformation within the boundaries of a regional imperial formation (in both respects, this regime differed from the more superficial 'Afro-Marxist' ones).

But it is the Cuban variant of the Soviet model that stands out as particularly significant. Whether it should be regarded as a Third World regime is a debatable point. Contrary to official myths, pre-revolutionary Cuba was not a typical case of underdevelopment, but rather an extreme case of disjointed development, and conditions differed in many ways from the conventional image of Third World societies. There is, however, no doubt that the Cuban precedent paved the way for comparable developments elsewhere; it also proved to be a more solid construction than the latecomers. Its specific characteristics are obviously the result of a fusion of Soviet and Latin American factors, and the latter ingredient is strong enough to set the regime sharply apart from the Soviet mainstream. The distinctively Latin American tradition of *caudillismo* has been a dominant factor from the outset. This pattern of political culture had both shaped the course of state formation in Latin America and left its mark on the indigenous revolutionary tradition; its concrete manifestations ranged from the most archaic forms of despotism to modernizing dictatorships which sometimes drew on Jacobin sources. The Cuban regime has obvious affinities with the latter type. In contrast to the autocracies which elsewhere grew out of the party-state apparatus, Castro was already firmly entrenched as a caudillo when he turned to the Communist movement and the Soviet model for institutional support. But this did not mean that the relationship between the two aspects of the regime was well-defined from the beginning: the question whether the caudillo would instrumentalize the apparatus or the apparatus absorb the caudillo led to major conflicts and was decided in favour of the former alternative during the 1960s. As a result, Cuba copied Soviet institutions but confined them to a more subaltern role than they had had in their original context. As Irving L. Horowitz (1982: 2) put it, the Cuban regime was to a significant extent characterized by 'routinization without institutionalization'. The synthesis of *caudillismo* and the Soviet model marked a break with another tradition which has been central to twentieth-century Latin American politics. The national-populist syndrome, as analysed by Touraine (1988), is based on the partial absorption of politicized social movements by a nationalist but structurally dependent state. Because of a weak state and a fragmented society, this pattern had failed to take root in Cuba; Castro's apparent commitment to it aided his rise to power, but his rejection of it was evident from the very moment of victory. The Soviet-inspired alternative was at first identified with a developmental project and expected to prove its superiority over national-populist policies in this regard, but the economic failures of the 1960s led the regime to redefine its goals and resign itself to economic underdevelopment while pursuing a military buildup that would enable Cuba to play an important if subordinate role in Soviet global strategy. No other Soviet-type regime has followed this path with comparable consistency.

Bibliography

Arnason, J.P. (1991) 'Modernity as project and as field of tensions', in A. Honneth and H. Joas (eds), *Communicative Action*, Cambridge: Polity Press, 181–213.

Avrich, P. (1972) *Russian Rebels, 1600–1800*, London: Allen Lane.

Balazs, E. (1964) *Chinese Civilization and Bureaucracy: Variations on a Theme*, New Haven: Yale University Press.

Barfield, T.J. (1989) *The Perilous Frontier: Nomadic Empires and China*, Oxford: Blackwell.

Bauman, Z. et al. (1984) 'Review-symposium on Soviet-type societies', *Telos* 60: 155–91.

Berdyaev, N. (1948) *The Origin of Russian Communism*, London: Geoffrey Bles.

Bergère, M.C. (1989) *The Golden Age of the Chinese Bourgeoisie*, Cambridge: Cambridge University Press.

Besançon, A. (1980) *Présent soviétique et passé russe*, Paris: Librairie Générale Française.

Bialer, S. (1986) *The Soviet Paradox: External Expansion, Internal Decline*, London: I.B. Tauris.

Bonnell, V. (1983) *Roots of Rebellion: Workers' Politics and Organization in St. Petersburg and Moscow, 1900–1914*: Berkeley: University of California Press.

Brown, J.F. (1988) *Eastern Europe and Communist Rule*, Durham and London: Duke University Press.

Brus, W. and Laski, K. (1989) *From Marx to Market: Socialism in Search of an Economic System*, Oxford: Clarendon Press.

Brzezinski, Z. (1967) *The Soviet Bloc: Unity and Conflict*, Cambridge, Mass.: Harvard University Press.

Bunce, V. (1985) 'The empire strikes back: the evolution of the Eastern bloc from a Soviet asset to a Soviet liability', *International Organization* 39(1): 1–46.

Carrère d'Encausse, H. (1978) *L'empire éclaté*, Paris: Flammarion.

—— (1990) *La gloire des nations ou la fin de l'empire soviétique*, Paris: Fayard.

Casals, F.G. (1980) *The Syncretic Society*, New York: M.E. Sharpe, (pseudonym for P. Campeanu).

Castoriadis, C. (1981) *Devant la guerre*, Paris: Fayard.

Cherniavsky, M. (1968) 'Ivan the Terrible as Renaissance prince', *Slavic Review* 27(2): 195–211.

—— (1970) 'Khan or Basileus: An aspect of Russian medieval political theory', in M. Cherniavsky (ed.), *The Structure of Russian History*, New York: Random House, 65– 79.

Chernov, V. (1924) 'Lenin', *Foreign Affairs* 2: 3, 366–72.

Clark, J. and Wildavsky, A. (1990) *The Moral Collapse of Communism: Poland as a Cautionary Tale*, San Francisco: Institute for Contemporary Studies.

Cohen, P. (1984) *Discovering History in China*, New York: Columbia University Press.

Collins, R. (1986) *Weberian Sociological Theory*, Cambridge: Cambridge University Press.

Dawisha, K. (1990) *Eastern Europe, Gorbachev and Reform: The Great Challenge*, Cambridge: Cambridge University Press.

Drewnowski, J. (ed.) (1982) *Crisis in the East European Economy: The Spread of the Polish Disease*, London: Croom Helm.

Ducellier, A. (1988) *Les Byzantins: Histoire et culture*, Paris: Editions du Seuil.

Eberhard, W. (1983) 'Die institutionelle Analyse des vormodernen China: Eine Einschätzung von Max Webers Ansatz', in W. Schluchter (ed.), *Max Webers Studie über Konfuzianismus und Taoismus*, Frankfurt/M: Suhrkamp, 55–90.

Eisenstadt, S.N. (1978) 'European expansion and the civilization of modernity', in H.L. Wesseling (ed.), *Expansion and Reaction*, Leiden: Leiden University Press, 167–86.

—— (1983) 'Innerweltliche Transzendenz und die Strukturierung der Welt: Max Webers Studie über China und die Gestalt der chinesischen Zivilisation', in W. Schluchter (ed.), *Max Webers Studie über Konfuzianismus und Taoismus*, Frankfurt/M: Suhrkamp, 363–411.

—— (1987) *European Civilization in Comparative Perspective*, Oslo: Norwegian University Press.

—— (1992) *The Political Systems of Empires*, New Brunswick, N.J.: Transaction Publishers.

Elvin, M. (1973) *The Pattern of the Chinese Past*, London: Eyre Methuen.

Fairbank, J.K. (1992) *China – A New History*, Cambridge, Mass. and London: Harvard University Press.

Feher, F. (1982) 'Paternalism as a mode of legitimation in Soviet-type societies', in T.H. Rigby and F. Feher (eds), *Political Legitimation in Communist States*, New York: St. Martin's Press.

—— (1985) 'Redemptive and democratic paradigms in radical politics', *Telos* 63: 147–56.

—— (1987) *The Frozen Revolution: An Essay on Jacobinism*, Cambridge: Cambridge University Press.

Feher, F., Heller, A. and Markus, G. (1983) *Dictatorship over Needs*, Oxford: Blackwell.

Garton Ash, T. (1989) *The Uses of Adversity: Essays on the Fate of Central Europe*, New York: Random House.

Gellner, E. (1991) 'Nationalism and politics in Eastern Europe', New Left Review 189: 127–34.

Geyer, D. (1987) *Russian Imperialism: The Interaction of Domestic and Foreign Policy, 1860–1914*, Leamington Spa: Berg.

Giddens, A. (1985) *The Nation-State and Violence*, Cambridge: Polity Press.

Gooding, J. (1992) 'Perestroika as revolution from within: An interpretation', *The Russian Review*, 51(1): 36–57.

Graham, A.C. (1989) *Disputers of the Tao: Philosophical Argument in Ancient China*, La Salle, Ill.: Open Court.

Grossman, G. (1977) 'The "second economy" of the USSR', *Problems of Communism* 26(5): 25–40.

Halliday, Fred (1992) 'A singular collapse: The Soviet Union, market pressure and inter-state competition', *Contention* 1(2): 121–41.

Halperin, Ch. (1987) *Russia and the Golden Horde: The Mongol Impact on Russian History*, London: I.B. Tauris.

Hammond, Th.H. (1975) 'The Communist takeover of Mongolia: Model for Eastern Europe', in Th.H. Hammond and R. Farrell (eds), *The Anatomy of Communist Takeovers*, New Haven and London: Yale University Press, 107–44.

Hankiss, E. (1990) *Eastern European Alternatives*, Oxford: Clarendon Press.

Hellie, R. (1977) 'The structure of modern Russian history: Towards a dynamic model', *Russian History* 4(1): 1–22.

—— (1982) *Slavery in Russia, 1450–1725*, Chicago: Chicago University Press.

Horowitz, I.L. (1982) *Cuban Communism*, New Brunswick, N.J.: Transaction Publishers.

Huang, Ph. (1991) 'The paradigmatic crisis in Chinese studies. Paradoxes in social and economic history', *Modern China*, 17(3): 299–341.

Jenner, W.J. F. (1992) *The Tyranny of History*, London: Allen Lane.

Jowitt, K. (1992) *New World Disorder: The Leninist Extinction*, Berkeley: University of California Press.

Kaminski, G. (1991) *The Collapse of State Socialism*, Princeton: Princeton University Press.

Katsenelinboigen, A. (1990) *The Soviet Union: Empire, Nation and System*, New Brunswick, N.J.: Transaction Publishers.

Keenan, E. (1986) 'Muscovite political folkways', *The Russian Review* 45(2): 115–81.

Klyuchevsky, V.O. (1965) *Peter the Great*, London: Macmillan.

Koenigsberger, H. (1977) '*Dominium regale* or *dominium politicum et regale*: Monarchies and parliaments in early modern Europe', in P. Gleichmann et al., *Human Figurations*, Amsterdam: Stichting Amsterdams Sociologisch Tijdschrift, 293–318.

Kornai, J. (1991) 'The Hungarian reform process. Visions, hopes and reality', in F. Feher and A. Arato (eds), *Crisis and Reform in Eastern Europe*, New Brunswick, N.J.: Transaction Publishers, 27–98.

Ladany, L. (1988) *The Communist Party of China and Marxism: A Self-Portrait*, London: C. Hurst & Co.

Lange, O. (1970) *Papers in Economics and Sociology*, London: Pergamon Press.

Laue, T. von (1966) *Why Lenin? Why Stalin? A Reappraisal of the Russian Revolution, 1900–1930*, London: Weidenfeld & Nicholson.

—— (1988) *The World Revolution of Westernization: The Twentieth Century in Global Perspective*, New York and Oxford: Oxford University Press.

Lévi, J. (1989) *Les fonctionnaires divins: Politique, despotisme et mystique en Chine ancienne*, Paris: Editions du Seuil.

Lewin, M. (1973) 'The disappearance of planning in the plan', *Slavic Review* 32(2): 271–87.

—— (1985) *The Making of the Soviet System*, London: Methuen.

—— (1988) *The Gorbachev Phenomenon: A Historical Interpretation*, London: Radius.

Lippit, V. (1978) 'The development of under-development in China', *Modern China* 4(3): 251–328.

Luttwak, E. (1983) *The Grand Strategy of the Soviet Union*, London: Weidenfeld & Nicholson.

McDaniel, Tim (1988) *Autocracy, Capitalism and Revolution in Russia*, Berkeley: University of California Press.

—— (1991) *Autocracy, Modernization and Revolution in Russia and Iran*, Princeton: Princeton University Press.

MacFarquhar (1974) *The Origins of the Cultural Revolution 1: Contradictions Among the People, 1956–57*, Oxford: Oxford University Press.

McNeill, W. (1964) *Europe's Steppe Frontier*, Chicago: Chicago University Press.

Malia, M. (1980) *Comprendre la révolution russe*, Paris: Editions du Seuil.

Mann, M. (1986) *The Sources of Social Power 1: A History of Power from the Beginning to AD 1760*, Cambridge: Cambridge University Press.

Markus, M. (1982) 'Overt and covert modes of legitimation in East European societies', in T.H. Rigby and F. Feher (eds), *Political Legitimation in Communist States*, New York: St. Martin's Press, 45–63.

Metzger, T. (1977) *Escape from Predicament: Neo-Confucianism and China's Evolving Political Culture*, New York: Columbia University Press.

—— (1984) 'Eisenstadt's analysis of the relations between modernization and tradition in China', *Li-Shih Hsueh-Pao*, 12: 345–418.

Meuschel, S. (1992) *Legitimation und Parteiherrschaft in der DDR*, Frankfurt/M: Suhrkamp.

Meyendorff, J. (1981) *Byzantium and the Rise of Russia: A Study of Byzantine–Russian Relations in the Fourteenth Century*, Cambridge: Cambridge University Press.

Monnerot, J. (1953) *The Sociology of Communism*, London: Allen & Unwin.

Morin, E. (1983) *De la nature de l' URSS*, Paris: Fayard.

Murakami, Y. (1987) 'Modernization in terms of integration: The case of Japan', in S.N. Eisenstadt (ed.), *Patterns of Modernity 2: Beyond the West*, London: Frances Pinter, 65–88.

Nelson, B. (1973) 'Civilizational complexes and intercivilizational encounters', *Sociological Analysis* 34(2): 79–105.

Obolensky, D. (1970) 'Russia's Byzantine heritage', in M. Cherniavsky (ed.), *The Structure of Russian History*, New York: Random House, 3–28.

Offe, C. (1991) 'Capitalism by democratic design? Democratic theory facing the triple transition in East Central Europe', *Social Research* 58(4): 865–92.

Pipes, R. (1974) *Russia under the Old Regime*, London: Weidenfeld & Nicolson.

—— (1990) *The Russian Revolution 1899–1919*, New York: A.A. Knopf.

Platonov, S.F. (1970) *The Time of Troubles*, Lawrence: Kansas University Press.

Polanyi, K. (1957) *The Great Transformation*, Boston: Beacon Press.

Presniakov, A.E. (1978) *The Tsardom of Muscovy*, Gulf Breeze, Fla.: Academic International.

Pye, L.W. (1985) *Asian Power and Politics – The Cultural Dimensions of Authority*, Cambridge, Mass.: Harvard University Press.

—— (1990) 'China: Erratic state, frustrated society', *Foreign Affairs* 69(4): 56–75.

Raeff, M. (1966) *Origins of the Russian Intelligentsia: The Eighteenth-Century Nobility*, New York: Harcourt, Brace & World.

—— (1983) *The Well-Ordered Police State: Social and Institutional Change through Law in the Germanies and Russia, 1600–1800*, New Haven and London: Yale University Press.

—— (1989) 'Un empire comme les autres?' *Cahiers du monde russe et soviétique* 30, 3–4: 321–28.

Riasanovsky, N. (1982) *The Image of Peter the Great in Russian History and Thought*, Oxford: Oxford University Press.

Rigby, T.H. (1982) 'Introduction: Political legitimacy, Weber and Communist mono-organisational systems', in T.H. Rigby and F. Feher (eds), *Political Legitimation in Communist States*, New York: St. Martin's Press, 1–26.

—— (1990) *The Changing Soviet System: Mono-Organisational Socialism from its Origins to Gorbachev's Restructuring*, Aldershot: Edward Elgar.

Riskin, C. (1991) 'Neither plan nor market: Mao's political economy', in William A. Joseph *et al.* (eds), *New Perspectives on the Cultural Revolution*, Cambridge, Mass.: Harvard University Press, 133–52.

Rittersporn, G.T. (1991) *Stalinist Simplifications and Soviet Complications: Social Tensions and Political Conflicts in the USSR, 1933–1953*, Chur: Harwood Academic Publishers.

Robertson, R. (1992) *Globalization – Social Theory and Global Culture*, London: Sage.

Rosenfeldt, N.G. (1978) *Knowledge and Power: The Role of Stalin's Secret Chancellery in the Soviet System of Government*, Copenhagen: Rosenkilde & Bagger.

Rostow, W.W. (1991) 'Eastern Europe and the Soviet Union: A technological time warp', in D. Chirot (ed.), *The Crisis of Leninism and the Decline of the Left: The Revolutions of 1989*, Seattle: University of Washington Press, 60–73.

Rothschild, J. (1989) *Return to Diversity: A Political History of East Central Europe since World War II*, Oxford: Oxford University Press.

Rywkin, M. (1989) *Soviet Society Today*, New York: M.E. Sharpe.

Sapir, J. (1990) *L'économie mobilisée*, Paris: Editions La Découverte.

—— (1991) *The Soviet Military System*, Cambridge: Polity Press.

Schrecker, J.E. (1991) *The Chinese Revolution in Historical Perspective*, New York: Praeger.

Schwartz, B. (1985a) *The World of Thought in Ancient China*, Cambridge, Mass.: Harvard University Press.

—— (1985b) *China's Cultural Values*, Occasional Paper no. 18, Arizona State University: Center for Asian Studies.

—— (1989) 'Thoughts on the late Mao: Between total redemption and utter frustration', in R. MacFarquhar (ed.), *The Secret Speeches of Chairman Mao*, Cambridge, Mass.: Harvard University Press.

Sgard, J. (1992) 'L'utopie libérale en Europe de l'Est', *Esprit*, no. 7, 62–83.

Shanin, T. (1986) *Russia 1905–07: Revolution as a Moment of Truth*, London: Macmillan.

Šimečka, M. (1984) *The Restoration of Order: The Normalization of Czechoslovakia 1969–76*, London: Verso.

Skilling, H.G. (1976) *Czechoslovakia's Interrupted Revolution*, Princeton University Press.

Starr, S.F. (1988) 'Soviet Union: a civil society', *Foreign Policy* no. 70, 26–41.

Strmiska, Z. (1983) *Sociální systém a strukturální rozpory společností sovětského typu* (*Social System and Structural Contradictions in Soviet-Type Societies*), Köln: Index.

—— (1988) 'The Prague spring as a social movement', in N. Stone and E. Stouhal (eds), *Czechoslovakia: Crossroads and Crises, 1918–88*, London: Macmillan, 253–270.

—— (1989) *Stagnation et changement dans les sociétés de type soviétique: Projet d'un cadre théorique pour une analyse théorique*, Köln: Index.

Szamuely, T. (1974) *The Russian Tradition*, London: Secker & Warburg.

Szporluk, R. (1991) 'The Soviet West – or Far Eastern Europe', *East European Politics and Societies* 5(3): 466–83.

Torke, H.J. (1974) *Die staatsbedingte Gesellschaft im Moskauer Reich*, Leiden: E.J. Brill.

Touraine, A. (1981) *The Voice and the Eye*, Cambridge: Cambridge University Press.

—— (1988) *La parole et le sang: Politique et société en Amérique latine*, Paris: Editions Odile Jacob.

—— (1990) *Stalin in Power: The Revolution from Above 1928–1991*, New York and London: W.W. Norton.

Tucker, R.C. (1987) *Political Culture and Leadership in Soviet Russia*, Brighton: Wheatsheaf Books.

Walicki, A. (1991) 'Notes on Jaruzelski's Poland', in F. Feher and A. Arato (eds), *Crisis and Reform in Eastern Europe*, New Brunswick, N.J.: Transaction Publishers, 335–93.

Wallerstein, I. (1974) *The Modern World-System 1: Capitalist Agriculture and the Origins of the European World-Economy in the Sixteenth Century*, New York: Academic Press International Edition.

Werth, N. (1990) *Histoire de l' Union Soviétique*, Paris: PUF.

Westoby, A. (1988) *The Evolution of Communism*, Oxford: Polity Press.

Wiles, P. (1977) *Economic Institutions Compared*, Oxford: Blackwell.

—— (1982) 'The worsening of Soviet economic performance', in J. Drewnowski (ed.), *Crisis in the East European Economy: The Spread of the Polish Disease*, London: Croom Helm, 143–63.

Williams, R.C. (1986) *The Other Bolsheviks: Lenin and His Critics, 1904–1914*, Bloomington: Indiana University Press.

Wittram, R. (1964) *Peter I. – Czar und Kaiser*, Göttingen: Vandenhoeck & Ruprecht.

Zaslavsky, V. (1982) *The Neo-Stalinist State: Class, Ethnicity and Consensus in Soviet Society*, New York: M.E. Sharpe.

Index